# THE HARDEST DRUG

# THE HARDEST DRUG,

## HEROIN AND PUBLIC POLICY

# JOHN KAPLAN

The University of Chicago Press
Chicago and London

John Kaplan is the Jackson Eli Reynolds Professor of Law at the Stanford Law School, Stanford, California. He is the author, with Jon R. Waltz, of *The Trial of Jack Ruby* (1965); *Marijuana—The New Prohibition* (1970); *Criminal Justice* (1973); with William Cohen, *The Bill of Rights* (1976); and *The Court Martial of the Kaohsiung Defendants* (1981).

The University of Chicago Press, Chicago 60637
The University of Chicago Press, Ltd., London

*Library of Congress Cataloging in Publication Data*

Kaplan, John.
    The hardest drug.

    (Studies in crime and justice)
    Includes bibliographical references and index.
    1. Heroin.   2. Narcotics, Control of—Government
policy—United States.   I. Title.   II. Series.
HV5822.H4K36   1983      362.2'93      82-17514
ISBN 0-226-42427-8

*TO MY BRIDE*

# CONTENTS

# FOREWORD

Heroin is one of the major blights of urban life in the United States and many other parts of the developed Western world. It creates addictions, contributes to crime, operates as one of many formidable obstacles to mobility out of city ghettos, overburdens the institutions of criminal justice, exacerbates problems of police corruption, and puts pressure on the adherence of law enforcement officials to constitutional values. Heroin never should have been invented.

But the existence of heroin and other physically and socially debilitating drugs of abuse cannot be wished away. Their existence and misuse pose basic questions about the relationship between individual liberty and social harm in modern Western democracy. The proliferation of heroin and its social costs raise practical as well as theoretical issues that call for hard-headed choices among unattractive policy options.

Yet cutting our losses goes against the grain of a major strain of American national character. If there are problems, there should be solutions: quick, simple, and complete. The gray area is suspect. The hard choice, even if it is the best course, is always viewed with suspicion. Need I add that most of the literature and policy debate about heroin in the United States have been innocent, fanciful, and informed more of ideology than data? On all sides, proponents of the "quick fix" to the problem of heroin in the United States seem to see the facts as they would wish them and fashion solutions as if their fantasies had been fulfilled.

This book is a well-informed, exhaustive, and worldly analysis of what the criminal justice system can and should do about heroin in the United

States. A decade from now and more, serious scholars and policy analysts will quote Professor Kaplan as a major authority and thank him for his efforts. His well-informed, stubborn refusal to uncomplicate the complicated and see the Promised Land will irritate many readers. Because of this, not in spite of it, his is an indispensable book for a thoughtful tour of a series of dilemmas involving criminal justice policy toward the "hardest drug."

A personal note: this is the second volume produced in the Studies in Crime and Justice since my supervisory involvement. Its publication is an occasion for rejoicing at the Chicago Center and at the University of Chicago Press. If there is anyone more meticulous than John Kaplan, I do not want to deal with him. Yet he never loses sight of the big picture. He has done scholarship and the national welfare a major service.

Franklin E. Zimring

# ACKNOWLEDGMENTS

This project was supported by Grant Number 76 NI-99-0113 awarded by National Institute of Law Enforcement and Criminal Justice, U.S. Department of Justice, under the Omnibus Crime Control and Safe Streets Act of 1968, as amended. I am required to state that the points of view or opinions stated in this document do not necessarily represent the official position or policies of the U.S. Department of Justice—though it would be good if they did.

Franklin Zimring read the entire manuscript more than once. He has my eternal gratitude. Several others have read parts of the manuscript and given me helpful advice. They know who they are, and I thank them all.

In addition, I would like to thank several Stanford students who helped on the footnotes. They are Dav Holzworth, Jon Cristy, and Dan Gonzales. Finally, I must thank Mary Tye and Judy Dearing who typed endless drafts of the manuscript into their overworked word processor.

# 1▪
# HEROIN AS A
# SOCIAL PROBLEM

*I*t is not at all clear why heroin should be the "hardest" drug. It is, after all, a white powder indistinguishable to the eye from cocaine, mescaline, various amphetamines and barbiturates, nicotine, and caffeine—some of which are "soft" and others not popularly considered drugs at all. It is true that heroin is addicting, but this complex property, as we will see, is shared by many other drugs we do not consider "hard" at all.

In all probability, the hardness of heroin, in the public view, stems from a combination of factors—the condition of those users who come to our attention; the public attitude toward the kinds of people who use the drug; the serious criminal penalties for its sale or use; the strong social disapproval it evokes; and the enormous social cost to the nation attributed to its use.

Regardless of heroin's hardness—whatever that may mean—there is no doubt that its use does constitute a social problem. To most, the drug is a destroyer of countless lives and the major cause of urban crime in the nation. Others recognize the existence of a social problem but regard it as self-inflicted by a national policy which has aggravated a relatively benign vice by forcing heroin users to steal to meet the grossly inflated cost of their drug habits.

Historians of social thought tell us that the concept of a social problem is only about two centuries old. Before then, individuals might have had difficulties, but even the sum of these did not amount to a matter of concern for the society or group as such. If things were bad, or worse than in earlier times, people did not think in terms of specific matters which could be separated from the rest of life and called social problems.

Today, however, we attempt to isolate particular groups of people, behavior patterns, or broad cultural trends from the great complexity of our society, and think of them as discrete social problems. And, since the term "problem" implies the existence of an answer, we tend to follow our isolation of the problem with a quest for its solution. The discussion then, focuses on how to solve the particular social problem in question, and on how to get those in power to undertake the appropriate remedies.

Analysis of the heroin problem has generally followed these lines. We regard the drug as a serious social problem, but one which could be "solved" were we able to surmount the political obstacles to rationality. If only it were so easy.

Heroin use in the United States, though perhaps a prototypical social problem, differs from many others in the extreme unreliability of the available data.[1] Six years ago the estimates of the number of heroin addicts in the United States varied from fewer than 150,000 to well over 1,000,000, with the majority of experts estimating (though this is no reason to assume that they were therefore correct) between one-half and three-quarters of a million. Since then we have been experiencing one of our periodic heroin droughts and most—but not all—estimators have lowered their estimate of the number of addicts by about 30 percent.[2]

We have been told that the percentage of heroin addicts in American metropolitan areas ranges from less than 0.15 percent of the population in Buffalo to 0.88 percent in San Francisco, with New York, supposedly the addict capital of the nation, at 0.75 percent, only slightly above the national average.[3] There is little reason to believe these more specific figures, and in fact we do not know how many heroin addicts we have in our population or how they are distributed. As we will see, we do not even know in many cases whom we should count as an addict.

Nor can we be any more confident about the total cost of heroin addiction to the nation. The most popular estimate is in the neighborhood of ten billion dollars a year, including the amounts stolen by addicts to support their habits; the cost of apprehending, processing, and imprison-

1. Researchers for the National Institute on Drug Abuse calculate a Heroin Problem Index for each of 24 metropolitan areas from five indicators—admission to treatment, emergency room visits, heroin involved deaths, heroin retail price, and heroin retail purity. Independent estimates of heroin addiction prevalence in two cities are used to establish a straight-line conversion of the HPI to a prevalence rate. Finally, these rates are converted to a nationwide estimated prevalence rate. For 1978, NIDA estimated between 432,000 and 508,000; for 1979, the estimate is 387,000 to 453,000.

2. Robert G. Demaree, Richard A. Hudiburg, and Bennett W. Fletcher, "Estimates of the Prevalence of Heroin Use in 24 Metropolitan Areas 1976–1979," report prepared for the National Institute on Drug Abuse, 12 March 1981. Mimeographed.

3. Ibid.

ing those whose offenses arise from the use or sale of heroin; and the sums spent on the treatment of addicts.[4]

As will be discussed later, these numbers may well be wildly in error; but even if they were correct, they would not by any means reveal the entire cost of heroin to our society. Nowhere do the usual calculations account for the erosion of civil liberties and the police corruption related to attempted enforcement of the heroin laws; the diversion of large profits to organized crime; the lowered quality of life in large areas of our cities; and the pain suffered by the families of addicts and, more directly, by the addicts themselves.

Of course, it simplifies the problem unduly to regard all these costs as attributable to one chemical, however hard. It is true that if there were no such thing as heroin (or its close pharmacological relatives) these particular costs would not have to be borne. On the other hand, each event has many causes. Our heroin problem is caused not only by the white powder but also by the fact that our society contains sizable numbers of people who are willing to use it in particular ways. In various other cultures, heroin or its relatives are available and, for the most part, are neither widely nor destructively used.[5]

In addition, a large part of the costs which heroin now imposes upon us are caused by the fact that our legal system does not seem very good at enforcing our national policy of complete prohibition of the drug. Certain other nations, for various reasons, seem to be far more effective at the task of preventing large numbers of their citizens from gaining access to it.[6]

Some of the factors which interact with heroin to impose costs upon us are perhaps within our power to change. Others lie considerably beyond our abilities, at least in the short run. However, before beginning a more detailed consideration of the many issues raised by heroin and our treatment of the drug, we should examine some basic pharmacology.

## THE POPPY

The opium poppy (*Papaver somniferum*) grows under a wide variety of conditions, though it seems to prefer a warm, dry climate. Its cultivation

4. This was the figure put forward by Robert L. DuPont, then director of NIDA, in "The View Around the Corner," an address given to the National Issues and Strategies Symposium on the Drug Abusing Criminal Offender, 21 April 1976, at Reston, Virginia. Mimeographed.

5. See, for example, Guido Belsasso, "Drug Abuse and Treatment in Mexico," and Alaeddin Akcasu, "Treatment of Drug Abusers in Turkey," in "International Survey," ed. John C. Ball, Jean Paul Smith, and Harold Graff, *Addictive Diseases* 3, no. 1 (1977): 21–23, 67.

6. Jean Chesnaux, *China: The People's Republic, 1949–1976* (New York: Random House, 1979), p. 40.

is illegal in most countries, including the United States, and in those where production is legal it is regulated by a network of international agreements.[7] Legally or not, however, the plant is grown on a large scale in several areas of the world.

In India, the poppy is grown lawfully as a cash crop for the medical drugs that may be obtained from it, and we are told that there is no large-scale diversion to the illegal trade.[8] The illegal market flourishes, however, in other areas where there is a shortage of police resources, a cultural tradition of opium growing, and a large supply of cheap, rural labor.

In central Turkey, the poppy is an important cash crop. Although the government, in theory, buys up the entire harvest for medical uses, the illegal market has paid enough of a premium to cause the diversion of a considerable but unknown amount. This diversion has been so serious, in fact, that the United States at one time expended a considerable amount of resources and goodwill to persuade the Turkish government—ultimately for only two years—to ban cultivation of the plant altogether.[9]

In Pakistan, Afghanistan, and the "Golden Triangle" of Laos, Burma, and Thailand, there exist areas that are, as a practical matter, outside the power of any of those embattled governments. In these, the poppy is grown by tribesmen both for local use and for the illegal market.[10]

The areas of poppy cultivation do not seem to be shrinking. Fifteen years ago very little was grown in Mexico. Then, with the interruption of the supply from Turkey, Mexico literally blossomed as an opium producer. Now, cooperation between American and Mexican authorities apparently has much reduced the amount of opium produced there.[11] On the other hand, the turmoil in Iran seems to have so weakened the control of the central government that that nation is reemerging as a major cultivator.[12]

7. For a discussion of the history of international narcotics control, see Adolph Lande, "The International Drug Control System," in The National Commission on Marihuana and Drug Abuse, *Drug Use in America: Problem in Perspective* (Washington, D.C.: Government Printing Office, 1973), app. vol. 3, *The Legal System and Drug Control*, pp. 6–132.

8. The Cabinet Committee on International Narcotics Control, "World Opium Survey 1972," in *Drug Use in America*, app., vol. 3, p. 410. Such opium as is diverted is apparently consumed locally.

9. Sibyl Cline Halper, *The Heroin Trade: From Poppies to Peoria* (Washington, D.C.: Drug Abuse Council, 1977), pp. 18–22.

10. Cabinet Committee, "World Opium Survey 1972," pp. 434, 440, 448.

11. Halper, *Heroin Trade*, pp. 5–8.

12. National Narcotics Intelligence Consumers Committee, *Narcotics Intelligence Estimate: The Supply of Drugs to the U.S. Illicit Market from Foreign and Domestic Sources in 1978 (with Projections for 1979-82)* (Washington, D.C.: Government Printing Office, 1980), pp. 33–34.

## THE OPIATES

Opium, a sticky brown gum, is the dried form of the exudate which oozes from the base of the mature poppy flower after that part of the plant has been lanced or cut. It has been known for several thousand years as a folk medicine, a healer of pain, and a giver of pleasure. Originally, it was drunk in various potions, but with the introduction from the New World of pipe smoking as a method of drug use, the opium pipe came into widespread service—the opium often being mixed with another New World import, tobacco.[13]

The major active ingredient of opium, responsible for most of its pharmacological effects, was first isolated in 1803. A white crystalline powder, it was named morphine after Morpheus, the god of dreams.[14] In 1893, heroin was commercially produced from morphine by a simple chemical manipulation.

Heroin was first marketed as a cough suppressant—its name apparently deriving from the German *heroisch*, meaning "powerful, with effect even in small doses."[15] Indeed, heroin was dramatically stronger than codeine, the opium derivative usually used for cough suppression.

Somehow, the legend has grown that the name "heroin" was intended to convey something far more grandiose—that the drug was originally thought to be a cure for morphine addiction. If that had been so, perhaps there would have been something heroic about the drug. There is little evidence supporting this theory, however. The drug was named heroin while its only known use was as a cough suppressant. While some early articles speculated that heroin might not be addictive, others at the same time warned of this possibility. Not only was there never a scientific conviction expressed that heroin was nonaddictive, it was never advertised as such.[16] Moreover, experience very quickly showed that it was every bit as addictive as morphine and that it was indeed *heroisch,* about two-and-a-half times more powerful than morphine on a per weight basis.

13. Gregory A. Austin, *Perspectives on the History of Psychoactive Substance Use*, National Institute on Drug Abuse, Research Issues Series, no. 24 (Washington, D.C.: Government Printing Office, 1978), p. 134.

14. In Greek mythology, Morpheus is one of the sons of Somnus, the god of sleep. He sends human shapes to the dreamer. See Ovid, *Metamorphoses*, book ll, lines 634–35, trans. Rolfe Humphries (Bloomington: Indiana University Press, 1955), p. 279. "And Sleep roused Morpheus from his thousand sons, Best of them all at imitating humans. . . . ."

15. United Nations, Department of Social Affairs, "History of Heroin," United Nations, *Bulletin on Narcotics* 5, no. 2 (April–June 1953): 3.

16. For a review of the earliest medical literature concerning the therapeutic use of heroin, see Charles E. Terry and Mildred Pellens, *The Opium Problem* (New York: Bureau of Social Hygiene, 1928), pp. 77–85.

The reason for this increased "strength" is somewhat complex. Heroin is not simply a concentrate of morphine—indeed a pound of morphine yields about one and one-fifth pounds of heroin. Heroin is not stronger than morphine in the same way that whiskey is stronger than beer as an intoxicant. Both opiates are used in such small quantities that the amount of time and effort needed to consume them is the same. In practice, the difference in strength means only that the user will adjust his dose so as to take less heroin than he would morphine to compensate for the difference in effect per milligram—or, more practically, that the heroin will be "cut" with a larger quantity of milk sugar, quinine, or other dilutant.

Moreover, despite the often heard remark that heroin is a more powerful medical painkiller than morphine—the implication being that our legal policies are causing increased agony to our medical patients—the evidence for such a proposition is quite weak. Although both heroin and morphine are used in Britain as painkillers, while only morphine can be used in the United States, careful double-blind studies have shown that the two drugs, in equivalent dosages, are equally effective in relieving pain and improving mood.[17]

The similarity of their effects is easily explainable; heroin is quickly converted into morphine in the bloodstream. The reason why heroin seems to be so much stronger than morphine is more interesting; it is a consequence of what is called the blood-brain barrier, the group of mechanisms which prevent many of the contents of the bloodstream from coming in contact with the sensitive brain. Although very little of the morphine in the bloodstream—perhaps one two-thousandth of the amount—is permitted to bathe the brain, heroin can cross the blood-brain barrier much more easily. If injected, some of the heroin reaches the brain before it is converted into morphine, and it is this fraction that accounts for the heroin's greater power.[18]

17. Robert F. Kaiko, Stanley L. Wallenstein, A. G. Rogers, P. Y. Grabinski, and R. W. Houde, "Analgesic and Mood Effects of Heroin and Morphine in Cancer Patients with Postoperative Pain," *New England Journal of Medicine* 304 (June 1981):1501–5. But see the contrary view expressed by Arnold S. Trebach in *The Heroin Solution* (New Haven: Yale University Press, 1982), pp. 59–84. Obviously this issue requires more study, but its resolution does not affect what is usually considered to be the social problem of heroin.

18. Jerome H. Jaffe and William R. Martin, "Opioid Analgesics and Antagonists," in *Goodman and Gilman's The Pharmacological Basis of Therapeutics*, ed. Alfred Goodman Gilman, Louis S. Goodman, and Alfred Gilman, 6th ed. (New York: Macmillan Co., 1980), pp. 506–7. W. H. Oldendorf et al., "Blood-Brain Barrier: Penetration of Morphine, Codeine, Heroin and Methadone after Carotid Injection," *Science* 178, no. 4064 (1 December 1972): 984–86. A. Herz et al., "On the Central Sites for the Antinociceptive Action of Morphine and Fentanyl," *Neuropharmacology* 9, no. 6 (November 1970): 542. Most likely the substance that most easily penetrates the blood-brain barrier is not heroin itself but a metabolite of heroin before complete conversion to morphine. It is even conceivable that certain receptors in the brain are activated by heroin or its metabolites and not by morphine.

Most patients cannot tell the difference between heroin and morphine in equivalent doses. However, those users who take their drug by intravenous injection tend to prefer heroin. Some value the slightly shorter time lag between administration and action, which only seems noticeable when the drug is injected into a vein, while others report that injections of morphine lead to an unpleasant tingling sensation in their fingers and toes. The high concentration of morphine near the site of the injection releases histamines, which, upon reaching the extremities, cause the tingling. Since intravenously injected heroin tends to be distributed by the bloodstream before it breaks down into morphine, it does not cause the release of significant amounts of histamines, and the user is spared the sensations he may find objectionable.[19]

The real reason why we consider ourselves to have a heroin rather than a morphine problem is due to the preference of the seller rather than that of the user. Heroin is chosen by the illegal trafficker because, being more concentrated, it can be concealed and smuggled more easily than can an equivalent dosage of morphine. It is primarily for this reason that heroin, not morphine, dominates the illegal market for opiates in the United States and in those other nations which make a serious but incomplete effort at law enforcement.

Technically, it is somewhat inaccurate to say that heroin dominates the illegal opiate trade. To be precise, heroin is encountered only in the laboratory. The substance we call heroin is, in fact, heroin hydrochloride, a salt of heroin itself, and also a white powder. Since heroin is insoluble in water and, hence, useless for injection, it is always converted into the hydrochloride form before it reaches the channels of commerce.

Until recently, chemists of the federal and local law enforcement agencies reported heroin assays based on the percentage of heroin itself rather than on that of the hydrochloride. Since the hydrochloride molecule has two additional atoms—hydrogen and chlorine—the maximum purity of heroin that could be found in any sample of the hydrochloride was 90 percent, even where the substance was otherwise pure. In 1969, however, the federal authorities changed their policy and began reporting the purity of seized heroin in terms of the heroin hydrochloride content. Local police chemists soon followed suit, thus raising by some 11 percent[20] the apparent purity of all samples assayed.

19. W. R. Martin and H. F. Fraser, "A Comparative Study of Physiological and Subjective Effects of Heroin and Morphine Administered Intravenously in Postaddicts," *Journal of Pharmacology and Experimental Therapeutics* 133. no. 3 (September 1961): 388–99.

20. William M. Lenck, Chief Counsel, Drug Enforcement Administration, letter of 12 September 1979 to author. Since the maximum purity of heroin, formerly 90 percent, now becomes 100 percent, the purity is increased by 10/90ths or about 11 percent.

In addition to morphine and heroin, the opiate family contains several other important members.[21] Codeine, an extremely valuable medicinal drug, is a relatively minor (5 percent) constituent of opium (though it is usually manufactured from morphine). Meperidine (Demerol) and methadone are both synthetic drugs quite close in pharmacological action to the natural opiates, though quite different in chemical structure. A host of less common opiates are also known. Some are up to one thousand times as powerful, on a per weight basis, as heroin[22]—probably because they are not broken down in the bloodstream and are far more able than morphine to cross the blood-brain barrier.

The term "opiate" covers all the family members, of which heroin is the most common in illegal street use. Pharmacologists also refer to the opiates as narcotics, from the Greek *narkosis*, meaning "benumbed." Scientists restrict this term to the opiates despite the fact that several other categories of drugs also produce numbness or sleep, and even though legislatures have often included within the narcotic classification both the stimulant, cocaine, and the tranquilizer, hypnotic, mild hallucinogen, or sui generis substance, marijuana.

## THE MODE OF ADMINISTRATION

Any effort to specify the effects of an opiate or, for that matter, of any other drug, runs immediately into a series of problems. Although we are accustomed to thinking that a drug has a definite set of effects, including side effects, in practice the matter is much more complicated than this. The effects of a drug vary, of course, with the amount taken. In addition, a given dosage of a drug may have quite different effects depending on its mode of administration.

Some drugs, such as coffee and alcohol, are typically used by only one route, drinking. Marijuana is usually smoked, but is sometimes eaten in brownies or spaghetti sauce. Tobacco is usually smoked today, but its active ingredients may be taken by a number of routes. The cigarette smoker absorbs his drug through his lungs. Most cigar smokers and those who chew tobacco take it through the lining of the mouth. In the United States as recently as 1910, more tobacco was taken in fine powder form through the gums or nasal membranes as snuff than was smoked in cigarettes.[23]

21. Jaffe and Martin, "Opioid Analgesics," p. 496.
22. D. R. Jasinski, J. D. Griffith, and C. B. Carr, Etorphine in Man, I. Subjective Effects and Suppression of Morphine Abstinence," *Clinical Pharmacology Therapeutics* 17 (1975):267–72.
23. Leonard M. Schuman, "Patterns of Smoking Behavior," in *Research on Smoking Behavior*, ed. Murray E. Jarvik et al., National Institute on Drug Abuse, Research Monograph No. 17 (Washington, D.C.: Government Printing Office, 1977), p. 37.

Cocaine is typically "snorted" in the United States today, though in years past it was more frequently injected. The inhabitants of the Andean highlands chew the coca leaf, the vegetable source of the drug, and we are told that in some areas such as Los Angeles, some of those in occupations such as the entertainment industry "free-base" it. They treat the crystalline powder with ether and then smoke the chemical derivative produced.[24]

Sometimes more unusual methods of drug administration—such as suppositories—have come to our attention. It is even reported that opera singers in late Czarist times took alcohol by enema, so that they could get drunk without endangering their vocal cords.[25]

Probably the most exotic means of drug administration was that by which the belladonna alkaloids (the products of *Datura*, or what in the United States is called jimsonweed) were taken during the Middle Ages. This drug, which contains scopolamine, often produces disorientation and the feeling that the user is flying through the air. Apparently, certain women would rub extract of *Datura* onto broomsticks and then, while naked, straddle the sticks and rotate them back and forth, absorbing the drug through the walls of the labia. This rather singular behavior, plus their stories of "soaring" drug experiences, seems to have given rise not only to the belief that they were witches but also to our present folklore that witches ride broomsticks.[26]

There are several reasons why the mode of its administration is important in determining a drug's effects. The effective concentration at the site of a drug's action may vary greatly, depending on whether it is slowly absorbed after eating or intramuscular injection, or whether it suddenly bathes the site of action after intravenous use. In addition, many of the harmful consequences of drug use may be directly traceable to its mode of administration. So far as we know, tobacco is not implicated in lung cancer unless the drug is smoked. Heroin use causes hepatitis only if the drug is injected, and causes collapsed veins and embolisms only if injected intravenously.[27]

The strength of a drug habit may also depend on the mode of administration. For some time we have known that behaviors may be produced and maintained by operant, or Skinnerian, conditioning. In

24. James H. Woods and David A. Downs, "The Psychopharmacology of Cocaine," in *Drug Use in America,* app., vol. 1, *Patterns and Consequences of Drug Use,* p. 130. See also, "Cocaine: Middle Class High," *Time,* 6 July 1981, p. 61.

25. Anecdote told by Yuri Cherkovin, Professor of Journalism at Moscow University, to Nathan Maccoby, Director, Institute for Communication Research, Stanford University. See also P. T. Furst and M. D. Coe, "Ritual Enemas," *Natural History* 86, no. 3 (March 1977): 88–91.

26. Michael J. Harner, "Hallucinogens in European Witchcraft," in *Hallucinogens and Shamanism.* ed. Michael J. Harner (New York: Oxford University Press, 1973), pp. 125-140.

27. Jerome H. Jaffe, "Drug Addiction and Drug Abuse," in *Goodman and Gilman,* p. 546.

simple terms, this means that a behavior which is rewarded will tend to be repeated, often long after the rewards have ceased and have been replaced by pain.

Numerous variables determine the persistence of a behavior shaped by operant conditioning. For our purposes here, it is important that one of these is the shortness of the time between the behavior and its reward. The persistence of both smoking and intravenous injection habits has been related in part to the short time between use of the drug and its effect. In the case of smoking, the lag between absorption of the active ingredients of tobacco or free-based cocaine through the lungs and their delivery by the bloodstream to the brain is about seven seconds. This is about the same time lag as when a drug is injected into a major vein in the arm.[28] Since a drug if eaten or drunk takes effect much more slowly than this, the conditioning effects tend to be weaker than when the drug is smoked or injected intravenously.[29]

Heroin addicts in the United States typically use the drug by intravenous injection. This method not only produces a pleasurable "rush," which we will describe later, but is the most efficient way to use the drug—a matter that is quite important in view of its high price.

Other methods of heroin use are also known. Although intramuscular injection seems to be used only for the medical delivery of opiates, subcutaneous injection, or "skin popping," is a common method of heroin use by experimenters or "tasters." Often they believe that addiction cannot result from this method of use—though later, to their sorrow, they may learn better.

Heroin also can be eaten, though this is quite inefficient since the action of the liver neutralizes most of the drug before it reaches the general circulation.[30] Smoking is more efficient, but still wastes a good deal, as does "chasing the dragon" (placing the drug on a sheet of tin foil, heating it from below and inhaling the vapor through a paper tube). Interestingly, in Iran and Hong Kong, where heroin, though illegal, is far cheaper than in the United States, the drug is much more frequently inhaled.[31]

In the United States, middle-class occasional users may take heroin through their nasal membranes by "snorting" it. The economic waste of

28. Department of Health, Education, and Welfare, *Smoking and Health: A Report of the Surgeon General* (Washington, D.C.: Government Printing Office, 1979), p. 16–. Bert S. Koppell and Jared R. Tinklenberg, "Pharmacology of the Opiates," in *Alternative Heroin Control Policies*, comp. and ed. Peter B. Bjorklund (Palo Alto, Cal.: Center for Planning and Research, Inc., 1979), vol. 2, app. A, p. 8.

29. Thomas J. Crowley, "The Reinforcers for Drug Abuse: Why People Take Drugs," *Comprehensive Psychiatry* 13, no. 1 (January 1972): 51–62. Abraham Wikler, "On the Nature of Addiction and Habituation," *British Journal of Addiction* 57, no. 2 (July 1961): 73–79.

30. Jaffe and Martin, "Opioid Analgesics," p. 505.

31. Thomas P. Shoesmith, "Chasing the Dragon: Narcotics in Hong Kong," *Drug Enforcement* 6, no. 1 (February 1979): 39.

methods other than injection may not be serious for them, since they use less and are likely to be wealthier than most other heroin users.

## SET AND SETTING

Two other important variables also help determine an individual's reaction to a drug. These are usually referred to as the user's "set" and the "setting" of use. The drug user's set includes, among other things, his biochemical and genetic makeup, and his expectation as to the drug's effect.

Although we know very little about such individual differences among users, these may be quite important. Some tobacco smokers were sickened by their first cigarette, others were unaffected, and the rest (a minority) enjoyed the experience. It is not unreasonable to expect that such differences affected the ease with which they took up the habit, though it is also clear that an unpleasant first experience is not enough to preclude subsequent regular use.

Reactions to other drugs show equally distinctive individual discrepancies. We have all noted the great variations in the effects of alcohol upon different drinkers. One careful, double-blind study of the reaction to caffeine among twenty coffee users showed that a given quantity of the drug disturbed the sleep of twelve but seemed to have no such effect on the other eight.[32]

A drug user's set includes not only his physical, but also his psychological state. The power of suggestion plays a significant part even in the medical use of drugs. Placebos, which have no pharmacological effect, are used solely for their interactions with the patient's set, and many a patient has derived relief from sleeplessness, tension, nausea, or pain through confidence in a completely inactive but impressively named pill.

In recreational drug use, as well, we often confound the pharmacological effect of a drug with the effect of the user's set. A number of interesting studies of alcohol separated these effects by using a drink which masked the taste of the drug. In one, where an experimental psychologist attempted to determine whether moderate alcohol consumption caused sexual arousal, he found that set was more important than pharmacology. Those subjects who thought they had received alcohol in their drinks were more sexually aroused than those who thought they had not.[33] Holding constant the individual's expectation, however, it turned

32. Avram Goldstein, Richard Warren, and Sophia Kaizer, "Psychotropic Effects of Caffeine in Man," *Journal of Pharmacology and Experimental Therapeutics* 149, no. 1 (July 1965): 156–59.
33. G. Terrence Wilson and David M. Lawson, "Expectancies, Alcohol, and Sexual Arousal in Male Social Drinkers," *Journal of Abnormal Psychology* 85, no. 6 (December 1976): 587–94.

out that those who did receive alcohol were no more sexually aroused than those who did not. In other words, the expectation of getting alcohol was sexually arousing, while the actual pharmacological effect of a moderate dose of the drug, Shakespeare to the contrary, made no measurable difference.

The set of a user may be an important determinant in separating the principal effect of a drug from what are regarded as its side effects. Just as a weed is any plant growing where it is not wanted, so a side effect is simply a consequence of drug use that the user does not want at that time. The set of the user may actually diminish unwanted effects and magnify desired ones by allowing him to select a very few moods or sensations produced by the drug, concentrate on them, and ignore any others.

The setting of its use also influences the effects of a drug. Persons who drink alcohol alone in their quiet homes may feel effects very different from those they would experience if they drank the same amount at a noisy cocktail party. Marijuana users are familiar with what is called the "contact high," where interaction with those using marijuana produces effects even in some who have not used the drug at all. By contrast, one early scientific report on the euphoric properties of marijuana was based on an experiment performed in the cadaver room of a hospital. Small wonder that the researcher found that marijuana use was generally regarded as unpleasant.

As we will see, a compounding problem in the study of heroin effects is that many of our studies of opiates are performed on hospital patients or experimental subjects in scientific settings. Heroin, when taken by an addict among his friends in familiar surroundings, may have quite different effects.

## THE PHARMACOLOGY OF THE OPIATES

Even though the mode of administration and the contributions of set and setting are important in determining the effects of a drug, we cannot neglect basic pharmacology. The relatively recent appreciation of non-drug variables has caused some commentators to do just this—resulting in an interesting drama, with sufficient attention paid to Laertes, Ophelia, Polonius, Gertrude, and Claudius, but without Prince Hamlet himself.

For medical purposes, the most important effect of the opiates is analgesia or pain relief. These drugs are unsurpassed for relieving the continuous dull pain of serious surgery. Opiate-induced analgesia seems to be quite selective. The drugs do little to reduce sharp pain and seem to inhibit dull pain without any lowering of sensitivity to touch, vibration, sights, or sound. One of the most remarkable things about opiates is that, according to many reports, the drugs do not remove the "feeling" of pain. Rather, in the words of one of the standard pharmacological texts, "patients frequently report that the pain is still present, but that they feel more comfortable."[34]

We know that a great part of the feeling of pain is caused by anxiety over the pain itself. (That is why medieval torturers exhibited their tools and described their procedures to their victims before beginning their work.)[35] To some extent opiates probably act to reduce pain by reducing anxiety. It certainly is true that the major opiates work as tranquilizers, in the ordinary meaning of the word. Though technically that term is reserved for other, quite different drugs, morphine and heroin produce tranquillity both in medical patients and in street users. In each case the drug allows its user to feel distant from and uninvolved in his own problems.[36]

The analgesic effect of the opiates is but one of several important medicinal effects. We have already mentioned the suppression of the coughing reflex, an important matter in patients recovering from abdominal surgery. More important even, to larger numbers of people, is the fact that opiates cause the smooth muscle of the gastrointestinal tract to contract. As a result, they are commonly used as a treatment for dysentery, diarrhea, and a whole series of digestive ailments. This accounts, in part, for their widespread use as a folk medicine in underdeveloped areas. Diarrhea is endemic in these regions because of poor sanitation, and opiates are still probably the most efficacious drugs for the control of this condition. The "tourist's friend," paregoric, for instance, is a solution of opium and camphor in alcohol.[37]

## TOLERANCE

For medical purposes, the most worrisome pharmacological properties of the opiates are the related effects of "tolerance" and "addiction." Tolerance to a consequence of drug use develops when the effect of a given dose diminishes with repeated use. As one becomes more tolerant he must increase his dosage to obtain a constant pharmacological effect. The phenomenon of tolerance is by no means unique to the opiates; it seems to characterize many psychoactive drugs. A novice smoker who tried to smoke two packs of cigarettes in a day would find himself very ill. Drinkers too develop tolerance to alcohol; we call this "learning to hold one's liquor."

34. Jaffe and Martin, "Opioid Analgesics," pp. 499–500, 512.

35. Amnesty International, Report on Torture (New York: Farrar, Straus and Giroux, 1975).

36. Norman E. Zinberg, "Observations on the Phenomenology of Consciousness Change," Journal of Psychedelic Drugs 8, no. 1 (January–March 1976): 67.

37. Jaffe and Martin, "Opioid Analgesics," pp. 509, 512–13.

Tolerance to some of a drug's effects may develop far more quickly
than tolerance to others. This differential can be quite dangerous in the
case of barbiturates because tolerance to sedation, the purpose for which
the drugs are usually taken, develops much more rapidly than does
tolerance to toxicity. As a result, those who frequently use barbiturates as
a sedative come closer and closer to taking a fatal overdose. Often they
die from the accidental ingestion of a relatively small additional amount,
either of the barbiturate or of its close pharmacological relative, alcohol.[38]

Tolerance to the effects of the opiates is less ominous, though also
uneven. The dose required to produce smooth muscle effects generally
increases more slowly than does that needed to produce most other
effects, making constipation a major complaint of heroin and methadone
addicts.[39]

We still do not understand much about the mechanism of tolerance to
the opiates, but it has been hypothesized that, generally, when foreign
substances upset the body's equilibrium, the body opposes these effects
by setting up processes to restore itself to its original condition. When
these invasions continue, the body gradually "learns" to become more
efficient at setting up these oppositional processes. Tolerance then
develops when more of the drug is required to override the increased
ability of the body to maintain its internal equilibrium. This, however,
leads to further opposition, which, in turn, requires yet more of the
substance to produce the original action.[40]

It appears that there are psychological as well as purely biochemical
elements in opiate tolerance. Tolerance to opiates builds up more quickly
in laboratory animals if a routine visible to them is followed before they
receive their injections. This has been explained as a case of classical, or
Pavlovian, conditioning.[41] What apparently happens is that the pairing of
the sight of the routine with the opiate administration is able to condition
the effects of the opiate very much as Pavlov conditioned salivation by
pairing the ringing bell with the presentation of food to his dog. Moreover,
the conditioned effects of the opiate include not only the direct pharmacological effects of the drug but also the oppositional effects. These
conditioned oppositional processes then, for reasons that are not clear,
gradually become stronger than the conditioned direct effects. They are,

38. Jaffe, "Drug Addiction and Drug Abuse," in *Goodman and Gilman's The Pharmacological Basis of Therapeutics*, ed. Alfred Goodman Gilman, Louis S. Goodman, and Alfred
Gilman, 6th ed. (New York: Macmillan Co., 1980), pp. 538–39.

39. Ibid., p. 547.

40. Huda Akil, "Opiates: Biological Mechanisms," in *Psychopharmacology: From
Theory to Practice*, ed. Jack D. Barchas et al. (New York: Oxford University Press, 1977),
p. 299.

41. Shepard Siegel, "Evidence from Rats That Morphine Tolerance Is a Learned
Response," *Journal of Comparative and Physiological Psychology* 89, no. 5 (July 1975):
499–501.

hence, available to oppose the pharmacological effect of the injected opiate, thus increasing the animal's tolerance.

Despite the importance of conditioning effects, we should note that there is also a clear pharmacological basis to the phenomenon of tolerance. Even in cases where no conditioning could occur, such as where an animal receives the drug with no warning, tolerance nonetheless develops, though probably at a slower rate.[42] In addition, we now have evidence that adaptation to morphine occurs at the cellular level. In the presence of morphine, the nuclear DNA manufactures more of various proteins which appear to lessen the effect of the opiate.[43]

## ADDICTION

The likelihood that the body develops processes opposing the effects of the opiates also seems to explain another major consequence of opiate use—addiction. If the same oppositional processes which cause tolerance themselves become fixed, they may in turn come to require the presence of the opiate to oppose them. The abrupt cessation of use will then leave the oppositional processes unopposed, and will thus precipitate a reaction, as if to another drug.

The image of two boys pushing against one another and one suddenly stepping out of the way is reinforced by several recent studies which have detected a type of rebound even after one dose of an opiate.[44] This apparently grows larger when the occasions of drug use are close enough so that each new dose takes effect before the consequences of the previous dose have ceased. The result of regular and frequent drug use, then, can be the development of a delayed, cumulative rebound—a set of full-blown withdrawal symptoms waiting only for the cessation of the drug use that is keeping them in check.

Whether or not this picture has any basis in reality, it is true that withdrawal symptoms—the reactions to ceasing regular use of an addicting drug—often seem to be the opposite of the drug's effects. Among the effects of opiates are constriction of the pupils, drop in blood pressure, a feeling of warmth, and constipation; while the symptoms of opiate withdrawal include dilation of the pupils, increase in blood pressure, chills, and diarrhea.[45]

---

42. Shepard Siegel, "The Role of Conditioning in Drug Tolerance and Addiction," in *Psychopathology in Animals: Research and Clinical Implications,* ed. J. D. Keehn (New York: Academic Press, 1979), pp. 146–50.

43. See "Evidence for Biochemical Adaptation in Morphine Tolerance Dependence," in E. Leong Way (ed.) *Endogenous and Exogenous Opiate Agonists and Antagonists.* Elmford, N.Y.: (Pergamon Press, 1980).

44. For a review of studies developing a physiological theory of addiction, see Jaffe, "Drug Addiction and Drug Abuse," pp. 541–42.

45. Siegel, "Role of Conditioning," p. 157.

Although all addictive drugs produce tolerance, the converse does not always hold. The regular user of LSD, for instance, does not risk addiction, but he will have to avoid using his drug too frequently in a short period, or else he will rapidly develop tolerance to its effects.[46]

## DRUG DEPENDENCE

For several reasons, the term "addiction" is in growing disrepute among drug authorities today. Pharmacologists have long argued that it is too emotion-laden a term, and that "physical dependence"—the presence of physical symptoms on cessation of drug use—means the same thing while being free of the emotional content.[47]

In addition, the events of the 1960s and '70s broadened the focus of those concerned with illegal drug use from the opiates to a much wider range of drugs—including marijuana, the amphetamines, and cocaine. Since it was not clear whether marijuana produced addiction, and since amphetamines and cocaine were thought not to do so, the World Health Organization's Expert Committee on Addiction-Producing Drugs changed its name to substitute the term "dependence-producing" for "addiction-producing."

There were several reasons for adopting this course. All of the drugs which concerned the Expert Committee shared the property that even though some of their users were palpably injuring themselves either physically or socially, they nonetheless continued their drug use. For opiate users, this continued use could be explained by the fact that cessation of use caused physical withdrawal symptoms; in other words, these users were addicted—physically dependent. Since no known withdrawal took place among the users of the other drugs, they had to be suffering from a different kind of drug dependence, equally real but psychological rather than physical in nature.

Authorities had noted another problem with relying on addiction as the cause of drug dependence. Some opiate and alcohol users who were clearly not addicted to these addiction-producing drugs nonetheless seemed dependent on them. Often opiate users who had gone through withdrawal and seemed completely free of any addiction relapsed into use again, despite their protestations that they wanted to avoid doing so. And many users of alcohol were problem drinkers who did themselves considerable harm, yet never became addicted. As a result, the Expert Committee classified the drugs producing dependence into those which produced physical dependence and those which merely produced psychological dependence. Alcohol and the opiates were placed in both catego-

46. Jaffe, "Drug Addiction and Drug Abuse," p. 566.
47. Ibid., pp. 535–36.

ries while the amphetamines, cocaine, marijuana, and the hallucinogens were held to produce only psychological dependence.

The dichotomy between physical and psychological dependence itself has come under attack. Although the presence of gross physical symptoms on cessation of use does differentiate some abused drugs from others, increases in our knowledge have blurred the Expert Committee's distinction. More careful measurements of users of various drugs we had thought caused only psychological dependence have revealed clear physical withdrawal symptoms.

Tobacco, for some time, was classified as habit-forming, causing phychological dependence, but nonaddictive. Recent investigations, however, have confirmed the complaints of many smokers that they felt physically ill when they attempted to stop, and have shown clear physical and biochemical changes occur to some as a consequence of nicotine withdrawal.[48] The same is the case with cocaine and its pharmacological relatives, the amphetamines. These drugs were once classed as nonaddictive because they produced no detectable physical withdrawal symptoms. Now there seems to be a biochemical and physiological basis for the depression and insomnia users suffer when they cease their use.[49]

As a result, many have argued that we should stop using terms like physical or psychological dependence and instead refer to drug dependence of the opiate, barbiturate, cocaine, or nicotine type. Further terms, such as "compulsive" or "weak," then, could be used to describe the strength of the particular individual's dependence —or, more precisely, the pain and inconvenience he is willing to endure in order to continue his drug use.

In discussing drug dependence, one might also specify the mode of administration and the set and setting of use since these variables are of considerable importance in describing the nature of a drug dependence. Cigarette smokers who inhale tobacco smoke find it far more difficult to give up smoking than those who do not inhale, while students commonly report that they feel a desire to use marijuana only when they are away at school or while listening to music.

Finally, a complete description of drug dependence might specify how harmful, in one way or another, the drug use is. For instance, if the effects of coffee turn out to be benign, the fact that the drug may produce a strong dependence in some of its users should be of no great concern.

There are several advantages to thinking about the matter this way. The concept of dependence focuses attention on the important observation that a user may continue to use a drug even though its use may cause him significant harm and even though he insists that he wishes to stop. The

48. Ibid., pp. 559–60.
49. Ibid., pp. 556–57.

subdivision of the concept of dependence by specifying the drug, the strength of the habit, and the harm it does its user emphasizes both the variability of the effects of drug dependence and the similarities in the motives for and consequences of various kinds of drug use. It is important to remember that the effects of many psychoactive drugs are far closer to one another than might be inferred from the large differences in their legal and social acceptability.

Finally, the concept of dependence allows us to talk in terms of greater or lesser degrees of dependence on a particular drug. We now know that even physical dependence, or addiction, is not an all-or-nothing condition but rather a continuum of rebound effects. As a result, we are not only unable to draw a sharp line between the addicting and the nonaddicting drugs, we cannot even draw one between addicted and nonaddicted users of a concededly addicting drug.

Some have objected to the term "drug dependence" on the ground that the term has a pejorative note and is a moral judgment on the behavior of some people—usually a minority—by others representing the majority. The argument is that when we assert that the drug-dependent individual does himself harm, we are merely making a value judgment upon the way people gain satisfaction from their lives. It is true that the concept of dependence is used mostly with respect to socially disapproved drugs. Although we rarely use the term in this context, more Americans are dependent on tobacco than upon all other drugs put together.

It is true that drug dependence is not a very helpful term. Entirely apart from any moral or political objection, it covers too variable a mixture of physical need, conditioning, search for pleasure, and desire for approval, as is indicated by the fact that many of its aspects seem to be common to behaviors other than drug taking. Thus, the dependence of some gamblers and some compulsive eaters looks strikingly like that of the most severely dependent drug abusers, and many of us are dependent on other things— such as TV, sex, the outdoors, jogging, newspapers, and Chinese food.

On the other hand, value judgment or not, large numbers of individuals do seem to display a kind of "drug-directed" behavior. Having suffered from various problems attributable to their drug use, they nonetheless seem to make strenuous efforts to procure and use their drug, often while pronouncing their wish to stop.

## OPIATE ADDICTION

Recognizing that the term "addiction" is in growing disfavor, we will continue to utilize it here. Its use is probably most defensible with respect to the opiates. Opiate addiction was the first such phenomenon discovered and described, and it is the opiates which most quickly cause the gross symptoms we associate with withdrawal from an addictive drug.

The symptoms of withdrawal from heroin or morphine have become part of the popular, as well as the medical, literature.[50] Beginning about eight to twelve hours after his last use, the addict's eyes begin to tear; he yawns and starts to perspire; his pupils dilate. Gradually, sneezing, weakness, depression, muscle cramps, nausea, vomiting, and diarrhea appear. Without treatment, the observable symptoms peak in two to three days and are over in a week to ten days. Biochemical and subclinical differences, generally unnoticed by the addict, last up to twelve additional months.[51]

A standard pharmacological text relates opiate withdrawal symptoms to our everyday language. One of these symptoms is a contraction of the muscles just underneath the skin, so that "waves of goose flesh are prominent, and the skin resembles that of a plucked turkey"—thus the origin of the expression "cold turkey" to signify abrupt withdrawal from opiates. In addition, according to the text, the muscle spasms in the long muscles of the leg produce kicking movements, "which may be the basis for the expression, 'kicking the habit' ";[52]

While the symptoms of withdrawal from opiates are quite impressive, those from alcohol and barbiturates are even more so. Although addiction to alcohol is generally slow to develop—heavy use over a period of about fifteen or twenty years is usually necessary to produce physical dependence—the withdrawal symptoms are extremely dramatic and dangerous. Unlike opiate withdrawal, which very rarely causes death, alcohol withdrawal, commonly referred to as delirium tremens or the DT's—and characterized by weakness, anxiety, cramps, vomiting and hallucinations—can prove fatal unless properly treated. Barbiturate withdrawal is also extremely dangerous and without proper medical management is often fatal.[53]

Though all the opiates produce both tolerance and addiction, there are considerable differences among the different members of this drug family. Tolerance and addiction to codeine, for instance, are comparatively slow to develop, and withdrawal is not very intense. In general, the shorter-acting opiates, such as morphine and heroin, tend to have more dramatic, though briefer, withdrawal symptoms than do their longer-acting relatives, such as methadone.[54] Nonetheless, the similarities among the opiates outweigh the differences. All opiates produce cross-tolerance to each other, i.e., tolerance built up by use of one opiate will apply to the

---

50. See, for example, Nelson Algren, *The Man with the Golden Arm* (Garden City, N.Y.: Doubleday, 1950), p. 56.
51. Jaffe, "Drug Addiction and Drug Abuse," pp. 547–48.
52. Ibid., p. 551, 553.
53. Ibid., p. 548.
54. Ibid., p. 541.

others as well, and one opiate can relieve the withdrawal symptoms caused by addiction to any other.[55]

## THE MECHANISM OF OPIATE ACTION

In recent years, considerable progress has been made in understanding how the opiates produce their effects in the body. We have long known of a set of compounds, called opiate antagonists, whose molecules are structurally quite similar to the opiates but which block their action and can precipitate immediate withdrawal symptoms in an addict.

It was postulated that there might be specific receptors in the brain which were designed to accommodate opiatelike molecules. The opiate antagonists presumably worked by occupying the space at the receptor sites, thereby denying the opiate molecules access to the receptors and hence preventing them from producing their usual physiological reactions. The theory pictured the opiate receptors as locks. The opiates were keys which could "unlock" the receptors and trigger their effects, while the antagonists were keys which could fit into the locks but would not turn. This theory was bolstered in 1971 by the discovery of a system of opiate receptors within the brain most concentrated in those areas associated with the feeling of pain and with emotional state.

The discovery of opiate receptors, in turn, caused speculation that they were used by some natural substance within the body. After all, it would be surprising to find in the human brain a receptor that seemed designed solely to accommodate a plant product unrelated to any internally produced chemical. Recently a number of "internal opiates," the endorphins, have been isolated and appear to be produced by both the brain and the pituitary gland.[56]

The scientific basis of acupuncture anesthesia may be related to the endorphins. Recent experiments have shown that acupuncture lessens the pain responses of laboratory animals and that animals which have been made tolerant to the opiates show less of this pain-relieving effect. This finding suggests that acupuncture causes the body to produce a painkilling substance cross-tolerant with the opiates—a suggestion supported by the finding that narcotic antagonists block the effects of acupuncture, just as they do of the opiates. Finally, acupuncture seems to be ineffective in lessening the pain of an animal whose pituitary gland has been removed, indicating that somehow acupuncture stimulates the pituitary to cause production of a natural, internal opiate.[57]

---

55. Jaffe and Martin, "Opioid Analgesics," pp. 497–99.
56. Huda Akil, "Opiates: Biological Mechanisms," pp. 300–02.
57. Avram Goldstein, "High on Research," *U.S. Journal of Drug and Alcohol Dependence* 1, no. 3 (April 1977): 6, 8.

A number of investigators have hypothesized that the body produces endorphins in response to pain. The adaptive purpose of the opiate receptors would then be to lessen any pain which might interfere with the functioning of the organism. Unfortunately, like many an elegant theory, this view has been brutalized by an ugly fact. It has recently been discovered that the feeling of pain is not increased by injection of narcotic antagonists—though this would be expected if the body produced an internal opiate to act as a painkiller.[58]

It is clear that the endorphin system is a complex one—indeed it seems to grow more complex with each successive investigation. Though the matter is far from well understood, endorphins seem to be involved in the body's reaction to pain and stress, and there is evidence that they influence certain types of learning. It has even been postulated that the endorphins play a major role in schizophrenia—though this aspect of their action is still very much in doubt.

The endorphins also help present a model for addiction. If the body requires these internal opiates for its normal functioning and simply produces less of them during opiate use, one would expect that the abrupt cessation of opiate administration would somehow leave the body unprepared to take up the slack. Withdrawal then would be caused by a sudden deficiency of both internal and external opiates—a condition seriously disturbing to the equilibrium of the organism.

## THE EFFECTS OF OPIATES ON THE STREET USER

Up to now, we have been considering the effects of the opiates as if laboratory and medical data were directly transferable to the nonmedical user. This, however, is not the case.

The first difference is in the drug itself. In the laboratory or hospital, the drug is pure. On the street, it not only is "cut" with milk sugar, quinine, or some other soluble substance; it often is contaminated with fiber as well.

The quantities used may also be very different. In laboratory studies of opiate addiction, the subject will be built up to a habit of perhaps 100 milligrams a day, while a street addict with a sizable habit will average less than one-third this amount.[59]

Since the severity of withdrawal symptoms depends, among other things, upon the amount of the drug regularly taken, we would expect that the street user who subsists on relatively small quantities of diluted heroin

58. Priscilla Grevert and Avram Goldstein, "Endorphins: Naloxone Fails to Alter Experimental Pain or Mood in Humans," *Science* 199, no. 4333 (10 March 1978): 1093–95.
59. Edward Preble and John J. Casey, "Taking Care of Business: The Heroin User's Life on the Street," *The International Journal of the Addictions* 4, no. 1, (March 1969): 14–15.

would have fewer and less painful withdrawal symptoms than the textbooks indicate. In fact, the quality of heroin available on the street has been so low in recent times that it has been years since most jailers have seen a full-blown case of heroin withdrawal in an arrested addict.

On the other hand, for reasons we do not fully understand, the withdrawal symptoms of patients who became addicted during medical treatment seem much less discomforting than those of the street addict. Probably this is in part because the pain of withdrawal, like most pain, increases with fear and anticipation, and street addicts clearly fear withdrawal more than do medical patients. In addition, the medical and street addicts interpret differently the reappearance of any pain which has been relieved by the opiate. Typically, the medical patient regards his discomfort not as withdrawal but as an additional consequence of his surgery or other underlying condition. The street addict, whose unhealthy life may have brought on many painful conditions, regards his newly unmasked suffering as part of his withdrawal pains.

## THE SUBJECTIVE EFFECTS OF HEROIN

The greatest differences between the medical and the street user appear with respect to subjective effects of the drug. The differences in the set and setting of use are so great indeed that it appears almost as if the two kinds of users were using different drugs. A standard medical text states that "when therapeutic doses of morphine are given to patients with pain, they report that the pain is less intense, less discomforting, or entirely gone. . . . In addition to relief of distress, some patients experience euphoria. . . . When morphine in the same dose is given to a presumably normal, pain-free individual, the experience is not always pleasant."[60]

The contrast with the street user could hardly be greater. Street users of heroin typically distinguish between two euphoric effects of heroin—the "rush" and the "high."[61] The rush comes almost immediately after intravenous injection and lasts only a minute or two. (In medical practice morphine is almost always given orally or by intramuscular injection.) It is caused by a sudden flood of the intravenously injected heroin bathing the brain before the drug has had time to be diffused through the bloodstream and changed to morphine. Usually the rush is described as a violent, orgasmic experience, somewhat like a sexual orgasm, "only vastly more so." Heroin users often emphasize that it does not seem localized but pervades the whole abdomen.

One researcher recently interviewed a group of illegal heroin users

60. Jaffe and Martin, "Opioid Analgesics," p. 499.
61. Edward M. Brecher, *Licit and Illicit Drugs* (Boston: Little, Brown & Co., 1972), pp. 12–13.

while they were under the influence of the drug. He summarized their description of the rush as a feeling "of great relief. Tension runs out of the body, the bones and muscles feel fluid and relaxed."[62]

After the rush comes the high, which can last up to four or five hours. It is an effect of the opiate diffusing from the bloodstream, through the blood-brain barrier, and does not depend on the method of administration. A user can get high not only from intravenous injection but from skin popping, smoking, or any other means that delivers enough of the opiate to the bloodstream.

The high is usually described as a warm, drowsy, extremely pleasant state where, in the words of many addicts, "all your wants seem to be satisfied." It involves a feeling of "lightheaded dizziness" and relaxation. The dizziness is pleasant and not severe.[63] In contrast to experience with the same level of euphoria from alcohol use, the opiate user has no trouble walking, for instance.

Related to this lightheaded feeling is a phenomenon called "mental clouding." Those under the influence of heroin show a significantly reduced performance on a variety of mental tests administered up to five hours after heroin use. Some of this effect is probably due to lowered motivation, but even apart from this, there appears to be a sharp drop in the speed of performance, without, however, any reduction in accuracy.

Along with the relaxation, the heroin high seems to be characterized by a dampening of stimuli from both within and without in a way that seems related to the medical effect of opiates in "distancing" a patient from his pain. One heroin user described the experience like this:

It's as if I'm all the way down a long tunnel. I see you and her and I listen to what you ask me but it would be just as easy not to. You seem to be moving around too quickly to be worth the effort of keeping up. I'm not much interested in what I'm saying either.

An investigator, after interviewing several heroin users, noted:

The tunnel or cave image occurred often when subjects attempted to describe the sense of distance from stimuli apparently characteristic of this group's response to the drug. Their descriptions are entirely compatible with experiments showing that people on morphine, though they feel no pain, know whether they have been brushed by a feather or stuck lightly or deeply with a needle. My subjects knew when an act or a conversation might be painful or anxiety-provoking,

62. Norman Zinberg, "Observations on the Phenomenology of Consciousness Change," p. 67.

63. Ibid.

but their consciousness was simply not invested in that response. They weren't interested.[64]

The euphoriant effects of heroin—the rush and the high—should be distinguished from the action of the drug in fighting off withdrawal. The latter effect will be noted only in those who are addicted—and will be experienced as an intense relief. Moreover, while only the most powerful opiates produce euphoria, any opiate, administered by a variety of methods, will help relieve the discomfort of withdrawal—though the most powerful opiates do the job most effectively, and intravenous injections act most quickly and efficiently on a per milligram basis.

For some time, it was believed that the addict's early heroin use brought him euphoria but that as addiction developed both the rush and the high gradually disappeared. It was therefore thought that the addict continued his opiate use solely to stave off withdrawal and to feel normal. Several investigators have concluded more recently that many long-time addicts continue to enjoy heroin use and continue to experience both the rush and the high, so long as they inject enough to overcome the drug tolerance they have built up.[65]

Other researchers have argued that an addict consuming large quantities of heroin gradually feels more unhappy, depressed, and hostile. He continues in part because each individual injection makes him feel somewhat better than he had just previously—though it only temporarily halts his increasing unhappiness and irritability.[66] Although this effect is noticeable in laboratory studies, it is not so clear that any street addicts use enough heroin to enter the range where increasing dosages become dysphoric.

Not only do the subjective effects of heroin differ substantially among addicts, but the effect of the drug on any one addict may be modified by changes in the myriad of "street variables." The set, setting, and pattern of drug use change like popular fashions in music, dress, and adolescent vocabulary. The way the user is treated by his peers and the society-at-large has not only changed over time but varies from place to place—even within a few blocks in a central city. As a result, the use of heroin, its consequences, and the social variables connected with it are in constant flux. What is true about one user may not be true about another, and what was true about most users a few years ago may not be true today.

64. Ibid.

65. William E. McAuliffe and Robert A. Gordon, "A Test of Lindesmith's Theory of Addiction: The Frequency of Euphoria among Long-Term Addicts," *American Journal of Sociology* 79, no. 4 (January 1974): 795–840.

66. Alfred R. Lindesmith, *Addiction and Opiates* (Chicago: Aldine, 1968), pp. 31–33, 94-n95.

Despite this, there are a number of enduring, basic facts about heroin use which are crucial to understanding the social problem we attribute to the drug. Perhaps the best way to begin is to examine and dispel five myths, each of which is important to the efficacy of one or another suggested solution, and each of which unduly simplifies the difficulties we face in adopting a rational policy. The first is what may be called the myth of the pusher.

## THE MYTH OF THE PUSHER

According to the popular view, the addict is most likely to have started heroin use because he was talked into it by a pusher, or drug seller, who supplied him with the drug and induced him to try it. Supposedly, the economic motivation of the pusher is clear; heroin is an addictive substance, and once the innocent is "hooked," his pusher can have a reliable and helpless customer who will have to purchase heroin from him at an inflated price.[67]

A well-known comedy record of the early fifties by Tom Lehrer expresses this view in a song about "The Old Dope Peddler" who

> even gives free samples
> Because he knows full well
> That today's young innocent faces
> Are tomorrow's clientele.[68]

In business terms, the theory is that the pusher, a salesman of heroin, makes gifts of the drug and persuades potential customers to try it, in the hope of recouping his sunk costs once they become addicted and are forced to buy from him. In economic terms this is not so farfetched. Indeed, under certain circumstances it can be a clever way to market a habit-forming substance—a fact appreciated by the cigarette companies which once gave away free packs on college campuses to induce prospective users to try their products.

Unfortunately, the necessary conditions for the theory to work are not present in the heroin market. Quite to the contrary, there are reasons to believe that sellers of heroin use considerably less pressure and inducement to market their wares than do most marketers of automobiles, detergents, toys, and breakfast cereals.

The relevant difference between the heroin pusher and the cigarette

67. See, for example, the accounts in Alwyn J. St. Charles, *The Narcotics Menace* (Los Angeles: Borden, 1952), pp. 29, 49, 63.

68. Tom Lehrer, "The Old Dope Peddler," in *The Tom Lehrer Song Book* (New York: Crown Publishers, 1954), pp. 51–53.

companies is that the companies had every expectation of staying in business for a long time and had the benefit of brand identification to help bind users to their product rather than to a competitors. A little thought should make one quite suspicious of such a scenario as applied to the street-level heroin seller.

The likelihood that an arrest or some other mishap will force the retail pusher to withdraw from business is such that he cannot expect to ply his trade long enough to recoup even a small amount that he might have given away. Moreover, though brand names are not unknown in heroin dealing, they are quite rare, subject to counterfeiting, and tend not to last very long. It would, therefore, be economically irrational for a seller to spend a substantial amount of his inventory or time in making new addicts who then might patronize someone else.

This is not to deny that the seller of heroin is a part of a large production and marketing system or that the making of new addicts is beneficial to that system as a whole. The point is that the system is unable, and apparently does not even try, to exercise the kind of discipline over its sellers that would make them invest part of their merchandise in developing new customers.[69]

Although the heroin trade is usually highly organized at the top of the pyramid (which involves the steps from purchasing the harvested opium to smuggling heroin into the United States), the degree of organization decreases through the kilogram dealers all the way down to the addict-retailers. These sellers typically are independent businessmen who purchase their supply for cash from someone higher up the chain.[70]

The financial risks for the wholesaler of entrusting consignments of heroin to a "pusher" are enormous. At any moment the street-level seller may be arrested and his supply confiscated; he may be "ripped off" by a potential customer; or he may simply develop a compulsive "run" and use up his inventory himself. As a result, at virtually all levels, dealers sell for cash to those lower in the distribution system.

In addition, giving free samples to nonusers is unwise for another reason; it would expose the heroin seller to a considerable additional risk of apprehension. The more he deals with nonusers, the greater his chances of involving himself with someone who has not learned the techniques of avoiding detection or with someone who might be forced by parents or police to inform on him. A pusher would be much better

69. Mark H. Moore, *Buy and Bust: The Effective Regulation of an Illicit Market in Heroin* (Lexington, Mass.: D.C. Heath & Co., 1977), p. 57.

70. Staff and editors of *Newsday, The Heroin Trail* (New York: New American Library, 1974), p. 205. See also Robert J. McGuire, "War on Narcotics: The State of Hostilities in New York," *Drug Enforcement* 6, no. 3 (October 1979): 7.

advised to deal only with experienced users; and virtually every study of heroin sellers confirms that they agree with this advice.[71]

The structure of the heroin market also militates against the "addictive sample" theory. Commerce in heroin is, for the most part, a seller's market.[72] The drug is generally in short supply because of law enforcement efforts, and the seller usually can unload all of his inventory on his regular customers.[73] Rather than give away the drug, he probably would use it himself, since at the retail level the seller is almost always also a user.

The "pusher" theory is objectionable on pharmacological, as well as commercial, grounds. Addiction does not develop after only one use of the drug. In the laboratory, it takes about two weeks of thrice daily use before noticeable withdrawal symptoms occur upon cessation, and, on the street, addiction is rare within six months of a user's first experience with the drug.[74] Moreover, as we will see, a street addict is not so much a slave to his drug as the popular mythology indicates, and hence he is often not a very reliable customer.

## How Heroin Use Spreads

These reasons should cause one to be extremely skeptical of the pusher theory, but there is an even better reason for rejecting it. There are literally dozens of investigations of the spread of heroin use—all of which show a remarkably consistent pattern, refuting the whole idea of the seller as a major inducer of new users.[75]

Most commonly, heroin use spreads within a peer group in areas where use is already endemic. Typically, these are the cores of our large cities where, as we will see, there are always more heroin users and sellers than police can apprehend or the courts process. In these neighborhoods there are many groups of "low riders" whose approach to authority and physical danger has long caused them to be seen as troublemakers. It is within these groups that heroin use usually spreads. The following story is not atypical:

71. See, for example, Patrick H. Hughes et al., "Social Structure of a Heroin Copping Community," *American Journal of Psychiatry* 128, no. 5 (November 1971): 48. See, generally, Moore, *Buy and Bust*, pp. 17–18.

72. J. Dean Heller, "The Attempt to Prevent Illicit Drug Supply," in *Drug Use in America*, app., vol. 3, p. 391.

73. Moore, *Buy and Bust*, pp. 54–58.

74. McAuliffe and Gordon, "Test of Lindesmith's Theory of Addiction," note 7, p. 799.

75. See Leon G. Hunt and Carl D. Chambers, *The Heroin Epidemics* (New York: Spectrum, 1976), chapter 1 and the literature cited therein.

H wanted to use heroin because he wanted to be like his brother-in-law, whom he idolized.

He first used heroin on a summer day when he was fourteen years old. He was working for his brother-in-law full-time, without pay, primarily to escape from his home. At work that day his brother-in-law told him that he had some "stuff" and that H could use some after work. H had used a lot of drugs before—he started sniffing glue when he was eleven and had used marijuana, LSD, and various pills—but he was very nervous about trying heroin, because he was fearful of becoming addicted and of getting sick. Nonetheless, he tried to appear cool and sophisticated, comforted by the fact that his bother-in-law was a user and he seemed happy—at least while he was on it.

In his brother-in-law's apartment, the two of them drank a few beers and then his brother-in-law injected him with heroin. H got violently sick and nearly blacked out—not enjoying the experience at all. However, shortly thereafter he reported to his brother-in-law that it had been great—thinking that this was what his brother-in-law would like to hear.

The next few times he tried heroin with his brother-in-law the same thing happened; but then he began to enjoy the drug. Thereafter he began bragging about it to his friends.[76]

Although often there is not quite such an intense relationship between the beginning user and his first source, the story is typical in that the most commonly reported source of an addict's first exposure to heroin is his "best friend." Probably the most common scenario of an addict's first heroin use is that he was walking or driving around with nothing much to do when he either ran into or visited a friend who, he discovered, was preparing to "shoot up." He was invited to join, perhaps by snorting or perhaps by injection, and, without thinking much about the matter, he accepted.

Why he used is a complex question, since there are many who refuse such offers. Perhaps he was bored or curious, but one common reason was that he came from an area where heroin was regarded as a nervy, "stand-up" thing to do.[77]

In our central cities, some extremely successful businessmen—pimps or gamblers—will often be known to have expensive heroin habits, along with their expensive cars, clothes, and women. The fact that they can afford all this adds to their status. These role-models may receive the

76. Sanford Okura, "Reasons for Initial Heroin Use," student paper, Stanford University, 19 May 1975, pp. 15–17.

77. Harvey W. Feldman, "Ideological Supports to Becoming and Remaining a Heroin Addict," *Journal of Health and Social Behavior* 9, no. 2 (June 1968): 131–39.

same admiration in the beginning user's peer group as would a successful rock musician or athlete among other groups of youth.

Finally, the euphoric effects of the drug are not to be underestimated. Virtually every youth in an area where heroin is available has heard someone talking of its virtues and the high pleasure it produces. Young people from many strata of our society are accustomed to taking risks for great pleasure, and both the user and his peer group tend to value just this kind of behavior. Interestingly, many addicts report that their first experience with heroin was not enjoyable, just as many do not enjoy their first cigarette.[78] Nonetheless, they continued either for the status or for the hope of future pleasure and eventually did come to enjoy the experience. Presumably, however, the minority of users who enjoyed heroin from the very beginning were even likelier candidates for continued use.

There is a dispute as to whether the first user in a group of youths is most likely to be the leader of his clique, a follower, or even one who is regarded as just marginally acceptable by the other members. It is clear, however, that a heroin miniepidemic begins when one member of the group is first introduced to heroin use, often through an older brother or friend outside the clique. Thereafter heroin use seems to spread with dramatic suddenness through the peer group.[79]

After his first few experiences with heroin, a user may arrange to earn a small supply of the drug in exchange for some service to a dealer or else he may scrape up some money and convince a seller that he is a reliable enough purchaser. In either case he will not require much of the drug because his tolerance has not yet developed. He has probably already bragged to his friends about his first heroin experience and now cannot keep the drug to himself; he must offer to share it as well.

Some psychologists have speculated that the beginning user's eagerness to share his drug is caused by a basic ambivalence toward his own use and a desire to have his actions approved by and practiced within his peer group. Regardless of the reason, it is often just a few days before four or five of his closest friends have also begun use.

The fear of addiction is not as much of a deterrent to trying heroin as one might think. As we will see, many addicts do not fit our stereotype but, rather, lead busy, exciting, and admired lives, at least for a while. The existence of downtrodden, emaciated, burned-out addicts nodding in doorways—a fate which is universally deplored—makes heroin use seem even braver. Though such addicts are not very much in evidence at the beginning of a heroin epidemic, there is reason to believe that enough of

78. William E. McAuliffe, "A Second Look at First Effects: The Subjective Effects of Opiates on Nonaddicts," *Journal of Drug Issues* 5, no. 4 (Fall 1975): 369–99.

79. Hunt and Chambers, *Heroin Epidemics*, p. 5.

them do accumulate after several years of widespread use to restrain somewhat the next generation's experimentation with the drug.[80]

Finally, the threat of addiction does not seem to deter beginning users because they believe, perhaps like soldiers going over the top, that they will be strong or lucky enough to escape the fate awaiting others. One study of twenty-six addicts in a treatment program asked each whether at the time he had first used heroin he had thought he might become addicted. One said yes, because he actually wanted to become an addict—for the increased status this would bring him in his high school. All the others said no, including one who did not think he stood any chance of addiction, even though this fate had already befallen his twin brother.[81]

Although we have fewer studies of the onset of heroin use in areas where use of the drug is not endemic, it seems that the pattern there is not dissimilar. One member of a small clique finds that, for one reason or another, he has access to the drug. He begins use himself and then introduces his friends, coming gradually under pressure from them to supply more of the drug or to provide access to his connection.[82]

Interestingly, virtually all of the studies indicate that a user introduces his friends to heroin only during a relatively short period. He tends to exhaust quickly his small circle of friends, and should his involvement with the drug persist for any length of time, he is likely to be drawn away from the "straight world," making more friends who are addicts themselves. If so, he will spend most of his time living the life of an addict, concentrating on maintaining his own supply of heroin and avoiding detection.[83]

The spread of heroin use has been likened, in public health terms, to an epidemic like flu or some other contagious disease, where one person introduces a few of his friends, who in turn introduce others, until all the "susceptibles" within a particular population have been "infected."[84] When looked at more closely, the large-scale heroin epidemics that have erupted in many areas since the mid-1960s seem actually to have been a sizable number of miniepidemics spreading rapidly through one clique after another, and between cliques through users with contacts in more

80. Ann F. Brunswick, "Black Youth and Drug Use Behavior," report prepared for the Center for Sociocultural Research on Drug Use, School of Public Health (Sociomedical Sciences), Columbia University, New York, April 1978. Mimeographed.

81. Okura, "Reasons for Initial Heroin Use," p. 30.

82. David B. Graeven and Andrew Jones, "Addicts and Experimenters: Dynamics of Involvement in an Adolescent Heroin Epidemic," California State University, Hayward, Adolescent Research Project, Research Report No. 1, Hayward, Cal. (Mimeographed).

83. Harold I. Hendler and Richard C. Stephens, "The Addict Odyssey: From Experimentation to Addiction," *The International Journal of the Addictions* 12, no. 1 (February 1977): 25–42.

84. Hunt and Chambers, *Heroin Epidemics*, pp. 12–13.

than one group.[85] After a relatively short time, such epidemics tend to "burn out," leaving in their wake a substantial number of heroin addicts, who constitute a major part of what we consider the heroin problem. Note how such a spread is inconsistent with the pusher mythology. If that mythology were true, the majority of users would have been introduced by sellers, each of whom would have had to introduce a large number.

There are other avenues to heroin use as well as the epidemic within the peer group, but these, too, refute the myth of the pusher who seduces innocent youths into trying the drug. A sizable number of the children of the white middle class center their lives upon the use of a variety of drugs—marijuana, alcohol, barbiturates, hallucinogens, cocaine, and amphetamines. Typically, they combine their drug use with a system of values and a life style in opposition to those of conventional society.[86]

Polydrug users often avoid heroin because of a fear of addiction, but some use that drug to add to their many drug experiences or because they find it a help in "coming down" from a "run" of using stimulants such as amphetamines or cocaine. A polydrug user then finds he likes the heroin experience or that it relieves a persistent unease. In any event, confident of his ability to handle any drug, he may continue using heroin until he becomes addicted.

Parenthetically, this may portend a new source of heroin addicts in the future. As cocaine use becomes more widely dispersed in our society, some fraction of the users of that drug can be expected to discover a need for heroin. These users, many of whom do not qualify as polydrug abusers—often using only marijuana and cocaine—may discover that cocaine use can easily get out of control, and that its cessation may be followed by a profound depression. Since heroin may be an obvious choice for self-medication at this time, some of these users, who already have access to illegal drug dealers, may find themselves "hooked."[87]

We have thus far referred to the heroin addict as "he," ignoring the sizable number of female addicts. Though this can be defended on the grounds that some three-fourths of all addicts are male, and that almost everything said will apply to addicts of both sexes, there is a major difference between the ways members of the different sexes are recruited into heroin use.

85. Patrick H. Hughes and Gail A. Crawford, "A Contagious Disease Model for Researching and Intervening in Heroin Epidemics," *Archives of General Psychiatry* 27, no. 2, (August 1972): 149–55.

86. Bruce D. Johnson, "Toward a Theory of Drug Subcultures," in *Theories on Drug Abuse*, ed. Dan J. Lettieri, Mollie Sayers, and Helen W. Pearson, National Institute on Drug Abuse, Research Monograph Series, no. 30 (Washington, D.C.: Government Printing Office, 1980), p. 117.

87. John Hubner, "Getting Straight," *San Jose Mercury News, Cal Today* (Magazine supplement), 14 February 1982, pp. 7–13.

Although use by young men is a peer group phenomenon, females are typically inducted into heroin use by their boyfriends. The fact that girls usually are involved with males older than they are explains the otherwise puzzling fact that the average age of beginning heroin use for females is somewhat below that for males. In a sense, then, the patterns of heroin use among women can be viewed as derivative of those involving their men—and still in no way supporting the pusher myth.[88]

## THE INEVITABILITY-OF-ADDICTION MYTH

The second myth we must refute is that the heroin user, after using the drug once or a few times, inevitably—or almost inevitably—becomes an addict. In the past, government officials have spread such a belief. In the mid-1960s, Henry M. Giordano, then head of the Federal Bureau of Narcotics, predecessor of the Drug Enforcement Administration, testified that according to that agency's research, anyone who used heroin more than six times would become an addict.[89]

Giordano based this conclusion on his interpretation of a careful study of drug use commissioned by the National Institute of Mental Health and published in 1967. This study, by Robbins and Murphy, reported the result of locating and interviewing a sample of 235 young, black men between the ages of thirty and thirty-five who had attended St. Louis public schools for at least six years. Twenty-eight members of this sample had used heroin, and, of these, twenty-two had become addicted. Of the six who had used heroin but avoided addiction, none had used the drug more than six times.[90]

The most interesting aspect of Giordano's use of this study, of course, is not what it tells us about heroin addiction. Rather, his conclusion that anyone who uses heroin more than six times inevitably becomes an addict is a commentary on the sophistication of the federal narcotics enforcement authorities in the 1960s. Happily, they understand a great deal more today.

Even at the time of Giordano's testimony, several studies were available which showed that those who had "tried" heroin far outnum-

---

88. Dean R. Gerstein, Lewis L. Judd, and Sumi Adachi Rovner, "Career Dynamics of Female Heroin Addicts," *American Journal of Drug and Alcohol Abuse* 6, no. 1 (1979): 1–23. Marsha Rosenbaum questions this 'conventional wisdom' in "Becoming Addicted: The Woman Addict," *Contemporary Drug Problems* 8, no. 2 (Summer 1979): 148. See also Marsha Rosenbaum, *Women on Heroin* (New Brunswick, N.J.: Rutgers University Press, 1981).

89. U.S., Congress, House, Committee on Appropriations, Oversight Hearings before a Subcommittee of the Committee on Appropriations, House, 90th Congress., 2d sess., 1968, testimony of Henry L. Giordano, Commissioner of Narcotics, Bureau of Narcotics, p. 623.

90. Lee N. Robins and George Murphy, "Drug Use in a Normal Population of Young Negro Men," *American Journal of Public Health* 57, no. 9 (September 1967): 1585.

bered those who became addicted. For the most part, authorities in the field explained this disparity by picturing the excess as consisting of those who used the drug a very few times and then stopped.[91]

This was plausible. We have long known of "experimenters" who had used heroin once or twice and then ceased because they did not like the effects of the drug, because they could not find any regular supply, or because they were afraid of addiction. We regarded them as those lucky ones who had played Russian roulette and lived to tell about it.

To be sure, the citation of any particular number of heroin usages as the inevitable cause of addiction was absurd—and deriving the number six from the Robbins and Murphy study was preposterous. Nonetheless, most authorities on the problem did tend to ignore the existence of "chippers"—long-term, occasional users of heroin who did not become addicted.

Although there were reports of nonaddicted, weekend users who had used heroin for years, they were regarded merely as on their way to addiction. It was felt that, sooner or later, without their realizing it, their occasions of use would become more and more frequent, until addiction had "sneaked up" on them. Though this certainly happens, we now know that it is by no means inevitable. In recent years, several investigators have begun to study numerous regular heroin users who space out their occasions of use so that they do not become addicted.[92]

These "successful" nonaddicted users tend to abide by rigid rules which control their drug use. Some use only on weekends. Often they use only in groups with other such users and derive considerable support from each other in limiting their intake. An almost universal rule among such groups is to shun addicts—both because they attract the attention of the police and because they are a threat to the values of the controlled user.

Though we know far too little about their numbers and the rules which govern their conduct, it is now clear that there exists a sizable population of nonaddicted but regular heroin users who seem well integrated into society and in many ways indistinguishable from the rest of the population. These users bear the same relation to heroin addicts as normal drinkers do to problem drinkers or alcoholics. In other words, the road to addiction is but one of several paths the heroin user may take.

It appears that the number of nonaddicted heroin users does not bear any constant relation to the number of addicts. In Robbins and Murphy's study, approximately 80 percent of the St. Louis youths who tried heroin once became addicted. In a study of a cross-section of American males,

91. Isidor Chein et al., *The Road to H: Narcotics, Delinquency, and Social Policy* (New York: Basic Books, 1964), p. 159.

92. Norman E. Zinberg and Richard B. Jacobson, "The Natural History of 'Chipping,' " *American Journal of Psychiatry* 133, no. 1 (January 1976): 37–40.

only one-third of those who had ever used heroin had used the drug daily
for any period. (Daily use is often used as a more easily quantifiable
substitute for the rather vague concept of addiction.) On the other hand,
of those who had used as often as once a month, 70 percent had also used
on a daily basis.[93]

Controlled heroin users are, of course, difficult to locate; since heroin
use is a serious crime, they do not advertise their existence. Nonetheless,
a number of investigators have concluded that the number of controlled
heroin users probably matches, and may even exceed, the number of
addicts at any one time.[94] In addition, there are indications that the
population of regular, controlled heroin users is rising quite rapidly, while
the number of addicts seems to be remaining relatively constant or even
decreasing.

## THE ONCE-AN-ADDICT-ALWAYS-AN-ADDICT MYTH

The next of our myths is that heroin addiction is a continuous, permanent
condition—that "once an addict, always an addict." In fact, heroin
addiction is neither continuous nor permanent. Furthermore, these two
concepts should be distinguished. Heroin addiction is *continuous* if a
person who is now addicted and was addicted a year ago has been
addicted during all the intervening time. The condition is *permanent* if
someone addicted during this year will be addicted for any period more
than ten years from now.

### The Continuity of Heroin Addiction

Despite our image of the heroin slave, addicts commonly go through
withdrawal and undergo considerable periods of voluntary—or semi-
voluntary—abstinence. One leading authority on addiction has emphasized this point in an article whose title, "Once an Addict, Seldom an
Addict," is only a pardonable exaggeration.[95] So far as we can tell, less
than half of the addicts who have been on the street for a year will have
used an opiate daily during the entire period.

Often the addict will go through voluntary withdrawal because the
build-up of his tolerance has made his habit too large and expensive. He
may decide that the heroin scene has become too much of a "hassle"—

93. Robins and Murphy, "Drug Use in a Normal Population of Young Negro Men," p.
1585. John A. O'Donnell, *Young Men and Drugs—A Nationwide Survey*, National Institute
on Drug Abuse, Research Monograph Series, no. 5 (Washington, D.C.: Government
Printing Office, 1976), p. 13.
94. O'Donnell, *Young Men and Drugs*, pp. 78–79.
95. Bruce D. Johnson, "Once an Addict, Seldom an Addict," *Contemporary Drug
Problems* 7, no. 1 (Spring 1978): 48–49.

especially if the drug is in short supply. Even if conditions on the street are not unusually taxing, the addict may simply need a rest from the strenuous life he has been leading. Finally, an addict may withdraw himself from heroin because he has an important engagement, such as a trial, at which he must not appear to be addicted.[96]

Contrary to popular view, the addict will not always require medical help in order to pass through withdrawal. Such assistance, however, is easily available and quite simple today. Addicts who wish it often appear at clinics or treatment programs for this purpose, usually claiming an intention to give up the drug permanently. Detoxification, the medical term for management of withdrawal (the name deriving from the days when withdrawal was thought to be caused by an accumulation of poisons in the body),[97] is usually accomplished by giving decreasing oral doses of a long-acting opiate such as methadone. After two weeks of this, the addict is usually opiate-free without having suffered any appreciable discomfort.

On some occasions, addicts simply detoxify themselves without medical aid. The rise of methadone maintenance programs has made available a certain amount of diverted methadone, with which the addict can do the job himself. Finally, many addicts go through withdrawal with no pharmacological help at all. They simply go to bed, telling their friends and neighbors that they have the flu, and suffer in relative silence.

Anyone who reads descriptions of withdrawal symptoms, in medical texts or in popular works such as *The Man With the Golden Arm*, cannot fail to be impressed with what a fearsome experience withdrawal must be. However, as mentioned before, the high price and low purity of the drug available on the street today guarantee that the great majority of heroin addicts in the United States have no such dramatic symptoms when they stop their use.

Even in its classic form, heroin withdrawal is not *that* serious. Pharmacologists compare it to a bad case of the one-week flu[98]—a considerable degree of pain and discomfort, but not so serious that it cannot be borne by someone with considerable determination, especially if he knows that the pain will be tolerable. Organizations such as Synanon insist that no medication be given to ease the withdrawal pains of those in their jurisdiction,[99] and, as mentioned earlier, fatalities (apart, perhaps,

96. Moore, *Buy and Bust*, pp. 8–9.

97. Vincent P. Dole, "Addictive Behavior," *Scientific American* 243, no. 6 (December 1980): 138–54.

98. Peter A. Mansky, "Opiates: Human Psychopharmacology," in *Handbook of Psychopharmacology*, vol 12, *Drugs of Abuse*, ed. Leslie L. Iversen, Susan D. Iversen, and Solomon H. Snyder (New York and London: Plenum Press, 1978), p. 158.

99. Lewis Yablonski, *The Tunnel Back: Synanon* (New York: Macmillan Co., 1965), p. 196.

from a small number of suicides) that can be traced to withdrawal from heroin are extremely rare.

The addict often will go through withdrawal with no real desire to give up heroin use permanently. He may fully intend to resume the life of the street addict after a rest from his "hustling" and pursuit of heroin, or after his tolerance is lowered enough so that he can resume use later at a lower, cheaper, and more euphoric level. At other times, the addict undergoing detoxification will fully intend to give up heroin permanently, though for various reasons he is likely to become readdicted after a period of abstinence.

## The Permanence of Heroin Addiction

Not only is heroin addiction not always a continuous condition, it is not always permanent either. The detoxified former addict may become readdicted but he also may not. Rather than remaining addicted permanently, many heroin addicts manage to give up all use of the drug.

It was once the conventional wisdom that, without treatment, heroin addiction was a permanent condition. Even if the addict stopped use for a while, it was thought that he would always drift back to use and addiction as long as he could gain access to the drug. Indeed, in more recent years an even more gloomy view has become widespread—that even with treatment, virtually all addicts relapse.[100]

At first, the rarity of addicts over forty was explained by the fact that the dangers of heroin use and of the addict life style caused almost all to die before that age. Gradually, as investigators followed up more carefully the addicts who had been treated, a somewhat different picture emerged, and addiction came to be regarded as a long-lasting, though perhaps not a permanent, condition. Although the death rate of heroin addicts was very high for their age group, many former addicts still lived but had "burned out," or "matured out," and given up heroin use.[101]

Until recently, the few known cures of addiction were held to support the relative, if not the absolute, permanence of that condition. Though these addicts had ceased their heroin use before the burn-out age, the changes they had made in their lives were usually so drastic that even

---

100. Brecher, *Licit and Illicit Drugs*, pp. 69–83.

101. Charles Winick advanced the idea of natural recovery from addiction in his study "Maturing Out of Narcotic Addiction," United Nations *Bulletin on Narcotics* 14, no. 1 (January–March 1962): 1–7. Winick's interpretation of his data was questioned by Dan Waldorf and Patrick Biernacki, "Natural Recovery from Heroin Addiction: A Review of the Incidence Literature," *Journal of Drug Issues* 9, no. 2 (Spring 1979): 281–83; but Waldorf and Biernacki accept the validity of the thesis. See their "The Natural Recovery from Opiate Addiction: Some Preliminary Findings," *Journal of Drug Issues* 11, no. 1 (Winter 1981): 68–69.

those who sincerely wanted to cease their heroin use could not be expected to undergo such transformations. Typically, they had cut off all contact with their former friends and moved to areas where they could not gain access to the drug. Often, in addition, they had undergone a religious conversion, married, or so changed their lives that they had found satisfactions which compensated them for their lack of heroin.

It now is clear that we have long been misled by the fact that those addicts who come to our attention and whom we attempt to cure are the stubbornest cases. It turns out that many addicts permanently give up heroin at an early age and after a relatively brief period of addiction.

For instance, in Robbins and Murphy's study of young black men who had been students in St. Louis high schools around twenty-five years earlier, only three of the twenty-two sample members who became addicted were still using heroin at the time of the study.[102] Similarly, of those in the cross section of American young men who had at one time used heroin on a daily basis, only 4 percent had used the drug in the twenty-four hours before their interview.[103] These two studies are quite unusual among investigations of heroin users and addicts because they involve what are called "normal samples." Unlike most samples collected from court or treatment records (which heavily overrepresent the most intractable cases), these samples consisted of those who had not been selected for any quality correlated with the difficulty of cure.

What was, to most, the surprisingly low rate of readdiction among the returned servicemen who had been heroin addicts in Vietnam is probably related to the higher cure rate in a more normal sample.[104] True, the two factors most often cited to explain this phenomenon are also very important. It is undeniable that the returned GIs could find in the United States nondrug satisfactions not open to them in Vietnam—one of which was simply being out of Vietnam. And, of course, it was also important that, except for those who returned to areas of endemic heroin use, they no longer had easy access to the drug.

Nonetheless, it is significant that large-scale urine testing of our soldiers in Vietnam had brought to our attention virtually all those addicted—not just those most visible and probably hardest to cure. And in the entire group, the cure rate could be expected to be far higher than among those who had the most difficulty giving up their drug use.

The low apparent cure rates for heroin addiction, in other words, are produced by the same statistical artifact that understates our cure rates

102. Robins and Murphy, "Drug Use in a Normal Population of Young Negro Men," p. 1586.

103. John A. O'Donnell, *Young Men and Drugs*

104. Lee N. Robins, John E. Helzer, and Darlene H. Davis, "Narcotic Use in Southeast Asia and Afterward: An Interview Study of 898 Vietnam Returnees," *Archives of General Psychiatry* 32, no. 8 (August 1976): 955–61.

for smoking and alcoholism. In all these situations, our view of the obstinacy of the condition is generally based on the most intractable cases—those who either have come for help or have been forced into treatment by others. The cure rates we hear about do not include the easier cases of those who cured themselves without coming to our attention. When these, too, are considered, it looks very much as if heroin addicts, like smokers and alcoholics, are not quite so intractable as we have thought.

Support for such a view comes from a recent analysis of a sample designed to represent an entire age cohort in a ghetto area of high heroin use. Of the group of black youths between twenty and twenty-three years old, some 16 percent had used heroin more than experimentally, while only 3 percent had used within the past year. Equally interesting, about half of those users were addicted for some period, of whom fully 50 percent ceased use with no treatment whatsoever.[105]

Interestingly, the follow-up data on Vietnam veterans also turned up a number of former addicts who still used heroin occasionally, and even some who regularly used the drug without becoming readdicted. Although there is considerable public dispute about whether an alcoholic can resume drinking but control his intake, there is enough documentation in the case of heroin addiction to make it quite clear that former heroin addicts can, at least in some circumstances, move to controlled, nonaddictive use.[106]

Apart from the dispute over moderate use, one must be struck by the resemblance between alcohol and heroin use. Some drinkers use alcohol moderately while others become problem drinkers and alcoholics; some use moderately for quite a while and then gradually seem to lose control over their intake; some, who are clearly problem drinkers or alcoholics, stop drinking completely but relapse again and again; while others give up alcohol permanently with or without social support. The analogy to heroin in each of these cases is striking.

## THE MYTH THAT WE CAN CURE ADDICTION

The "once an addict, always an addict" myth bears a complex relation to the next myth—that we can cure addiction. The former myth denies that addicts can cure themselves; the latter argues that outside forces can cure them. Although both myths involve the permanence of heroin addiction, the latter is much more complex. The reason is that it involves not so

105. Brunswick, "Black Youth and Drug Use Behavior."
106. Lee N. Robins, *The Vietnam Drug User Returns*, Special Action Office Monograph Series A, No. 2 (Washington, D.C.: Government Printing Office, 1974), pp. 58, 63.

much an objective description of the addict's drug use as a view of our power to influence his conduct.

The belief in this myth has had important consequences for our national policy toward heroin. When the Harrison Act was passed in 1914, establishing our national policy of prohibiting heroin supply, the Congress was assured that a revolutionary new method had been discovered to cure opiate addiction.[107] This turned out to be the product of wild overoptimism—a trait we have encountered on many subsequent occasions when this or that treatment was discovered and popularized.

Part of the problem is contained in the wording of the myth itself. The use of the word "cure" implies that heroin addiction must be a sickness or disease. But if it is a disease, it is not a typical one.

The debate over the disease model of heroin addiction is almost as lengthy and heated as the corresponding argument over alcoholism, the problem in both cases being that conditions in the real world do not come labeled "disease" or "not disease." These are names that human beings, for their own reasons, place on existing situations.

In cases where we have not already reached an agreement on the appropriateness of the term, none of the dictionary definitions of disease are at all helpful. Rather, we seem to regard something as a disease, depending on whether the similarities to the conditions that we do recognize as diseases are seen to outweigh the differences, or whether the advantages for our purposes of so labeling the condition are seen to outweigh the disadvantages. Various commentators on what we call mental disease have pointed out the difficulties our use of the disease concept causes in that context.[108] There are even greater problems in the case of heroin addiction.

A disease seems, at base, to have three characteristics. First, it is something which is bad to have and which it would be good to have go way, or be cured of. Second, it must be a condition over which the sufferer has no control at the time—even though some diseases, such as gonorrhea or syphilis, may have been originally brought on by the sufferer's own "misbehavior." Finally, a disease is a condition which we regard as primarily within the domain of the medical profession to try to cure or alleviate.

It is not clear whether heroin addiction meets the first criterion of a disease. Although we take it for granted in the case of those conditions which are clearly diseases that the sufferer wishes to be cured, this does not seem to be the case with many heroin addicts. In fact, on this criterion, cigarette smoking is more clearly a disease, since cigarette

107. David F. Musto, *The American Disease* (New Haven and London: Yale University Press, 1973), pp. 78–82.

108. Alexander D. Brooks, *Law, Psychiatry and the Mental Health System* (Boston: Little, Brown and Co.; 1974), pp. 21–88.

smokers almost always report that they would like to stop but cannot, while heroin addicts are often "righteous" about their addiction.[109]

Interview data might lead us to exaggerate this difference, however. The two types of drug use are probably more similar in this regard than they seem. The heroin addict may not wish to stop his use, but he does want to have the circumstances surrounding his life—such as the unavailability of cheap heroin or his harassment by the police—changed. The cigarette smoker also wants to continue his use—but without danger to his health. It may well be that because his danger seems decreed by nature rather than by man, the smoker does not even consider continuing smoking without risking harm to himself as a possibility worth talking about—though he will often switch to lower tar cigarettes in an effort to lessen his danger.

The second of our criteria for a disease is that the condition, regardless of what brought it on, is, once established, beyond the control of the sufferer. With respect to heroin addiction, this also raises problems. All of the many kinds of drug abuse raise complex issues as to the extent the abuser can control his actions. Indeed, drug dependence is not the only behavior involving us in the quagmire of free will versus determinism. Compulsive gambling, obesity, and various sex behaviors raise similar issues.

Certainly, some heroin addicts—as well as some cigarette smokers and some alcohol drinkers—act as if they cannot control themselves. But, as we have seen, others manage quite well, once they decide that they want to. Often it is only after we note whether they have changed their behavior that we reach any conclusion as to whether they could do so.

Nor does the third criterion for a disease seem to be any more applicable to heroin addiction. It is hard to see any intrinsic reason why the medical profession should be charged with the primary responsibility for the cure or alleviation of heroin addiction. It is true that physicians are responsible for treating the serum hepatitis and embolisms caused by heroin injection, just as we charge them with the task of treating the emphysema caused by smoking, or the liver cirrhosis caused by excessive drinking. Still, the underlying conditions of heroin addiction, cigarette smoking, or alcoholism seem no more in the competence of the physician than in that of the moralist, the existential philosopher, the behavioral psychologist, the teacher, or the policeman. Some indication of this is the fact that we could quite easily regard the two-pack-a-day cigarette smoker, the alcoholic, or the heroin addict as not suffering from an illness but from a "social disorder," or a "bad habit." Rather than regard him as a patient, we could call him a sinner, the practitioner of an "alternate life

109. Alan G. Sutter, "The World of the Righteous Dope Fiend," *Issues in Criminology* 2, no. 2 (Fall 1966): 178.

style," or various other things—each of which would focus upon aspects of the problem that might be as important as are the consequences of the disease model.

Nonetheless, the disease concept of heroin addiction has gained considerable acceptance for several reasons. First, no institution of vigor and status comparable to that of the medical profession has shown much interest in the area. Indeed, in recent years, the medical profession has claimed authority over a larger and larger range of conduct, from nutrition and exercise to sexual adjustment.

Seventy years ago, when the ministry was among our most dynamic institutions, alcoholism was regarded as much more in the domain of morals. And, of course, until the medical profession became both powerful and interested enough in the problem to demand a major share, it was the police who claimed narcotics as within their domain.

There are several practical reasons why the medical profession has been granted primary responsibility for those aspects of heroin addiction not allocated to law enforcement. First of all, if drug abuse is a sickness, resources may be made available for its alleviation in government health budgets and in private insurance policies—without its having to compete for a share of our more strained law enforcement budgets. In addition, physicians quite naturally come in contact with addicts. The management of withdrawal—the beginning of an addict's cessation of use—is far more easily accomplished with medical aid; several of the programs attempting to cure heroin addicts involve the administration of therapeutic drugs— traditionally the domain of the medical profession; and the health complications of addicts often force them to seek medical assistance. In all these cases, once contact is made with the addict, the physician becomes the obvious conduit for other kinds of help and control.

The disease model as applied to both heroin addiction and alcoholism has several additional consequences which, depending on our view of the appropriate attitudes, may be good or bad. Once we consider something to be a disease, we no longer try to punish the sufferer but rather do our best to help him. Displacing responsibility from the sufferer onto those who are treating him also may make him more willing to accept treatment. After all, it is easier to say, "I'm sick, treat me," than to say, "I have a destructive behavior pattern, stop me." In addition, the alcoholic or addict who feels he has a disease may be better able to cope with the guilt over his prior behavior because he cannot blame himself for being sick. This may be quite important practically, since the drug user's guilt over his past behavior may indirectly stimulate his further drug use.

On the other hand, the disease concept may have practical disadvantages as well. Because they regard their drinking or drug use as a disease, some alcoholics and addicts may decide that they need not accept responsibility for controlling it and—perhaps more important—for the harm they do to others. The acceptance of both kinds of responsibility, however, may be a necessary condition of any change.

Our ambivalence toward the disease concept of heroin addiction is indicated by our legal treatment of that condition. This can only be called, by analogy to another disease, schizophrenic. Though the state cannot legally punish someone for having the "disease" of heroin addiction, it can punish the addict for certain behaviors that flow automatically from his disease.[110] Thus, it may punish the "sick" heroin addict for two of his "symptoms"—possession of and use of heroin. If we really thought heroin addiction were a disease, this would be as logical as punishing someone for running a temperature, while refusing to penalize him for having the flu.

In any event, our whole attitude toward what might be called "excessive behaviors" is illogical. While many regard heroin addiction or alcoholism as a disease, few think the same of habitual cigarette smoking, eating too much, or compulsive gambling—though it is by no means easy to articulate any relevant differences among these.


The Stubbornness of Addiction

Whether or not one regards heroin addiction as a disease, the fact remains that a high percentage of addicts persist in their heroin use under conditions which, so far as we can tell, give them every reason to wish to stop. Part of the reason for the stubbornness of heroin addiction, of course, is the very fact that heroin is addictive and that an addict must continue to use the drug or he will go through withdrawal. Even when it does not exhibit the full-blown, classic symptoms, withdrawal is unpleasant. Its psychological aspects, though less dramatic, are perhaps more important than its physical effects. Withdrawal, even from a habit of relatively modest strength, produces a depression and, as addicts describe it, a "craving" for heroin.

It is likely that the addict's knowledge that he can gain relief by shooting up aggravates this craving. Certainly this is the case with many coffee drinkers. If they are on vacation or otherwise distracted, they may omit their afternoon cup and suffer only the mildest discomfort. But if coffee is readily available, the coffee drinker who wishes to skip his cup faces considerable difficulty. Often the closest he can come to abstinence is a long argument with himself during which he must decide that he doesn't really need coffee; that he will quit some other day; and that he will have one cup, just this time.

The psychological stresses suffered by the heroin addict in withdrawal are, of course, much greater than those which affect the coffee drinker.

110. This was the principle enunciated by the Supreme Court in *Robinson v. California* 370 U.S. 660 (1962).

They are more comparable to those of the smoker attempting to give up cigarettes—though the physical symptoms of withdrawal from tobacco are not nearly so gross as those from heroin.

Withdrawal symptoms, however, are only part of the problem. The conditioning effects of heroin use are also extremely important. Not only do these processes exert their force long after withdrawal symptoms have ceased, but they may outweigh the threat of withdrawal even for some of those still addicted. We have already seen that classical, or Pavlovian, conditioning is significant in the buildup of tolerance to opiates. We cannot understand the stubbornness of heroin addiction, however, unless we also understand another kind of conditioning—operant, or stimulus-response, conditioning.

Operant Conditioning

Although operant conditioning seems to be based on the commonsense notion that people will do something more often if they gain a reward or satisfaction from doing it, the process is a great deal more complex than this. Much of the research in this area has produced conclusions which are by no means obvious—and even when conditioning may be expected on commonsense grounds, the strength of the effect may be surprising.

For instance, much of the difficulty of giving up cigarettes is explainable by operant conditioning. The two-pack-a-day smoker takes several hundred puffs per day—each one of which, absorbed through the lungs, strikes his brain several seconds later as a separate jolt of nicotine. To the extent that this jolt is psychologically rewarding, it strongly conditions not only the act of drug taking but the ritual of taking out the cigarette pack, removing a cigarette, lighting it, and drawing each puff.

Though the heroin addict injects only three or four times a day, he is using an extremely rewarding substance. Even if the drug does not produce euphoria—and it does for many—the addict will be rewarded by feeling his injection fight off the beginnings of withdrawal. In fact, some addicts are known to postpone their heroin injection until withdrawal has begun, "the way you may wait to get especially hungry before you have a good steak dinner." Moreover, the addict's own preparations before shooting up will call forth the classically conditioned processes opposing the effect of heroin within his body, which, in turn, will make it more likely that he will experience his heroin use as relief from withdrawal.

Underlying conditions in many addicts may increase the rewarding effect of heroin. The drug's ability to produce peace and tranquillity may have made the addict unused to coping with feelings of discomfort and frustration—other than through the use of heroin. The rewards of heroin use, then, include the lessening of these feelings, which may be a regular part of the addict's life.

Similarly, the painkilling effect of heroin may relieve the discomfort caused by conditions which may have antedated heroin use, or have accumulated during the addict's unhealthy life on the street. This pain may not necessarily be physical in origin. One recent study has indicated that a significant percentage of addicts use their heroin as a kind of self-medication for mental problems. They continue use in part because when they stop, their symptoms of depression, and in some even schizophrenia, return.[111] Interestingly, it may be that this type of addict can be most easily cured by medical intervention. If the rewards of using heroin can be lessened by either curing the underlying medical problem or treating it with a better drug—such as an antidepressant or a major tranquilizer—the patient may find it much easier to give up heroin completely.[112]

Use of heroin by intravenous injection produces especially strong conditioning effects. Not only is the rush extremely rewarding, but the short time between the drug taking and its reward increases the strength of the operant conditioning.[113]

It is not only the use of heroin that is conditioned by these rewards; the whole injection ritual is subject to operant conditioning as well. As a result, the addict attempting to stop use misses not only the effect of heroin but the whole process of "shooting up"—heating the water-filled spoon to dissolve the drug, tying off his vein, drawing up some blood into his needle, and, finally, pressing home the plunger. No wonder that some addicts go through the motions of shooting up when no heroin is available and even inject water into their veins.[114] This behavior is not unlike that of the "reformed" cigarette smoker who now holds a pencil like a cigarette and sucks at its end.

An often neglected aspect of operant conditioning that may be of extreme importance is what is called the schedule effect. It turns out that the strength of conditioning—the persistence of the behavior which has been rewarded—is very much dependent on the schedule of rewards. Moreover, among the most powerful schedules in this regard is what is called intermittent reinforcement—wherein the behavior is rewarded only some of the time—without the subject's being able to "know" in advance whether a reward will follow his actions. The most dramatic example of the stubbornness of the behavior which intermittent reinforcement may

111. Such theories are reviewed by Gerald J. McKenna in "Psychopathology in Drug Dependent Individuals: A Clinical Review," *Journal of Drug Issues* 9 no. 2 (Spring 1979): 197–204.

112. Howard Wishnie, "Opioid Addiction as a Masked Depression," in *Masked Depression*, ed. Stanley Lesse (New York: Jason Aronson, 1974): 350–67.

113. Travis Thompson and Roy Pickens, "Drug Self-administration and Conditioning," in *Scientific Basis of Drug Dependence*, ed. Hannah Steinberg (New York: Grune & Stratton, 1969), pp. 177–98.

114. David G. Levine, " 'Needle Freaks:' Compulsive Self-injection by Drug Users," *American Journal of Psychiatry* 131, no. 3 (March 1974): 297–300.

produce is probably that of the compulsive gambler—though any behavior which is satisfying only on random occasions may prove extremely persistent.[115]

The use of heroin by street users meets this requirement. Sometimes the injection is extremely rewarding, while at other times the potency of the drug may have dropped, or the user's tolerance increased. In these cases, the reward would be less, without the user's foreknowledge.

Indeed, the addict lives in a world of intermittent reinforcement. Sometimes his hustling produces money and sometimes it does not; sometimes his money allows him to "cop" heroin and sometimes it does not; and sometimes his heroin injection produces the feelings he desires and sometimes it does not. As a result, it may even be that intermittent reinforcement conditions not only the drug use but the entire hustling behavior of the addict.

Operant conditioning may also account for a major part of the greater stubbornness of the opiate habit in the street user as compared with the medical patient. To understand this we must remember two facts. First, since it is the history of past rewards for a behavior which conditions the behavior, operant conditioning takes place only where the subject engages in a behavior which is rewarded. Second, the street addict injects himself while others, typically nurses, administer drugs to the medical patient. While this distinction might not seem important, it means that the medical patient has no behavior to be "maintained" by operant conditioning.[116]

Whether or not they are caused by conditioning, pharmacology, or some other factor, there are striking similarities in the behavior of those trying to break a cigarette habit and those trying to break a heroin habit. Though both heroin and cigarette "addicts" may be able to summon up the effort to begin their withdrawal, something often makes the process so painful that many change their minds midway in the effort—and thereafter may not even try again for some time. Both kinds of dependent drug users will often go to considerable lengths to secure their respective drugs. The smoker, to be sure, will find it far less difficult, in physical terms, to gain access to his drug because of its widespread legal availability. But the heroin addict, being more used to duplicity and cunning, will usually have fewer scruples about the means by which he continues his quest.

## The Problem of Readdiction

Despite the difficulties, cessation of heroin use is not the major obstacle in the way of cure for most addicts; most have stopped for considerable

115. Thompson and Pickens, "Drug Self-administration and Conditioning," p. 186.
116. John R. Nichols, "How Opiates Change Behavior," *Scientific American* 212, no. 2 (February 1965): 80.

periods more than once. Since medical help has become easily available
to them for this purpose, they generally report that it was not even very
uncomfortable once they had made up their minds. Basic to the problem,
then, is the phenomenon of readdiction.

We have long known that it is far easier to bring an addict through
withdrawal than it is to keep him from becoming readdicted. Even before
the Harrison Act, when addiction was regarded simply as a personal
medical problem, it had been noted that the relapse rate among those who
had sought or been coerced into treatment approached 100 percent.[117]

Nor was the criminal law a more effective agent of cure after 1914.
Although incarcerated addicts appear to go completely through their
withdrawal within the first few weeks after incarceration, something does
seem to persist. It was noted early that the great majority of those
imprisoned for years, who had sincerely resolved to give up heroin as the
cause of their misfortunes, nonetheless returned to heroin use, often
within a few hours of their release.[118] Often they reported afterward that
they had not missed heroin while in prison—but that when they arrived
back on the streets they were immediately seized by a craving for heroin,
which they did not understand but which they had to satisfy.


The Craving for Heroin

Several scientists have postulated a biochemical mechanism to explain
the "craving" phenomenon. According to this theory, opiate use causes a
permanent change in the biochemistry of the addict which persists long
after the withdrawal symptoms have disappeared. This results in periods
of tension, depression, anxiety, and craving for opiates—all of which
make it virtually impossible to effect any permanent cure.[119]

There are several problems with this theory, however. While we can
measure subtle physiological changes for some months after withdrawal,
there is no evidence that these have anything to do with a return to heroin
use, and we do know that addicts imprisoned for far longer periods often
return quickly to heroin use. Moreover, we do know of substantial
numbers of former addicts who have cured themselves despite these
alleged changes.

On the other hand, it may be that some biochemical change caused by
addiction increases a user's proneness to readdiction, once he starts using
heroin again. It has been noted that heroin tolerance seems to build up

117. Musto, *American Disease*, p. 74.

118. This phenomenon is mentioned by C. P. O'Brien, "Experimental Analysis of
Conditioning Factors in Human Narcotic Addiction," *Pharmacological Reviews* 27, no. 4
(December 1975): 533.

119. Vincent P. Dole, "Narcotic Addiction, Physical Dependence and Relapse," *New
England Journal of Medicine* 286, no. 18 (4 May 1972): 988–92.

faster in a former addict than in a neophyte. Workers in the field also have the distinct impression that becoming addicted is much easier the second time around.[120]

## Conditioning and Relapse

The high relapse rate among heroin addicts and particularly the "craving" for heroin are better explained by two different psychological conditioning theories, each of which is supported by a good deal of experimental evidence. The first of these theories involves operant conditioning. As we have seen, the addict's injection of heroin has been intermittently rewarded over a long period and, as a result, has become quite stubborn.

Moreover, it turns out that conditioning exerts its strongest force under circumstances that most approximate those in which the behavior was rewarded. Psychologists call these circumstances "discriminative stimuli" because the organism discriminates in their presence and "recognizes" the circumstances as appropriate for the previously rewarded behavior.[121] The word "recognizes" is in quotation marks because this may not be a conscious process. Human beings may be acted upon by discriminative stimuli without their knowing it, and the phenomenon affects not only monkeys and rats but salamanders as well.

For our purposes here, it is important that the behavior of heroin injection has been rewarded under certain specific conditions. It was rewarded in the addict's "copping area," among his friends and in sight of particular landmarks. Moreover, the addict's use of heroin was most rewarding when it fought off the beginnings of withdrawal, as he was feeling the onset of discomfort and a vague depression.

Unfortunately, all these discriminative stimuli, or "cues"—those of the streets and the feelings of discomfort—are common in the ex-addict's life. External cues may increase the power of the conditioning when he returns to his copping area, sees an addict friend, or looks at a "works." Moreover, as the ex-addict struggles to earn a living and reestablish his personal relationships, his circumstances will often depress him. This internal cue may act most powerfully just when the addict is least likely to have the willpower to abstain.

Research on operant conditioning also suggests why this mechanism can exert an effect so long after the addict's last heroin injection. Failure, for one reason or another, to perform a previously rewarded behavior

120. Animal studies indicate that tolerance diminishes little simply with the passage of time. Joseph Cochin and Conan Kornetsky, "Development and Loss of Tolerance to Morphine in the Rat after Single and Multiple Injections," *Journal of Pharmacology and Experimental Therapeutics* 145, no. 1 (July 1964): 1–10.

121. Roy Pickens, Richard A. Meisch, and Travis Thompson, "Drug Self-administration: An Analysis of the Reinforcing Effects of Drugs," in *Handbook of Psychopharmacology*, vol. 12, p. 23.

does not extinguish the conditioning. Only engaging in that behavior over a long period without rewarding consequences can do this.[122]

As a result, lengthy abstention from heroin use—even in the presence of the cues to previous use—may not guarantee that the former addict can continue to stay off heroin. The addict may exert his willpower for long periods on the street, but the task may not become easier; and then, in the presence of especially strong cues, he may "fall."

Operant conditioning is not the only psychological mechanism implicated in the ex-addict's sudden craving for heroin and his return to heroin use. Classical, or Pavlovian, conditioning seems to be a major factor as well. We have already seen an example of this type of conditioning in the case of the laboratory animals whose sight of the beginning of the injection ritual became paired with their internal oppositional responses to the injected opiate. Gradually the sight of the ritual came to provoke the oppositional response, even before the drug entered the body.[123]

For our purposes here, we are interested in the Pavlovian conditioning of the withdrawal syndrome itself. During his life on the street, an addict will often suffer a heroin deficit and feel the onset of withdrawal. Gradually the stimuli of the street—the sight of a "works," a friend "shooting up," the sights and sounds of the copping area—become paired with the beginnings of withdrawal. These stimuli, then, acquire the power to elicit the feelings, and even the physical symptoms, of withdrawal, just as the sound of a bell, which Pavlov had paired with the presentation of food, developed the power to elicit the dog's salivation, Thus, a former addict, abstinent for years in prison, or even under a maintenance dose of methadone, may suddenly experience all the symptoms of opiate withdrawal when he returns to his home area, reads about addiction, or experiences some feeling which had been paired with his earlier heroin use. He not only interprets his discomfort, as a craving for heroin, but, in fact, he can relieve it by a heroin injection.[124]

There is no inconsistency between the explanation of heroin craving relying on operant conditioned responses to the discriminatory stimuli of the copping area, and that based on the classical conditioning of withdrawal symptoms. It is likely that both effects play a part in the phenomenon, probably together with others that we have not discovered.[125]

122. C. P. O'Brien, "Experimental analysis of conditioning factors in human narcotic addiction. *Pharmacology Reviews* 27, (1975) pp. 533–43.

123. Siegel, "Evidence from Rats That Morphine Tolerance Is a Learned Response," 503–4.

124. Roger E. Meyer and Steve M. Mirin, *The Heroin Stimulus: Implications for a Theory of Addiction* (New York and London: Plenum Medical Book Co., 1979), pp. 233, 240–44

125. Charles P. O'Brien et al., "Conditioned Narcotic Withdrawal in Humans," *Science* 195, no. 4282 (11 March 1977): 1000–1002. See also William A. Hunt, L. Walker Barnett, and Laurence G. Branch, "Relapse Rates in Addiction Programs," *Journal of Clinical Psychology* 27, no. 4 (October 1971): 455–56.

## The Addict as a Human Being

Our explanations for the extreme difficulty of curing heroin addicts have, up to now, proceeded from the mechanistic view that addicts were passive only—in other words, controlled by biochemical drug effects or conditioning mechanisms. These ways of looking at the matter are not necessarily invalid, but there is another dimension which we should not forget.

Though some may regard this view as unscientific because it treats a human being—and more particularly a heroin addict—as more than a collection of macromolecules and conditioned responses, heroin addicts are human beings, and, by and large, they use heroin because they like it. The neglect of this basic truth has caused us to make many errors in the past.

We must not forget that for many people heroin use is extremely pleasurable. Perhaps the author of a book about heroin entitled *It's So Good, Don't Even Try It Once* has exaggerated the euphoria, but there is no doubt that many addicts speak in almost reverential tones of the pleasures of heroin use.[126] Some feel that, despite the many disadvantages, social, legal, and medical, of heroin use, the pleasure they derive from the drug makes their use worthwhile.

The nonpharmacological satisfactions stemming from heroin use may also be extremely important to the addict. Typically, his friends are also addicts and he is embedded in their culture. Perhaps some have taught him the necessary street lore, even something so basic as how to use the drug, and perhaps he has taught others. We must remember that most of us, if presented with a package of heroin and a "works" (an eye dropper, a needle, a spoon, and a piece of rubber tubing), would not know what to do with them—even if we had decided to use heroin.

The addict's drug use permits him to enjoy his friends' company and esteem. Since his peer group consists of other addicts who share his perceptions about the worthwhile nature of heroin use, he will derive fellowship and psychological support from them.

In short, the addict, like the football fan, the bowler, and the member of a college history department, may have a high regard for the activity in which he and his peers engage. He is likely to have acquired a whole set of beliefs and values respecting heroin use—including the views that people who don't use drugs are unbearably "square" and that those who use drugs other than heroin are simply babies who are just playing around. To such addicts and their friends, only heroin users have the status that they desire and reward with approval.[127]

126. These are the words of Emmanuel, a young middle-class addict, in *"It's So Good, Don't Even Try it Once:" Heroin in Perspective*, ed. David E. Smith and George R. Gay (Englewood Cliffs, N.J.: Prentice-Hall, 1972), epigraph.

127. Robert S. Weppner, "An Anthropological View of the Street Addict's World," *Human Organization* 32, no. 2 (Summer 1973): 115.

Such views may be reinforced, not diminished, by the evident disadvantages of the addict's life. Once he has suffered for his views, strong dissonance mechanisms come into play, which help convince him that his views must be correct—or else why would he have suffered so much for them? To support such an opinion, he will exaggerate to himself the advantages of his condition and downplay the disadvantages.

The addict's peer group not only gives psychological support to his heroin use; it discourages his abstinence. The reformed addict represents a threat to the group's values, and cases are quite common where group members have used persuasion, temptation, and sometimes even intimidation, to bring an abstinent addict back to their ranks.

## The Life Style of the Addict

Though the rewards of peer approval and of conformity to what the addict values as proper behavior should not be underestimated, heroin addiction holds another attraction. For many addicts, both the drug effects and the peer approval are secondary. It is the life style of the heroin addict that they find most attractive.

For some, being a heroin addict is one enormous game.[128] The addict, after all, has a license to steal, in the sense that both he and society accept as an explanation that he must do so in order to support his habit. In other words, his stealing or selling drugs is no sin over and above that of being addicted to begin with. The most common self-image of the heroin addict is that of an outlaw. (The alcoholic's, on the other hand, tends to be that of a failure.) And outlaws are regarded as living exciting, romantic lives.[129]

The addict, moreover, has no problems of existential choice. He knows who he is; he is an addict. He knows what he is going to do from the moment he gets up in the morning until the time he goes to sleep at night; he is going to try to "score" heroin and to steal or hustle enough to do so. There are no distractions for this kind of addict. He has a far simpler life than we do. He is consumed with a single-minded and, in many ways, a very interesting and exciting game. Though we may think his situation unenviable, he may prefer it to any other he could attain. If he were not an addict, he might be unemployed—that is to say, nothing—or he might be a casual day laborer, a dishwasher, or a worker in any one of a large number of unpleasant, ill-paid, and low-status jobs. Knowing the menial alternatives available to him, the addict is hardly in a frame of mind conducive to cure.

Moreover, once he has stopped using heroin, these problems may intensify. Free of his identity as an addict, the former addict will still have

---

128. Dan Waldorf, *Careers in Dope* (Englewood Cliffs, N.J.: Prentice-Hall, 1973), p. 141.
129. Preble and Casey, "Taking Care of Business," pp. 22–23.

to cope with the world. Now he may have to experience the life and status of the busboy, the messenger, the dishwasher, or the unemployed. Whatever physical pain or depression his opiate use had suppressed will return to add to his general dissatisfaction with life. After considerable success in avoiding heroin use, he may suddenly feel a craving he cannot resist; or he may simply decide that bad as it was, his life as an addict was better. Some of the reasons should be familiar to those who have taken up cigarette smoking again after a long period of abstinence.

At a moment of high tension or after an upsetting event, such as the loss of his job or a fight with his wife, the addict may be able to convince himself, "What the hell. Just one won't hurt." Guilt over his behavior, plus an awakening of all the conditioning mechanisms that support addiction, often result in his subsequent use and readdiction. Regardless of the particular trigger, the addict may be "hooked" once more, and the whole cycle of detoxification, temporary abstinence, and our attempts to cure him may begin again.

## HEROIN AND CRIME

The last of our myths about heroin addiction is that heroin causes its users to become thieves who commit a great percentage of this nation's property crime. The term "myth" may be inappropriate here, since this view, though a considerable exaggeration, is to some extent true. The connection between heroin and crime is under intensive investigation at present and we cannot yet reach any firm conclusions about it. Nonetheless, it now looks as if the causal connection between heroin and property crime has been grossly overestimated in the past.

This is not to deny that heroin addicts commit a great deal of property crime in some areas. In Manhattan, for instance, about 25 percent of those arrested for the nondrug felonies (mostly burglary, grand larceny, and robbery) in 1971 were heroin addicts, and another 25 percent were heroin users who were not addicted at the time.[130] Unless one makes the very unlikely assumption that heroin users are vastly more likely to be caught for their crimes than are nonusers, this must mean that about half of the street crime in New York was committed by heroin users.

At one time, figures such as these were explained by the supposition that heroin produced an effect on the brain which led to moral weakness and crime.[131] If an intelligent citizen were asked today whether heroin use

130. Majda I. Sajovik and Sandra Karpis, "Crime Committed by Narcotic Users in Manhattan," in *Staff Working Papers of the Drug Law Evaluation Project: A Companion Volume to the Final Report of the Joint Committee on New York Drug Law Evaluation*, Department of Justice, National Institute of Law Enforcement and Criminal Justice, Law Enforcement Assistance Administration (Washington, D.C.: Government Printing Office, 1978), pp. 100–101.

131. Musto, *American Disease*, pp. 74–75.

caused crime, he would answer, "Of course. How else would addicts be able to afford the heroin they need?" In other words, although the well-known criminality of many heroin addicts is now accounted for by the external conditions associated with addiction, the belief remains that heroin addiction causes its users to become criminals.

It is true that many aspects of the drug and its treatment in our society make it very difficult for an addict to hold steady and legitimate employment. If an addict were a highly paid rock-music star, as we are told some are, he could probably afford his addiction without too much difficulty. Or, if he were a peasant in an agricultural society where the drug was cheap, and the demands his employment placed upon him were limited, he could remain addicted and support himself without stealing. But in our culture he is typically neither of these.

The addict usually is not very skilled in a society that tends already to demand more occupational qualifications than he possesses. His quest for heroin every six hours requires a considerable portion of his time and energy. The constant variation in the availability and potency of the drug on the street makes it difficult for him to stabilize his dosage enough to perform much useful labor. Holding steady employment is difficult when one tends to alternate between a lazy euphoria shortly after one injection and a feeling of heroin deprivation before the next.

In addition, arrests and other types of law enforcement harassment add to his difficulties in maintaining any kind of steady employment. And, of course, even if the typical street addict could hold down a steady job, he probably could not earn enough from it to afford his addiction at the high prices which the illegal market demands.

Nonetheless, the amount of predatory crime committed out of need to support heroin addiction seems not to be nearly so great as has been thought. Former calculations attempted to determine how much an addict spent on his habit and ascribed the total amount to the proceeds of street crime. Such estimates were widely accepted until someone compared the amounts allegedly stolen by addicts in New York City with the reported losses from crime there—and revealed that addicts alone were said to have stolen about ten times as much as was stolen in all the thefts reported to the police.[132] Obviously something was very wrong with the usual reasoning.

Nor can we explain the discrepancy between the amounts attributed to thefts by addicts and the total theft statistics by the fact that the latter figures are based upon police reports which considerably underestimate the total amount of victimization. The disparity is far too large for that; careful recent studies indicate that the underestimate in the theft figure is

132. Max Singer, "The Vitality of Mythical Numbers," *Public Interest* 23 (Spring 1971): 3–9.

by no more than a factor of three—and against this we must weigh the obvious fact that not all property crime is committed by addicts.

Probably the largest single cause of the exaggeration in the amount of theft by addicts was the considerable inflation of the average habit size and hence the sum of money that an addict had to raise.[133] Investigators took the word of addicts as to their habit size, not realizing that addicts consider a large habit a status symbol and, hence, are prone to exaggeration. According to one addict, "When they ask me the size of my habit, they're really asking me whether I'm a real man or a pipsqueak."

Moreover, investigators tended to neglect the fact that many addicts do not maintain their "average" habit size for long. Although many addicts at some point in their careers develop truly "ferocious" habits, most of them do not continue to use at such a high rate even while they remain addicted. Indeed, since tolerance to the effects of heroin in fighting withdrawal does not develop very quickly, and not nearly as quickly as tolerance to the euphoric effect of the drug, a sizable number of addicts continue to use heroin primarily to prevent withdrawal and continue to do this at relatively low dosages for substantial periods. The usual calculations, moreover, accepted the once-an-addict-always-an-addict myth, multiplying the average daily habit by the total time elapsed since the onset of addiction. This, of course, failed to take account of the fact that most addicts remain abstinent for various periods during their street life.

Another major fallacy in the addict theft figures was the investigators' assumption that the addict could gain no funds through legitimate employment and therefore that he had to steal the full price of his heroin habit. However, even street addicts sometimes earn some money through casual labor, especially in periods when their habits are under control. And a sizable number—though a minority—of addicts are able to hold continuous employment while addicted; indeed, some manage for years.[134] Presumably such addicts are more likely than most to have lower and more stable habits and to be less involved in the addict life style and values. One can only say "presumably" since no investigator has yet carefully studied this type of user.

The assumption that the addict could not work at all was compounded by the even more misleading belief that he had to raise all his funds from property crimes such as burglary, theft, and robbery. This is wrong on several grounds. First of all, many middle-class addicts do not commit any property crime—except perhaps for victimizing their parents or other relatives. Perhaps they simply lack the "street skills" which a thief must possess. Moreover, even the more common lower-class addict often has

133. Preble and Casey, "Taking Care of Business," pp. 17–21.
134. David Caplovitz, *The Working Addict* (White Plains, N.Y.: M. E. Sharpe, 1976), pp. 7–8.

sources of income which are neither earned nor illegal, such as welfare
payments and help from his family. And even the illegal earnings of
addicts do not all derive from thefts. Addicts raise almost as much
through nonvictim crimes—prostitution, pimping, and, most importantly,
selling heroin—as they do through property crimes.[135]

While the profits at the top of the heroin distribution pyramid are taken
by nonaddicts, a major share of the price of heroin on the street is the cost
of distribution at the lower levels. These profits are earned mostly by
addict pushers to support their own habits. Computing the price of a
heroin habit and assuming that an addict must steal all of this amount,
therefore, involves a kind of double counting. The price of heroin includes
the sizable profit at the retail level, which goes to feed the habits of the
many addicts who sell the drug.

Despite this, there is no doubt that heroin addicts are much more likely
to commit property crimes than are most other categories of individuals
that one could name. The problem is in determining to what extent the
demands of a heroin habit are responsible for the difference.

At first glance, it would seem that his addiction would have to be the
major cause of whatever theft the addict commits, since the cost of his
habit is typically the addict's major expense. On the other hand, and
although at first it seems counterintuitive, one can make a strong
argument that heroin use is not a major factor in turning addicts into
criminals. The alternative explanation is that criminality causes heroin
addiction instead of the other way around, or, more precisely, that both
heroin addiction and criminality are caused by the same thing.

This is more than merely an assertion that heroin addicts commit so
much crime because a great many criminals use heroin. In sociological
terms, the view is that in the black and the Spanish-surname lower-class
urban American subcultures, heroin use has acquired a meaning and a
symbolic value which is tied to particular deviant groups.

These crime-prone groups use heroin for a host of purposes. Heroin use
sets off their members further from the rest of society; emphasizes the
negation of, and superiority to, the dominant society's values; binds their
members more closely to each other through shared experiences; ensures
the resentment and hostility of their members toward the law enforcement
apparatus; and helps socialize and attract new members into the groups.

Such an explanation of the relation between heroin and crime is
consistent with several things that we know about heroin addicts. It has
often been observed that the criminalistic heroin addict was most likely a
criminal before he became a heroin addict. Virtually every study of the

135. William H. McGlothlin, "Drugs and Crime," in *Handbook on Drug Abuse*, ed.
Robert L. DuPont, Avram Goldstein, and John O'Donnell (Washington, D.C.: Government
Printing Office, 1979), p. 359.

onset of addiction shows that, on the average, the addict's first arrest precedes his first use of heroin by about one-and-a-half years.[136]

The view that, rather than causing crime, heroin use has merely been adopted by various criminalistic groups is also consistent with the wide variations between different areas of the nation in the percentage of arrested criminals who are heroin addicts. This variation exists even among places where the cost and extent of heroin addiction are about the same. If addicts were merely financing their habits through crime, one would expect that the amount which they had to raise would be the primary determinant of their criminality. The large variations in the criminality of addicts from place to place, however, may be more consistent with the criminal subculture theory.

The subcultural view also helps explain the extremely high percentage of those arrested for property crimes who have used heroin but are not currently addicted.[137] These users are under no compulsion to finance their habits, yet they continue to engage in criminality. Under the subcultural view, this is not surprising. The nonaddicted user may maintain ties to the heroin-using subculture but, instead of stealing to feed his heroin habit, may steal to indulge a taste for clothes, cars, women, or anything else that requires money.

If we focus on the amount of crime committed by most heroin addicts, rather than on whether they commit crimes, a different picture emerges. A considerable amount of evidence indicates that the amount of property crime an addict commits is related to the size of his habit. We have long known that even among those who were delinquents before they used heroin, there tends to be a jump in criminal activity after addiction.[138] Now three separate studies indicate that some addicts steal a great deal more while in a "run" of heroin use than they do while abstinent or using the drug only intermittently. When we chart the amount stolen by an addict together with his periods of highest use (from self-reports confirmed by other data), there appears to be a very sizable correspondence—and the amounts stolen are often prodigious.

For instance, one investigator asked two different samples of what would have to be called "hard-core" California addicts to recall their periods of daily heroin use. He then checked their arrest records and discovered a far higher arrest rate during those periods both for property

136. C. Jack Friedman and Alfred S. Friedman, "Drug Abuse and Delinquency," in *Drug Use in America*, app., vol. 1, p. 409.

137. William I. Barton, "Heroin Use and Criminality: Survey of Inmates of State Correctional Facilities, January 1974," in *Drug Use and Crime: Report of the Panel on Drug Use and Criminal Behavior*, National Institute on Drug Abuse and Research Triangle Institute (Washington, D.C.: Government Printing Office, 1976), app., pp. 419–40.

138. Chein et al., *The Road to H*, pp 61–62.

TABLE 1

Mean Individual Arrest Rates and Self-Reported Behavior During Daily and Other-Than-Daily Narcotic Use

| | 1st Sample N = 198 | | 2d Sample N = 109 | |
|---|---|---|---|---|
| Variable | Daily Use | Other Than Daily Use | Daily Use | Other Than Daily Use |
| Arrest rates/ nonincarcerated man-year | | | | |
| Drug offenses | 1.09 | .50 | 1.09 | .49 |
| Property offenses | .72 | .35 | 1.07 | .40 |
| Self-report data (nonincarcerated time) | | | | |
| Criminal activity (% time) | 47 | 17 | 52 | 12 |
| Number of property crimes/man-year | 104 | 25 | 155 | 17 |
| Income from crime ($1,000/man-year) | 91 | 17 | 113 | 10 |
| Drug dealing (% time) | | | | |
| With profit | 23 | 7 | 21 | 5 |
| Without profit | 35 | 9 | 37 | 13 |
| Employment (% time) | 39 | 69 | 39 | 58 |

and for drug offenses. More relevant here, the addicts' self-reports of criminality were far higher for their daily use periods (see table 1).[139]

Another recent study, of a number of Baltimore addicts, emphasized the incredible volume of crimes committed by the sample members. According to the study, the 237 members of the sample committed more than 500,000 crimes during their average of eleven years on the street. The addict's rate of criminality was six times as great while he was using heroin daily as during his periods of abstinence or occasional use.[140] Finally, a study of a sample of Miami addicts also showed a prodigious rate of property criminality—which was at its highest rate during daily heroin use.[141]

Several less precise studies confirm this type of relationship. In general, they tend to show an extent of criminality between two and six

139. William H. McGlothlin, M. Douglas Anglin, and Bruce D. Wilson, "Narcotic Addiction and Crime," *Criminology* 16, no. 3 (November 1978): table 6, p. 309.

140. John C. Ball et al., "The Criminality of Heroin Addicts When Addicted and When Off Opiates," study prepared for the National Institute on Drug Abuse, 9 October 1980. Mimeographed.

141. James A. Inciardi, "Heroin Use and Street Crime," *Crime and Delinquency* 25, no. 3 (July 1979): 335–46.

times as great during a run of heroin use as when the addict is abstinent or using heroin intermittently.[142]

The solid majority of drug treatment studies confirm this general point by showing a sizable drop in property criminality along with the decrease in heroin use during treatment.[143] Though this finding has come under considerable attack on methodological grounds and does not seem to be universal, it is supported by virtually all of the careful participant observation and interview studies of those under treatment.

The methadone studies, particularly, conclude that, for a sizable percentage of addicts, entry into treatment is marked by a cessation of hustling and criminal activities. For another group, treatment is accompanied by a sharp drop in property crime while the hustling that continues tends to revolve about selling some of the prescribed methadone.[144]

Though there are formidable methodological problems in drawing conclusions from studies of overall crime rates, even these tend to support the view that the cost of heroin during a "run" is an important determinant of an addict's criminality. The better designed studies show a short-run positive correlation between increases in the price of heroin and increased property crime, as well as broad relations over time between the number of addicts and the property crime rate.[145]

In other words, there is empirical support for the commonsense view that the pressure to come up with the price of his heroin habit is a major determinent of the number of crimes committed by many heroin addicts. However, we cannot conclude on present evidence that heroin addiction is the only or even usually the most important factor in the addict's criminality. Nor can we relate the contribution of heroin addiction to the total volume of property crime in the United States—except to say that it is far less than the popular literature has portrayed.

Finally, we should note that virtually all of our studies of addict crime are based on the samples of addicts who come to our attention. These far-from-normal samples are usually composed of addicts arrested for crimes or those who have appeared for treatment, and their friends. It may well be that the criminality of most addicts is very much less. They may have fewer, shorter, or less intense runs of heroin; or they may cope with their

---

142. See Robert P. Gandossy et al., *Drug Use and Crime: A Survey and Analysis of the Literature*. U.S. Department of Justice, National Institute of Justice (Washington, D.C.: Government Printing Office, 1980), pp. 82–87.

143. McGlothlin, "Drugs and Crime," in *Handbook on Drug Abuse*, pp. 361–62.

144. Edward Preble and Thomas Miller, "Methadone, Wine and Welfare," in *Street Ethnography: Selected Studies of Crime and Drug Use in Natural Settings*, ed. Robert S. Weppner (Beverly Hills, Calif.: Sage Publications, 1977), p. 236.

145. George F. Brown, Jr., and Lester P. Silverman, "The Retail Price of Heroin: Estimation and Applications," *Journal of the American Statistical Association* 69, no. 347 (September 1974): 603–5.

runs differently. What we do know is that some addicts are extremely prolific criminals who, on a per-person basis, commit a staggering amount of crime during their periods of heavy heroin use. Moreover, we also have reason to believe that such addicts are numerous enough in many areas to constitute at the least a considerable nuisance and probably a significant social problem.

The precise strength of the connection between heroin use and property crime is a matter of considerable importance in determining the advantages and disadvantages of various governmental policies toward the drug. Any effect of a legal policy which strengthens this connection by raising the price of heroin should be accounted a cost of that policy—to be weighed against any benefits it produces.

However, the connection, whatever it is, between heroin and crime is only one of the areas where our law influences the social problem of heroin use. It might be said that the largest costs imposed by heroin today are those due, directly and indirectly, to our use of the criminal law to enforce the prohibition of the drug. For this reason, it is essential that we examine in greater detail the nature and consequences of our legal policies. This will be the subject of the next chapter.

# 2 ■■
# HEROIN PROHIBITION

$T$he effects of the criminal law upon the heroin problem arise mainly from two categories of governmental actions—those aimed at the supplier and those aimed at the user of the drug. Law enforcement efforts of the former type attempt to lessen the availability of heroin; those of the latter kind try to prevent or reduce the use of heroin by people who manage to gain access to the drug.

In this chapter we focus on the former efforts, leaving the latter for discussion in chapter 5. It is the policies aimed at supply which determine most of the characteristics of any drug prohibition. In the United States, Prohibition itself, during its fourteen-year reign, did not even forbid the use of alcohol; rather, it was only the manufacture and sale of beverage alcohol that the Volstead Act and most state laws made criminal.[1] And, though we cannot expect the reader to take it on faith at this point, it will turn out that legal restrictions on use are relatively unimportant in limiting consumption. Before describing our present prohibition of heroin supply, however, it will be helpful to sketch out a bit of history.

## THE HISTORY OF AMERICAN OPIATE LEGISLATION

Vigorous attempts to prevent opiate use are of relatively recent origin. It has long been known that opium is addicting, but, until the nineteenth

---

1. Austin, *Perspectives on History*, p. 128.

century, use of the drug was conceived of as a personal weakness rather than a social problem.[2]

Probably the first nation to become concerned with the social consequences of opium use was Imperial China. During the eighteenth and nineteenth centuries, Chinese exports—tea, pottery, silks and the like— were enormously prized in Europe. Because China was virtually self-sufficient and needed few of Europe's products, it demanded payment for its goods in gold and silver. European merchants and their governments, as a result, searched for some way to ease their growing and frightening imbalance of trade.

In the latter part of the eighteenth century, the British discovered a sizable market in China for Indian-grown opium, and gradually encouraged the production and shipment of more and more of that drug. The Chinese authorities soon became alarmed, although not primarily on public health grounds. It is true that opium smoking was regarded as a vice, very much as cigarette smoking is today (or was until the Surgeon General's report of 1963 put the matter on a much firmer public health foundation). However, the Chinese government worried primarily about the increasing drain on their foreign exchange.

It was this concern that moved China to attempt to shut off opium importation—an effort which, as every student of colonial history knows, led to the Opium War of 1840–41. There it was decided by force of arms that China could not prevent the Western nations from paying for its goods with opium.

Chinese imports of opium rose from 340 tons per year during 1811–21 to 6,500 tons in 1880. Domestic consumption increased even faster, since in the 1860s China attempted to save its foreign exchange by repealing its own ban on opium cultivation.[3] Over the same period, missionaries, many of whom were American, began to protest the opium trade on grounds of morals, public health, and Chinese sovereignty. Although their campaign against Western shipment of opium into China was discernible much earlier, it did not attract much support in the United States until after the Spanish-American War.

In 1898, with the annexation of the Philippines, the United States for the first time acquired an Asian colony. Opium, there, was regarded as both a social and a health problem, and the American public began

2. Brecher, *Licit and Illicit Drugs*, pp. 6–7.

3. Leonard P. Adams, "China: The Historical Setting of Asia's Profitable Plague," in Alfred W. McCoy and Cathleen B. Reed, *The Politics of Heroin in Southeast Asia* (New York: Harper & Row, 1972), app., pp. 367–69. For the modern Chinese version of these events, see Compilation Group for the "History of Modern China" series, *The Opium War* (Peking: Foreign Languages Press, 1976), pp. 4–5, 8–10, 17–18.

increasingly to listen to the sermons on the evils of the international opium trade.[4]

## THE PROBLEM IN THE UNITED STATES

The United States had had its own problems with opiates before this, though the public did not connect them with the international opium trade. During the Civil War, the relatively new drug, morphine, injected by the still more novel hypodermic syringe, was used—promiscuously by today's medical standards—to treat large numbers of battlefield injuries. As a result, after the war, the nation was left with a sizable population of morphine addicts. This problem, however, was treated almost exclusively as medical in nature—yet another kind of war injury. Morphine, the drug which not only caused but also alleviated the symptoms of the addiction, remained freely available.[5]

The next major development in the American awareness of opiates came in the wake of one of the nation's recurrent racial problems. The Chinese coolies, who in the 1860s had been brought to build the western railroads, stayed on to compete with white Americans for jobs. Perhaps because of this, a series of unpleasant practices were ascribed to them, and their smoking of the exotic drug opium received a considerable share of the attention.

The prohibition of opium smoking had several attractions for those caught up in the anti-Chinese feeling. It stigmatized a practice associated with that despised minority. Insofar as opium provided the Chinese with their energy and ability to tolerate hardship (a very different view of the drug's effects than is generally held today), its prohibition was seen as depriving the aliens of an unfair advantage over American workmen.[6] Finally, many hoped that the Chinese, deprived of access to their drug in the United States, might simply go back to China.

The first major American legislation in the narcotics field was responsive to the resentment against the Chinese. Beginning with a San Francisco ordinance of 1875 forbidding the keeping of opium dens, prohibitions on opium smoking were gradually adopted and extended in one western state after another. Congress joined in as well, raising the tariff on smoking-opium (a prepared, relatively mild form of the drug) in 1883; prohibiting the importation of such opium by Chinese in 1887; and prohibiting completely its importation in 1909.

4. Joseph D. McNamara, "The History of the United States Anti-Opium Policy," *Federal Probation* 37, no. 2 (June 1973): 15–16.

5. Terry and Pellens, *The Opium Problem*, p. 69. This thesis has come under criticism recently; see Austin, *Perspectives on History*, pp. 199, 203–4.

6. Austin, *Perspectives on History*, pp. 210–14.

The effect of these laws has never been investigated carefully. It has, however, been argued that their two principal consequences were to shift use to the still-legal morphine from smoking-opium, and to create a class of illegal opium smokers among those who clung to the use of that drug.[7]

Although the stridency of the campaigns against opium smoking continued to grow, the general outlines of our present narcotics policy were laid down in the Harrison Act of 1914, in response to quite different pressures. Because China had been the leading target of American missionaries, we had developed a unique relationship with that country, in which religious groups were far more vocal, and perhaps even more powerful, than commercial interests. Because of the missionaries' agitation against the opium trade, the United States had taken a major part in the international negotiations which resulted in The Hague Convention of 1912, outlawing the international nonmedical opium traffic.[8]

It was realized then that the United States itself, apart from its restrictions on smoking opium, exercised virtually no comprehensive control of its own internal traffic. Opium smoking was a relatively minor cause of opiate addiction here, but "tonics" and patent medicines were virtually unregulated, and many contained opiates. It was said that the largest group of addicts consisted of southern white women who did not even know they were addicted. They knew only that their "tonic," taken regularly, prevented the sickly feeling that came on whenever they missed their medicine.[9] Obviously this situation was inconsistent with a major thrust of the Progressive movement. Patent medicines containing morphine or opium were dangerous, and it was the function of government to protect the consumer from harmful foods and drugs. It is perhaps no coincidence that the Harrison Act was passed approximately midway between the Pure Food and Drug Act (1906) and Prohibition (1920).

Finally, the rise of the medical profession also played a part. Just around the turn of the century, physicians began upgrading their profession. More stringent educational and licensing requirements became part of this as knowledge of physiology and medicine expanded, until according to one authority: "Somewhere between 1910 and 1912 in this country, a random patient, with a random disease, consulting a doctor chosen at random, had for the first time in the history of mankind, a better than fifty-fifty chance of profiting from the encounter."[10] Patent medicines were a major competitor of professional medical treatment, and in the

7. Brecher, *Licit and Illicit Drugs*, pp. 42–46.

8. Musto, *American Disease*, pp. 24–53.

9. Brecher, *Licit and Illicit Drugs*, pp. 3–7, 17–19.

10. Lawrence J. Henderson, quoted in *Familiar Medical Quotations*, ed. Maurice B. Strauss, 1st ed. Little, Brown and Co., 1968), p. 302. See also Herrman T. Blumgart, "Caring for the Patient," *New England Journal of Medicine* 270 (1964): 449.

physician's view, a most inferior one. As a result, the American Medical Association campaigned vigorously for the prohibition of opiates outside of medical channels.

## THE HARRISON ACT

In any event, the Harrison Act of 1914 made illegal the importation, sale, or possession of opiates except within medical channels. Such drugs could be obtained legally only if pursuant to a physician's prescription, and pharmacists were required to keep detailed records to prevent diversion.[11]

Even more important than the Harrison Act itself were its implementing policies and regulations. The language of the statute could be read either as permitting a physician to prescribe narcotics to fulfill an addict's need or as forbidding this practice. The legal issue involved the interpretation of an exception to the general prohibition on the supply of opiates. Such drugs might be prescribed by a physician "in the course of his professional practice and where said drugs are dispensed or administered to the patient for legitimate medical purposes," and the question was whether this language permitted the physician to prescribe opiates solely to prevent his patient's going through withdrawal. The authorities enforcing the law immediately took the position that the language of the Harrison Act did not comprehend mere maintenance of addicts on opiates, and began prosecutions of physicians who acted according to a contrary interpretation.[12]

The first case reaching the U.S. Supreme Court affirmed the validity of these prosecutions, and although the Court later changed its mind about the meaning of the Harrison Act, the American policy forbidding prescription of opiates to maintain addicts had already been firmly laid down. From then on, it was enforced by medical associations, state laws, threats of federal prosecution, and a whole range of governmental and nongovernmental sanctions; nor was it disputed by the vast majority of medical practitioners, who regarded narcotics addicts as extremely difficult and unsatisfying patients.[13]

The effect of this was not only to eliminate the "scrip doctors" who promiscuously gave out prescriptions for opiates, but also to deter those who would have maintained addicts under careful medical supervision. For a while, the authorities tolerated, indeed encouraged, the organiza-

11. Austin, *Perspectives on History*, p. 203.

12. David F. Musto, "Evolution of American Narcotic Controls," in *Drug Use in America*, app., vol. 3, pp. 340–42.

13. Alfred R. Lindesmith, *The Addict and the Law* (Bloomington: Indiana University Press, 1965), pp. 3–34. See also Trebach, *The Heroin Solution*, pp. 126–31.

tion of specialized clinics out of the control of individual private practitioners to maintain addicts on opiates. Gradually, however, even these
were closed down.

It is by no means clear even today whether this occurred because of
abuses that cropped up in the clinics or because the federal authorities
held to a generally prohibitionist philosophy. In any event, by 1923, with
the closing of the last remaining maintenance clinic (in Shreveport,
Louisiana) there were no legitimate sources of opiates for maintaining
addicts.[14]

From then until the 1960s, the national narcotics policy changed only in
the direction of progressive increases in the penalty structure. Indeed, the
only significant modifications made since have been the repeal of certain
mandatory minimum sentences and the allowance, under many restrictions, of methadone maintenance.[15]

## THE EFFECTS OF THE HARRISON ACT

The consequences of sixty years of opiate prohibition are subject to some
dispute. Several facts are clear, however. First, the type of addict has
changed dramatically from the pre–Harrison Act days. Then, opiate
addicts tended to be middle-class and middle-aged women from rural
areas or small towns. They took their morphine or opium orally and
certainly were not regarded as particularly criminal—though their use was
not without problems, as pictured in Eugene O'Neil's autobiographical
Long Day's Journey into Night.

Within fifteen years after the passage of the Harrison Act, the addict
was much more likely to be male, urban, lower-class, and young.[16] He
was typically an injector of heroin, and regarded as a serious criminal
problem not only with respect to the violations of the drug laws inherent
in using a prohibited substance but with respect to property crimes as
well.

A considerable part of this transition can be explained by the change in
the legal treatment of opiates. Because of the difficulties of smuggling and
concealment, more potent opiates such as heroin became favored over

---

14. Dan Waldorf, Martin Orlich, and Craig Reinarman, *Morphine Maintenance: The
Shreveport Clinic, 1919–1922* (Washington, D.C.: Drug Abuse Council, 1974) pp. 2–18.

15. Musto, "Evolution of American Narcotic Control," pp. 343–46. Michael X. Morrell,
"Maintenance of Opiate Dependent Persons in the United States: A Legal Medical
History," in *Drug Use in America*, app., vol. 4, *Treatment and Rehabilitation*, pp. 552–53.

16. Terry and Pellens, *The Opium Problem*, pp. 474–75, 481–86. This trend has continued
since; and addicts are more likely to be ethnic minorities. See John C. Ball, "Two Patterns
of Opiate Addiction," in *The Epidemiology of Opiate Addiction in the United States*, ed.
John C. Ball and Carl D. Chambers (Springfield, Ill.: Charles C. Thomas, 1970), pp. 93–94.

morphine and—even more so—over opium. Similarly, injection grew to be favored over drinking in a "tonic" because of the greater effectiveness of the former means of administration per milligram of opiate.

Because all their legitimate sources of opiates had been cut off, those who remained addicted could receive drugs only from criminals. To derive social support for their use, to maintain their supply, and to avoid detection, they were forced to join a comparatively tight, drug-using subculture. Since opiate users were already stigmatized and in close contact with criminals, opiates themselves acquired a criminal meaning and their use came to be seen as a way of defying the mores of the wider society.[17]

Finally, the price of opiates had increased so enormously that to sustain a habit required considerably more than many addicts could earn through honest work. This was especially so since the search for a continuous drug supply consumed a great deal of their time and effort.

There are those who assert that these changes are outweighed by the likelihood that the percentage of opiate addicts in the population has been markedly reduced since the Harrison Act. Though this is probable,[18] it is by no means certain, since the estimates of the number of addicts before 1914 are even less reliable than our data as to the number today.[19] Moreover, even if addicts constituted a higher percentage of the population before 1914 than today, addiction was then so much less personally destructive and socially costly that the balance is clear. It is hard to deny that opiates have become a far greater social problem since the passage of the Harrison Act.

## LAW ENFORCEMENT TODAY

The transformation in the nature of the addict has not been the only change in the opiate problem since the Harrison Act. For some time after the passage of the Harrison Act, the resources put into law enforcement were minimal.[20] A relatively small number of prosecutions, together with

17. Edwin M. Schur, *Narcotic Addiction in Britain and America: The Impact of Public Policy* (Bloomington: Indiana University Press, 1962), p. 145. John A. O'Donnell, *Narcotic Addicts in Kentucky*, United States Public Health Service Publication 1881 (Washington, D.C.: Government Printing Office, 1969), pp. 242–43.

18. Brecher, *Licit and Illicit Drugs*, p. 62.

19. For a review of the morass of conflicting statistics, see Terry and Pellens, *The Opium Problem*, pp. 1–52.

20. Musto, *American Disease*, p. 184. "Expenditures for narcotic enforcement rose from about $270,000 in Fiscal Year 1919 to slightly more than $500,000 in Fiscal Year 1920, and for several years thereafter it ranged between one-half and three-quarters of a million dollars annually." There were about 170 agents in 1920 and only about 270 from 1929 through the Depression.

the ever-present threat of others, were all that was necessary to intimidate the vast majority of private medical practitioners, and no great police and prosecutorial energy was needed to close the maintenance clinics that sprang up. Gradually, however, as the nature of the addict changed, so did the supply system and the government response to it until, at present, the attempt to make heroin unavailable requires a great deal of energy and resources.[21]

To understand more about the restrictions on heroin supply, we must look more carefully at how the law and its agents go about their tasks and why they manage to do as well or as badly as they do. In all this discussion, the dominating fact will be that law enforcement is a contest against an intelligent and highly motivated adversary. Every improvement in the techniques of heroin enforcement will be met by a change in the drug supplier's tactics tending to offset the police advantage. Similarly, progress in the traffickers' art will tend to be countered by changes in law enforcement techniques. Thus, the enforcement of heroin prohibition tends to change even more rapidly than does the pattern of drug use on the street—though, of course, the two influence each other.[22]

Despite the volatility of the subject, let us organize our consideration of law enforcement efforts to reduce the availability of heroin into three major activities—eliminating the production of heroin, preventing its entry into the United States, and stopping its sale to the ultimate user.

## PREVENTING PRODUCTION ABROAD

### Enforcement Abroad

There are several reasons why one might regard attempts to prevent the production of heroin as preferable to either of the other strategies. First of all, it is generally true that the closer law enforcement can get to the origin of a prohibited material, the easier the task of suppression becomes. Often this is because the illegal market can best be seen as a pyramid, with the smallest number of traffickers closest to the source. The place of greatest vulnerability to law-enforcement effort is often where the market is most concentrated.

It is likely that in the heroin market the highest level of concentration occurs where the morphine base—the opium product which is usually smuggled out of the poppy-growing region—is processed into heroin. Our

21. One estimate of the amount spent on enforcement of the heroin laws in 1975 was $620 million. See Robert L. DuPont, Director SAODAP, "Social Cost of Drug Abuse," in *Federal Drug Enforcement*, Hearings before the Permanent Subcommittee on Investigations of the Committee on Government Operations, Senate, 94th Cong., 1st sess., 1975, Part I, p. 255.

22. Moore, *Buy and Bust*. pp. 15–47, 128–78.

efforts to take advantage of this assumed vulnerability have been disappointing, however. French and American law enforcement officials were apparently able to break the "French connection" and to destroy the famous Marseilles laboratories, which then manufactured a great part of the heroin destined for the American market. But it turned out that the necessary level of technology was not very high and that labs could be set up elsewhere with little difficulty. Indeed, they were set up again in Marseilles. For five years after the major crackdown in 1973, there were no indications that heroin laboratories still existed in France. Then, between 1978 and 1980, enforcement authorities seized three in the Marseilles area.[23]

The problem is that heroin can be manufactured with simple and easily available chemical equipment. Except for the morphine base, the necessary raw materials are cheap and widely available. Acetic anhydride, the primary chemical used in converting morphine into heroin, costs about 15 cents per pound, and, in the United States alone, production amounts to over 700,000 tons.[24]

On the other hand, the idea of interfering with heroin trafficking at its source is not necessarily faulty. Although manufacture turns out to be difficult to suppress, the cultivation of the poppy raises different opportunities. It takes place in the open, where the plants are visible for a considerable period before their opium can be harvested. Airplanes and helicopters permit surveys from the air, and a high-technology industry has developed—with Department of Justice encouragement—the Multispectral Opium Poppy Sensor, capable of spotting clandestine poppy fields with considerable accuracy.[25]

One would think that once the opium fields were discovered, it would be a relatively easy matter to destroy those producing for the illegal market. This view is buttressed by our feeling that, despite the sizable demand for heroin in the United States, the nation seems to produce no illegal opium. One can argue from this that the job can be done, and from the fact that few resources are necessary to do it, that it can be done cheaply as well.

To be sure, recent experience with marijuana in the United States may have eroded our confidence in the ease of suppressing illegal cultivation. Fifteen years ago, law enforcement agencies were confident that virtually no marijuana was grown in the United States. Indeed, there was a statutory presumption that any marijuana found within the United States

23. John Bacon, "Is the French Connection Really Dead?" *Drug Enforcement* 8, no. 1 (Summer 1981): 19.

24. Cabinet Committee, "World Opium Survey 1972," pp. 415–16, 419–20.

25. Irwin C. Swank, "North American Heroin," *Drug Enforcement* 4, no. 1 (February 1977): 8–9.

had been illegally smuggled in from abroad.[26] (The presumption was struck down by the United States Supreme Court in 1969 on constitutional grounds.) Though the bulk of the nation's supply still seems to come from abroad, a goodly and growing fraction of its enormous consumption of marijuana today (estimates run about 10 percent) is being grown in the United States. Sizable marijuana plantations have been discovered in rural areas of California and Hawaii;[27] and there are strong indications that even greater areas of domestic cultivation have not yet come to police attention. If the United States is unable to suppress the growing of marijuana within its own territory, it may not be as easy as had been thought to root out the opium poppy in less developed nations.

## The Difficulty of Enforcement Abroad

The main problem is not the lack of a technical ability to suppress opium cultivation. There are enough airplanes and defoliants available for that. The problems go much deeper. We are dealing here with sovereign nations, whose willingness to let American airplanes spray defoliants on their own people is likely to be limited at best. And the repercussions of doing so over their objections are, at the international political level, unthinkable.[28]

Even where nations have cooperated fully with the United States in suppressing their opium cultivation, the results have not always been completely satisfactory. The Mexican government recently has made use of American technical assistance—planes and defoliants—to wipe out many of its illegal poppy fields.[29] It is disputed whether the United States government urged it to do the same to marijuana cultivation, but it is clear that the Mexican government has seen fit to attempt to defoliate its marijuana fields as well.[30]

One difference between marijuana and opium, however, is that large parts of the marijuana plant can be smoked, while only the resinous exudate of the poppy flower is used in heroin production. As a result, though the sprayed opium poppies die before they can produce their

26. See the discussion of this presumption in *Leary v. United States*, 395 U.S. 6, 37–43 (1969).

27. Joseph Flanders, "Sinsemilla Harvest," *Drug Enforcement* 7, no. 1 (March 1980): 36.

28. McCoy and Reed, *Politics of Heroin*, pp. 358–60.

29. Swank, "North American Heroin," pp. 3–12.

30. Peter Bensinger, head of the Drug Enforcement Administration, in his answers to written questions from Senator Culver, denied American urging or financing of the operation. See U.S., Congress, Senate, Committee on the Judiciary, *The Mexican Connection,* Hearings before the Subcommittee to Investigate Juvenile Delinquency of the Committee on the Judiciary, Senate, 95th Cong., 2d sess., 1978. On United States efforts to halt heroin importation: *Eradication and Enforcement in Mexico-Southwest Border Control*, pp. 45–46.

opium, the marijuana plants can still be harvested quickly and sent to market. The smoking of marijuana contaminated by the defoliant paraquat may cause lung injury and other consequences out of proportion to any penalty either that the law would impose for their activity, or that the drug enforcement authorities—at least at the higher levels—desire.[31]

Moreover, Mexico is an atypical opium producer. Though it seems to lack the capability to enforce its law on the ground, the Mexican government does seem to be concerned about an indigenous opiate problem, and perhaps even more with diversion of the proceeds of some drug sales to clandestine antigovernment activities. Most of the nations in which the poppy is cultivated do not think of themselves as having a problem with opiates—and they do have many other problems that they regard as genuinely urgent, such as health, education, and industrial development.[32]

Alhough opium cultivation is not crucial to the overall economies of these countries, the poppy is often quite important to farmers in particular regions, both as a cash crop and for local use. Frequently, the central government has little force at its disposal to bring to bear on these relatively inaccessible areas, and it worries about promoting insurgency by alienating the poppy growers—who can be quite numerous.

In Turkey, for example, an estimated 40 percent of farmers raised the poppy in 1971. The plant has been cultivated for centuries in the highlands of Anatolia and is the basis of the local cuisine. Its leaves are eaten in salads and the oil from its seeds is as important in cookery there as is olive oil in the cuisine of Spain. No wonder American interest in the suppression of opium cultivation has been so much greater than that of the Turks. For a while Turkish cooperation was purchased by the United States with various forms of persuasion and inducement—costing some 35 million dollars in one year—but their ban on cultivation turned out to be only temporary.[33]

Another major problem with attempting to suppress cultivation in a nation with a sizable indigenous market is illustrated by the Iranian experience. For hundreds of years, opium had been used in rural areas of Iran, especially among more traditional, older citizens. For various reasons, the government decided to prevent nonmedical opiate use and, hence, prohibited cultivation of the poppy. So far as we can tell, within a few years; the Iranians were successful at enforcing this ban but their

31. The dangers of paraquat are still in dispute. For a compendium of information, see U.S., Congress, House, Select Committee on Narcotics Abuse and Control, *The Use of Paraquat to Eradicate Illicit Marihuana Crops and the Health Implications of Paraquat-Contaminated Marihuana on the U.S. Market*, 96th Cong., 2d sess., 1980.

32. Jesse Kornbluth, "Paraquat and the Marijuana War," *New York Times Magazine*, 13 August 1978, reprinted in *The Mexican Connection Hearings*, pp. 152–53.

33. Cabinet Committee, "World Opium Survey 1972," pp. 431–51.

neighbors, Afghanistan and Turkey, continued to allow opium production. Various groups soon sprang up to smuggle foreign opium into the country, across the large, sparsely settled and rugged border areas; and heroin, being more concentrated and easier to transport, began to gain a foothold in the Iranian markets. When it appeared, after a few years, that executing the drug smugglers they caught had no measurable effect on the problem, the Iranian authorities decided that the cure was worse than the disease and repealed their ban on opium cultivation.

Since most nations that grow the poppy also have a domestic market for opium, the threat of drug smuggling from abroad provides them with an additional reason not to prohibit cultivation by their own farmers.[34] Indeed, it may well be that laws against opium cultivation are too costly to enforce within one nation unless it has only a small domestic market, or is isolated by geography or law enforcement from other producing regions.

## Crop Substitution

For some years, a major component of the United States' international heroin policy has been the introduction and encouragement of crop substitution programs in other nations. These programs have had the dual purpose of enlisting the self-interest of the opium farmer in the reduction of his opium acreage and of lessening his opposition to laws prohibiting poppy cultivation. The American effort to induce Turkish farmers to replace opium poppies with wheat and barley has thus far been the most publicized such attempt, though similar measures are being tried in Thailand and other countries. During the two years that the Turkish ban on cultivation was in effect, farmers there protested that the compensation—or as much as reached them of the cash paid their government—was inadequate; and the extent of their actual crop substitution during that period was probably much exaggerated. In Thailand, we are informed, the process—if it ever succeeds—will take generations.[35]

The basic problems again and again have been both the inertia of rural populations toward replacing a commercially and culturally important crop, and the unsuitability of opium growing regions for the cultivation of anything else. It often turns out that the land is not fertile enough to grow other crops, or that the distance from markets is too great for economic production of whatever can be grown. In short, despite American efforts, cultivation of opium will continue for some time to come to earn many farmers by far the highest income per acre of their land.

## The Size of the American Market

Probably the most important reason for pessimism over American efforts to prevent the production of opium abroad is the comparative smallness

---

34. Ibid., pp. 436–37.
35. Halper, *The Heroin Trade*, pp. 17–20.

of the illegal market in the United States. It is estimated that the entire American consumption of heroin in 1979 was less than five tons. Perhaps the figure is unnaturally small since the nation may have experienced not a permanent lowering of heroin use but, rather, merely one of its periodic and temporary shortages. Let us take for comparison the figure in 1971 during a heroin glut. The American consumption then amounted to about ten tons.[36] Compare this amount to the 1979 estimated production of opium in various nations. Inasmuch as the bulk of heroin traffic in the United States during the 1960s and early 1970s was sustained by Turkish opium production of only 80 tons, the result is more than merely striking (see table 2).

TABLE 2
Production of Opium in Tons

| Burma | 500 |
|---|---|
| Thailand | 50 |
| Laos | 50 |
| Mexico | 50 |
| Afghanistan | 800–1000 |
| Pakistan | 800–1000 |

Since a quantity of opium may be refined into about one-tenth its weight of heroin, the opium production listed in table 2 is over twenty times American consumption. The table does not even mention Iran, for which no reliable estimate is available but which has clearly emerged as a major producer. Iranian opium production now not only provides for that nation's own large domestic consumption and, hence, has dumped its former suppliers upon the world trade, but also has added a considerable but unknown amount of heroin to the illegal markets in other countries.

The calculation in terms of area is even more depressing. The entire illegal American market could be satisfied by the production from twenty-five square miles of land.[37] As a result, American efforts to prevent the growth of illegal opium would have to be successful, not only in areas such as Turkey, India, and Mexico—where the governments have a reasonable degree of control over their populations—but also in areas such as Afghanistan and the Golden Triangle of Thailand, Laos, and Burma, where the plant is cultivated by tribes uncontrolled by any government.

Even if the United States could accomplish it, the complete suppression of opium cultivation might not prevent widespread addiction. Modern chemistry has created several families of synthetic opiates—two of

36. *Narcotics Intelligence Estimate*, p. 4. Heller, "The Attempt to Prevent Illicit Drug Supply," p. 384.
37. *Federal Strategy for Drug Abuse and Drug Traffic Prevention*, p. 39. *Narcotics Intelligence Estimate*, p. 40.

which, the etonitazenes and the Bentley compounds, contain members about five hundred times as potent as heroin on a per weight basis. Many of these drugs, properly "cut," would probably do about as well as heroin from the user's viewpoint. Some are not enormously difficult to synthesize from widely available industrial chemicals and the stronger ones, as one might gather, are much easier than heroin to conceal and smuggle. The most likely result, then, of our cutting off the supply of natural opiates would be the production, in the United States or elsewhere, of artificial opiates for the illegal market. That this has not yet happened may be some indication that law enforcement efforts against heroin itself have not yet been effective enough to call into being a market for a substitute drug.[38]

Finally, the suppression of poppy cultivation would in some ways be harmful. The products of the poppy—opium, codeine, morphine, and, in some nations, heroin itself—are extremely useful in medicine. To some extent, synthetic opiates such as methadone and meperidine (Demerol) might substitute for them—but the substitution would not be a completely satisfactory one and medical care would suffer noticeably if physicians were forced to do without natural opiates.

Regulation of Production

The medical importance of natural opiates, plus the enormous political difficulties of gaining and enforcing a complete ban on poppy cultivation, has caused American foreign policy to veer toward a less ambitious goal. The United States has sometimes sought agreements under which opium cultivation could be subjected to regulations aimed at allowing production for medical purposes and for indigenous use but preventing diversion to the illegal market.[39] The problem here is that once the existence of opium fields does not, in itself, show criminal production, law enforcement must work at the much more difficult problem of preventing the diversion to the illegal market of relatively small amounts of an easily concealable substance.

Turkey's experience with what is called the "poppy straw" method of opiate production provides a textbook illustration of the difficulties of this approach.[40] If, instead of being lanced to produce opium, the pods of the opium flower are allowed to remain in the field until they are completely dry, the technology of producing opiates from this poppy straw becomes a great deal more complicated, and a sizable factory becomes necessary for economic production.

38. Apart, of course, from that which presently existed for diverted methadone. See also Heller, "The Attempt to Prevent Illicit Drug Supply," p. 385.

39. Ibid., pp. 386–87.

40. *Narcotics Intelligence Estimate*, p. 38.

In the 1974–75 crop year, when the Turkish government repealed its brief prohibition on poppy cultivation, it attempted to prevent diversion by forbidding the traditional harvesting of opium and requiring that the dried pods, no longer usable in the illegal traffic, be sold to the government for domestic processing, or export. Unfortunately, it turned out that the Turkish poppy straw did not have quite the composition of alkaloids which foreign processors desired. In addition, the processing capacity within Turkey was so limited that large amounts of poppy straw had to be stored in the open outside the facilities and left vulnerable to the weather. The Turkish government is presently building a new processing plant, but the capacity of this will only be twenty thousand tons of poppy straw per year—with a fifty thousand ton stockpile already on hand. As a result, the government has been forced to incur a significant degree of unpopularity by reducing the acreage allotment for poppies and it is not clear to what extent farmers are simply disobeying the new government rules.

In all those nations which lack sufficient police apparatus to exert a high degree of control over the behavior of their citizens, preventing diversion as a practical matter is next to impossible. Indeed, even in the relatively well-policed United States, diversion of legally manufactured drugs, such as barbiturates and amphetamines, has been a serious problem.[41] When we try to impose rules preventing diversion on a resistant peasant population far from the seats of governmental power, the results are predictable. Moreover, national pride being what it is, it is hard to imagine that many nations could be induced to admit that they are unable to prevent diversion and hence should ban cultivation completely—or that some acceptable system could be set up to adjudicate the matter.

It has been suggested—apparently quite seriously—that with relatively little active support from the opium growing nations the United States could choke off the supply of illegal opium at its source simply by buying up the entire crop. At present prices this would cost far less than is now spent on the enforcement of the heroin laws.[42] Unfortunately, as American agriculture clearly demonstrated during the 1950s, guaranteed government purchase is an agricultural subsidy which acts to induce farmers to raise more and more of the subsidized crop.

Moreover, the chances are that no matter how high a price opium producers were offered for their crop, the criminal drug traffickers could simply bid higher on the relatively small amount they require. We must remember that what the farmer gets paid is less than 1 percent of the price of heroin on the street.[43] No matter how much, within reason, a

41. *Narcotics Intelligence Estimate*, app. D, p. 131, estimates that 250 million dosage units of controlled substances were diverted at the retail level in 1978.

42. McCoy and Reed, *Politics of Heroin*, p. 358.

43. Cabinet Committee, "World Opium Survey 1972," p. 427.

government paid opium farmers for their crop, they would still maximize their income by withholding enough to supply the illegal market, and delivering the rest of their production to the official opium-purchasing agency.

## The Importance of Enforcement Abroad

Despite the many difficulties in preventing the production of opiates at their sources, this prevention strategy will remain important so long as we take the view that a lesser amount of heroin coming into the United States is better than a greater amount. The amounts that can be suppressed in this manner are substantial. Though the political and practical obstacles are severe, the method is probably still the most cost-effective means of lowering the availability of heroin in the United States.

Thus, the Mexican crop-spraying program is generally credited with the sizable drops in heroin availability in the United States that have occurred in several recent years. Although Mexico apparently has remained the single largest heroin supplier to the American market, its contribution has dropped sharply. As a result of the crop spraying, the total amount of the drug entering the United States fell by about 35 percent between March of 1976 and March of 1978. In that two-year period the average purity of seized heroin samples in the United States decreased from 6.6 percent to 3.5 percent, with the price of street heroin rising proportionately. It is inconceivable that this kind of an effect could have been achieved by any other means of enforcement.[44]

Entirely apart from the amounts involved, if opium production outside the United States were completely uncontrolled, American customs authorities would then have to worry about shipments and passengers from many areas—rather than about imports along a relatively few known, though admittedly changing, routes.

In addition, the capital requirements for entry into the business of producing and importing heroin would be considerably reduced, and nationals from many more countries would have the contacts to commence large-scale trafficking. This would, in turn, spread the opportunities to deal in the drug to many more groups within the United States. In short, the fewer the places opium can be cultivated for the illegal market and the less the total amount grown, the lower the volume of heroin there will be to reach the United States, and the more practicable will be the task of law enforcement in interfering with the rest, both at the borders and within the United States.

Still, we cannot expect enforcement in producing countries to do much more than periodically disrupt the production of opium for this country's

44. The Strategy Council on Drug Abuse, *Federal Strategy for Drug Abuse and Drug Traffic Prevention* (Washington, D.C.: Government Printing Office, 1979), p. 10. *Narcotics Intelligence Estimate:* pp. 12–13.

market. The poppy can be cultivated in a sizable number of nations and there is no reason to think that any long-term shortage in the supply for a market as small as that in the United States will not be made up by production somewhere. This may occur fairly quickly through changes in the international pattern of supply whereby producers not affected take up the slack. Or, the shortage may be made up in a somewhat longer time by new cultivation in an area which had not previously grown the poppy.[45]

## The Politics of Enforcement Abroad

Although enforcement in other nations has notable benefits, it is dangerous to rely too heavily on this technique of suppressing heroin. As a political matter, it is almost too easy. There is an ever-present pressure upon American political officials to adopt policies which, if they fail, can be blamed on other countries rather than upon their own. And the immediate costs of changes in behavior such as cessation of cultivation will appear to be borne by those in other nations—Turkish farmers, Burmese government officials, etc.—rather than by Americans.

To some extent, this type of enforcement is attractive because so many of its costs to the United States are hidden. Most people understand that the governments of the opium growing nations do not have as much incentive to attack the problem as does the United States government, and that the United States must therefore make such enforcement worth their while. What most people do not realize is that American efforts to export enforcement of its heroin prohibition will appear on the books to be a great deal cheaper than in fact they are. The understandable tendency of those involved in any activity to underestimate the cost of their efforts pushes them toward attaching to other budgets as many as possible of the necessary payments. As a result, costs of American heroin enforcement often are labeled military or economic aid.

This kind of solution becomes even more attractive when, as often happens, there is no bureaucratic opposition to the misaccounting, because no government outlay of funds is required. Where American payments to other nations consist of trade concessions or other nonpecuniary benefits bestowed by the world's richest and most powerful nation, they do not appear to cost anything at all. Or where American officials make threats which they may not have to carry out, they may seem to have gotten their way costlessly.

These policies do have costs, of course. In various ways payment must be made for the benefits one nation bestows upon another and the persuasion—some call it bullying—a nation uses may not only cost it goodwill but may be quite expensive in the long run.

45. Heller, "The Attempt to Prevent Illicit Drug Supply," pp. 384–85.

An often-ignored cost related to American attempts to suppress opium growing abroad has been the constraint this has introduced upon the nation's domestic marijuana policy. The legalization and licensed sale of marijuana is a policy option currently receiving some attention in the United States. Regardless of whether one supports it or not, it clearly should be within the realm of political debate.

Nonetheless, it has been argued that the international repercussions of any move toward legalization would be so serious as to make this course impossible. Many of the nations the United States depends on for aid in suppressing opium also consider themselves to have a marijuana problem, and their view of that drug is far less benign than that even of many conservative Americans. As a result, it is contended that if the United States "breaks the line" on marijuana it will forfeit the cooperation of many other nations in the more important task of coping with its heroin problem.[46]

## PREVENTING SMUGGLING

The second major law enforcement strategy against heroin is preventing the smuggling of the drug into the United States. Here the importance of policing is indicated by the sharp increase in the price of heroin once it has crossed the borders of the United States. According to drug enforcement agency figures, in late 1978 a kilo of heroin sold in Bankok for less than $4,500, while on the other side of the border, in Hawaii, the price was $120,000.[47]

Nonetheless, enforcement at the borders is every bit as beset with difficulties as is enforcement in the opium producing nations. This time, instead of comparing United States heroin use to world opiate production, we must compare the nation's consumption of less than ten tons with the yearly total of 100 million tons of freight brought into the United States. And, if we also consider the fact that a staggering 250 million individual border crossings into the United States take place each year, the magnitude of the task of preventing smuggling becomes clear.[48]

46. U.S., Congress, Senate, Committee on the Judiciary, *Marijuana Decriminalization*, Hearing before the Subcommittee to Investigate Juvenile Delinquency, Committee on the Judiciary, Senate, 94th Cong., 1st sess., 1975, statement of Donald E. Miller, Chief Counsel, Drug Enforcement Administration, pp. 25–27.

47. *Narcotics Intelligence Estimate*, p. 20.

48. United States Bureau of the Census, *Statistical Abstract of the United States: 1980 (101st ed.)* (Washington, D.C.: Government Printing Office, 1980), pp. 253, 673, 677. U.S., Department of the Treasury, Customs Service, *Update '75* (Washington, D.C.: Government Printing Office, 1976), p. 9. See also Office of Drug Abuse Policy, *Border Management and Interdiction—An Interagency Review*, 4–10 (Washington, D.C.: Government Printing Office, 1977).

The consequences of a serious attempt to prevent smuggling along just one of the United States' borders have been shown dramatically. Although the famous Operation Intercept of October 1969 was primarily a method of bringing pressure on the Mexican authorities by demonstrating the American government's concern about the drug problem, it also revealed the difficulties of expending great efforts to stop drugs at the borders. For the three weeks the operation lasted, when all persons and vehicles crossing into the United States from Mexico were searched, traffic was hopelessly snarled, great economic dislocations ensued, and Mexico not only protested vehemently but threatened retaliatory action.[49]

The task, moreover, is not limited to examining the people and freight legally entering the United States. A great amount of marijuana is brought in each year by private airplanes which illegally cross the borders and land at out-of-the-way airstrips, and we have no idea how much comes ashore from fishing boats and launches at deserted beaches.[50] If contraband of far less value per pound can enter the United States so easily, we have virtually no chance of stopping those impelled by the much greater profits of heroin smuggling.

This is not to say that we cannot improve our performance in this task. A number of studies have suggested that means should be found to improve coordination among the ten agencies involved in controlling the United States borders (the Customs Service; the Immigration and Naturalization Service; the Drug Enforcement Administration; the FBI; the Bureau of Alcohol, Tobacco and Firearms; the Department of Defense; the Federal Aviation Administration; the Coast Guard; the Department of Agriculture; and the Public Health Service).[51] Nonetheless, the estimate is that at present about 5 percent of the heroin entering the United States is seized at the borders.[52] We can perhaps do better than this, but it is hard to believe that law enforcement agents can more than double or triple the percentage seized without causing intolerable inconvenience to those legitimately entering the United States or else paying for a vast increase in the technology and manpower devoted to preventing smuggling.

If such an investment would correspondingly increase the dangers of

49. Cabinet Committee, "World Opium Survey 1972," p. 457.

50. *Narcotics Intelligence Estimate*, chapter 11. "Stopgap: How Much Marijuana Can Be Prevented From Entering the U.S.?" *Drug Enforcement* 7, no. 1 (March 1980): 38–39.

51. Comptroller General of the United States, *Report to the Congress: Gains Mode in Controlling Illegal Drugs, Yet the Drug Trade Flourishes*, General Accounting Office, 25 October 1979 (Washington, D.C.: Government Printing Office, 1979), p. 66.

52. Customs seized 1029 lbs. of an estimated 6–7 tons of heroin entering the U.S. in 1975. Testimony of Vernon D. Acree, Commissioner of Customs, U.S. Customs Service, *Oversight Hearings on Narcotics Abuse and Current Federal and International Narcotics Control Effort*, Hearing before the Select Committee on Narcotics Abuse and Control, House, 94th Cong., 2d sess., 1976, p. 427.

apprehension to the organizers or financiers who mount heroin smuggling operations, improvements in detection at the borders might be very important. If the risks of the business could be significantly raised, the amount of the drug entering the United States might be lowered considerably.

Unfortunately, the smugglers who are detected at our borders are generally merely "mules," paid for undergoing these very risks. They are not very knowledgeable about the overall operation and hence are unable to assist much in police investigations. As a result, even a considerable increase in the rate of interdiction of heroin at our borders would not have much effect on the major traffickers in the drug. Their only extra costs would be the loss of the additional heroin seized and the higher wages needed to compensate their mules. Since heroin has far less value outside the United States before it is smuggled in, the value of the material lost at the border would still be low compared to the profits of successful smuggling; and the mules are usually of such low economic status and desperate financial need that compensating them for the increased risks they might bear would still be quite inexpensive.

In short, though enforcement at the borders obviously removes some heroin from the United States market and imposes some costs upon traffickers, it is unlikely that any conceivable increase in the efficiency of this strategy could greatly change the illegal market for heroin. Indeed, smugglers could probably tolerate many more seizures at the borders without significantly lowering their importation of heroin.

## ENFORCEMENT WITHIN THE UNITED STATES

While efforts in other countries and at the borders are aimed at reducing the quantity of heroin reaching the American market, law enforcement within the nation has a more complex effect. To some extent, of course, this area of police activity reduces the total amount of heroin accessible to the ultimate consumer. Its more interesting functions, however, are structuring the heroin market and controlling which potential customers have access to the drug and which do not. In other words, law enforcement within the United States helps determine not only the amount of heroin used, but the distribution of users as well.

Any detailed picture of the way law enforcement acts to accomplish these tasks will necessarily be quite complex, since to an even greater extent than at the borders, various enforcement agencies within the United States have overlapping jurisdictions, act independently of each other, and sometimes work at cross purposes. Federal enforcement officials work within the United States as well as abroad and at the borders, and often their investigations within the nation are the result of leads developed in foreign countries or of a find during a border search. Theoretically, they concentrate on major traffickers, and thus aim more at the total supply of heroin, but in many cases small-time operators are swept into their net.

State enforcement agents may be employed by a division of the state police or a statewide drug enforcement agency, and occupy an intermediate position between affecting the total supply of the drug and influencing the areas of availability and unavailability within their jurisdictions. Finally, local enforcement officers, who may be either members of the drug squad or simply beat-patrol policemen, primarily affect which areas and even which individuals have access to heroin.

Each police agency regards itself as having some specific mission and expertise in an area of narcotic enforcement—though considerable overlap and rivalry may develop among them and the particular interest of an agency may change over time. Generally speaking, federal agents consider their specialty the mounting of long undercover and conspiracy investigations in an effort to suppress relatively high-level dealing and to put whole organizations out of business.[53] At the other end of the spectrum, the patrolman is more likely to be concerned with not letting narcotic sales get too far out of hand and too visible on his beat.[54]

## The Local Police Function

The importance of the beat patrolman, and the local police in general, cannot be overestimated. What can happen when they fail to "keep the lid on" is shown in the experience of New York City in December 1976. At that time the law enforcement resources usually spent to drive low-level heroin dealing underground seemed to disappear, and a genuine metamorphosis took place in the heroin market.

What appears to have happened is that heroin sellers, seeking to avoid the high penalties threatened by the recently enacted "Rockefeller Drug Law," began to employ for the riskier jobs juveniles not subject to that law. At about the same time, the juvenile branch of the criminal justice system became so overloaded that the police simply stopped arresting juveniles for heroin offenses.

As a result of these developments, a new level of distribution appeared, whose sellers no longer had to make themselves inaccessible to the police and could therefore become publicly available to potential customers. The *New York Post* told the story with its customary verve:

> The heroin bazaars are out in the open. Street peddlers hustled back and forth from car to car, touting their wares.

53. U.S., Congress, House, Select Committee on Narcotics Abuse and Control, *Second Interim Report, New York Hearings: Drug Law Enforcement*, 95th Cong., 1st sess., 1977, p. 17.

54. James Q. Wilson, *Varieties of Police Behavior* (Cambridge: Harvard University Press, 1968), p. 31.

. . .There are few cops to be seen. Most of the pushers appeared to be between the ages of 12 and 15—hired by older dealers. . . .

My first buy was made on the corner of 147th St. and Eighth Ave., a mini-market, where a group of teenagers stood huddled together to ward off the cold. . . .

One ran briskly over and served a man in a car that had pulled up just before mine. The driver was white and drove a car with New Jersey plates. Residents in the community say many whites buy drugs at this market—particularly from New Jersey—because it is close to the George Washington Bridge. . . .

One of the teenagers asked me what I was looking for.

"Dope," I said.

He pulled out a wad of cellophane bags wrapped in a rubber band and asked, "How many?" He called the dope "Death Boy" and each bag had a little red stamp to identify the brand.

"How much is it?" I asked.

"Ten dollars a bag," he said, running his thumb over the stack of packets, each the size of a Sweet 'n Low, with the deftness of a card hustler.

"I'll take two," I said, handing him the money as he handed me the dope. "Is it any good?"

"Sure it's good; do you want to taste it?" he said. . . .

Next, I went to an open air market at 114th St. and Lenox Ave. As I drove up, I was spotted by a young pusher who was standing among a group of men and women warming themselves next to a garbage can that held burning rubbish.

He winked at me. I nodded at him and he strolled over to the car window.

"We're selling quarters and ripdowns of the Brown Bomber," he said with an easy smile. "A quarter sells for $50 and a ripdown for $25."

"What is a ripdown?" I asked.

"Where have you been?" he said with a look of disbelief on his face.

"I've been out of town for awhile."

"Well, a ripdown is half of a quarter or about three and a half spoons of dope. A quarter is seven spoons," he replied, rattling off the information like a stockbroker quoting the ticker.

"I'd like a ripdown."

He pushed off the car, into which he had been peering through the open window, and walked to the corner where a fast-moving courier handed him something. When he came back he had a bag of dope that had been ripped in half. He gave me the dope; I gave him the $25.

"Is the dope any good?" I asked.

"This is the best brown dope around," he replied. . . . [55]

---

55. John L. Mitchell, "It's Easy to Score at the Corner Drug 'Store,'" *New York Post*, 9 December 1976, reprinted in *New York Hearings*, pp. 31–32.

After considerable public outcry, the necessary criminal justice resources were made available—diverted from what other crimes we do not know—and the New York police suppressed the open-air heroin markets. Of course, this did not end retail heroin dealing, but it did considerably lessen the availability of heroin to newspaper reporters and other potential customers from outside the area.

The fact that the newly applied police resources drove the heroin selling back indoors is important. To see the significance of this we must appreciate that the police constitute only one of the two major restraints on heroin dealing. The other is predatory crime.

## The Heroin Dealer as Crime Victim

It has often been pointed out that law enforcement works best when it is alerted by the victim of a crime, as in a robbery or rape, or where tangible evidence of the crime remains behind for examination and study—as in embezzlement or homicide. Where all the parties to a transaction not only make no effort to report it to the police but do all they can to hinder investigation, and where, in addition, guarantees of privacy inhibit police evesdropping, wiretapping, and intrusive searches, the police are at a particular disadvantage. Of course this is the case with respect to all "nonvictim" or "consensual" crime, where, by and large, the police are singularly ineffective at preventing illegal transactions between willing buyers and sellers.[56]

What even moderate police effort can do, however, is to drive that dealing underground. Heroin dealers, for instance, do not sell openly on the street in most areas. Nor do they generally sell from accessible, publicized locations—for the obvious reason that if they do, they may be observed by the police and arrested.

The law then forces the dealers to move into back apartments, hallways, and other areas that tend to be free of police presence, both because of constitutional restrictions and because of insufficient police resources. It is here that dealers run a severe risk from predators. Heroin is an extremely valuable commodity, and since the seller is unable to complain to the police that his stock in trade was stolen, he becomes fair game for the numerous thieves and musclemen that abound in just those areas where heroin is most available.

The heroin dealer is extremely vulnerable to losing his profits and working capital as well as his heroin. Though he may be in a somewhat stronger position to complain to the police if he is robbed of money rather than of an illegal drug, the disadvantages of attracting police attention and

---

56. Herbert L. Packer, *The Limits of the Criminal Sanction* (Stanford: Stanford University Press, 1968), p. 151.

having to answer embarrassing questions about the source of his wealth are generally enough to deter his complaint.

The loss of his property in a robbery is not all the heroin dealer must fear. He may be robbed by an acquaintance or someone he can identify. This kind of robbery is among the most dangerous we know of, since the robber must realize that some form of retaliation will follow unless he acts to prevent it. As a result, robbery by someone known to the victim is very often accompanied by execution, and is a major factor in our surge of what are now commonly called "drug related" killings.

Nor is the risk of violence to the heroin seller confined to robbery and its aftermath. In certain circumstances he may be subjected to the violent efforts of competitors to gain a larger market share by putting him out of business.

Of course, the heroin seller can lessen his risk by hiring protection in the form of his own musclemen and bodyguards. However, this not only increases his costs but also exposes him to the danger that his protectors may decide that they can handle his enterprise without him.[57]

Admittedly, there is a rough analogy between the risks of violence or theft in the chain of heroin distribution and those in the legal marketplace. Hijacking of legal liquor, cigarettes, or jewelry is hardly unknown, and sometimes the means of competition in legitimate industries become overvigorous. Nonetheless, the difficulties of complaint to the police or other enforcement agencies by both buyers and sellers; the necessity of doing business in places where the police cannot intervene directly; the inability to make long-term, enforceable supply or sales contracts; the many disputes caused by the constant disruption of the market; and the fact that most of the participants in the activity must be constantly armed and alert—all abound in the case of heroin suppliers and escalate both the costs of physical protection and the risks to life and property.

Some indication of the high level of violence in heroin distribution can be gleaned from the Detroit murder statistics. In 1975, Detroit took first place in the homicide statistics—to replace Atlanta as the murder capital of the United States—and retained this position for 1976 as well. The next year the murder rate dropped by 27 percent, in part, the police said, because the narcotics squad's manpower was greatly increased. Since a high percentage of the killings were "narcotics related," the homicide rate could be lowered much more effectively by exerting additional pressure on the heroin dealers than by strengthening the homicide squad.[58]

The predation in the heroin area affects the buyer as well as the seller. It is true that the further up the chain of distribution one goes, the greater are the rewards of relieving the buyer of his cash, either through armed

57. Moore, *Buy and Bust*, pp. 23–24, 43–44.
58. Uniform Crime Reports, Federal Bureau of Investigation, 1974, 1975, 1976.

robbery or by selling him an inactive powder instead of heroin. Nonetheless, the user at the bottom of the chain faces in lesser degree most of the very same dangers of predation that inhibit the seller.[59]

Indeed, this very danger has been cited by one investigator as a major reason for the low "relapse" rate of GI's who had been addicted in Vietnam:

> Today in the United States almost anyone, middle class or otherwise, is only two handshakes away from a reasonably safe, dignified "connection" to buy marijuana. Buying heroin, as many returnees have discovered, is a very different matter. If you are not familiar with a heroin-using group, you have to go cold to one of the roughest parts of town and search around. Your chances of getting gypped, beaten up, or "ripped off" are excellent.[60]

## The Effect of Law Enforcement

Law enforcement, of course, does more than merely increase the danger of violence and theft in heroin trafficking. At all levels of heroin marketing, the constant risk of apprehension requires that dealers take expensive precautions over and above those they must take to guard against predation.

Every seller of heroin, whatever his level, must try to protect against the possibility that his customer may be an undercover federal agent or a "flipped" informer, whom the agents have already caught and have "turned" to help them make cases. Suppliers must guard against their telephones being tapped or their conversations bugged; and they are forced into what may be expensive and difficult methods of hiding their wares from police searches. All of these precautions, which make police detection more difficult, both raise suppliers' costs of doing business and make it more difficult for them to find and be found by possible customers.[61]

Finally, law enforcement does have a direct effect. It seizes a significant amount of heroin—though less than does enforcement outside the United States and at the borders. And it puts a certain number of suppliers out of business—at least temporarily.[62]

59. Richard Woodley, *Dealer* (New York: Holt, Rinehart & Winston, 1971), pp. 5–7.

60. Norman E. Zinberg, "Rehabilitation of Heroin Users in Vietnam," *Contemporary Drug Problems* 1, no. 2 (Spring 1972): 290.

61. Moore, *Buy and Bust*, pp. 15–23.

62. See Carol A. Atkinson, "The Effects of Law Enforcement Activity on a Population of Opiate Abusers," in *Problems of Drug Dependence 1980: Proceedings of the 42nd Annual Scientific Meeting, The Committee on Problems of Drug Dependence, Inc.*, ed. Louis Harris, National Institute on Drug Abuse, Research Monograph Series, no. 34 (Washington, D.C.: Government Printing Office, 1981), pp. 199–205.

The Difficulty of Law Enforcement

Despite the effect of both law enforcement and predation on the heroin market, the fact is that heroin is still widely available in the United States. Addicts and users in great numbers have access to it with varying degrees of difficulty; and, in some areas, it is easily available to almost any resident. As a result, we must ask why we do not do a great deal better in choking off the supply of heroin to its users. We have seen the obstacles to doing this with respect to enforcement in other countries and at the borders, but the question remains why the job cannot be done simply through application of the criminal law within the United States.

Often it is contended that we could do this if only the police concentrated on high-level traffickers and ignored the far-easier-to-catch but correspondingly more numerous street-level dealers. The argument is that if there were no large-scale suppliers there would be nothing for the small dealers to sell, and that jailing street-level heroin sellers in our urban ghettos is—to use the usual analogy—like bailing out the ocean with a bucket.

Part of the problem is that until the higher levels of the trade are suppressed, low-level dealing will continue to exert a claim on police resources. We have seen in New York's experience with the open-air market the effect of ignoring the street-level dealers. More important, law enforcement must not only concentrate on the high-level suppliers but must identify and catch them as well, a task of extreme difficulty considering their incentives to take precautions. Indeed, a major reason why the police arrest lower-level operatives in the heroin market is the hope that various forms of pressure on these arrestees will make them "turn" and provide evidence against their suppliers. The problem is that to get any substantial number of such leads the police must strain their resources by arresting a large number of lower-level dealers, in search of a lucky break that will lead them further up the chain.[63]

Those in the heroin supply business are often quite intelligent and, at least at the higher levels, make large enough profits to allow them to be very cautious in preventing the police from finding out about their activities. Indeed, their objective may be even less demanding than keeping their identity from discovery by law enforcement agents. They may really need only to prevent the police from building a provable case against them.

Some traffickers make sure they deal only in long-term relationships with those whom, because of family ties or previous experience, they can trust not to yield to police pressure.[64] Often their intermediaries are so

63. James Q. Wilson, *The Investigators* (New York: Basic Books, 1978), p. 42.
64. Moore, *Buy and Bust*, pp. 23, 45–47.

eager for a share of the profits that they are willing to accept the risks of detection—and, being heroin traffickers themselves, they make unreliable witnesses if ever they should decide to testify against their employers.

Other traffickers make the police task difficult by remaining in the business only for a relatively short period. They may make their quick profit and then get out—often into another area of criminality—to be replaced by someone else before the police have had time to build their case. Moreover, even if the police do catch them, relatively little is accomplished. The profits are so huge that the risk seems worthwhile to others contemplating the venture; and since such part-time operators are in business only for a short time, the imprisonment of even a significant number of them has little effect on the overall market.[65]

In their effort to escape punishment, traffickers are aided by two major constraints upon the police—the constitutional protections of the privacy of the citizen and the shortage of police resources. Actually, these two police problems are connected because compliance with the constitutional restrictions on their activities greatly increases the amount of time and effort the police must expend in developing their cases.

Although, as we will see, the police often break the rules, they do not usually ignore them entirely. As a result, some heroin suppliers will inevitably be so careful or lucky that the constitutional protections of their (and our) privacy will make it impossible for the police to catch them. It may be that the escape of a certain percentage of heroin traffickers is simply part of the price we pay for the rules under which we live—but that does not make the job of law enforcement any easier.

For the most part, however, the constitutional protections do not insulate heroin suppliers from the law but merely require the police to build their cases the hard way and spend their resources in time-consuming, difficult investigations. The difficulty here is that the police often lack the resources to do this. At the higher levels, investigations can be enormously expensive and time-consuming; while at the lower levels, where cases are much easier to make, there are so many suppliers that the police cannot arrest them fast enough.

## Deterrence and Isolation

Part of the problem is that, with anything like the resources we currently devote to law enforcement, neither deterrence nor isolation, the two most important mechanisms by which the criminal law acts to repress crime, work at all well here.

The theory of deterrence is simple: if we catch and punish a high enough percentage of wrongdoers, the rest will be unwilling to risk the

65. Ibid., p. 101.

same fate and, hence, will behave themselves. Unfortunately, law enforcement is unable to make the chances of apprehension so great that no rational criminal would undertake trafficking in heroin. At the higher levels of trade, the risk is too low and the profits too large. The 1971 border price for smuggled heroin at the Port of New York City was about $10,000 per kilogram while the wholesale price in New York was $22,000 per kilogram. At these prices, a wholesaler could turn a quick profit of over half a million dollars on a suitcase full.[66]

Even if the chances of apprehension and severe punishment were enough to frighten most people out of engaging in the heroin trade, many might still take the risk. Some are simply more reckless and optimistic about their cleverness in escaping detection than others may be. Or they may regard the rewards in money, in excitement, and in life style as worth the danger. Moreover, as law enforcement drives more competitors out of the market and makes the drug more scarce, both the price of the drug and the profits from dealing in it rise. Thus, each imprisonment of a trafficker acts not only to deter others but also to increase the financial rewards for those entering the business.[67]

Nor is the input of police resources very effective in deterring dealing at the lower levels of the heroin traffic. To a sizable extent, those lower in the chain are addicts whose need for heroin makes them much harder to deter at any given level of risk. And there are so many of them that it would take enormous police resources to catch enough to deter most of the rest.[68]

The other major mechanism of the criminal law is isolation. This is premised on the commonsense view that we make our society safer by apprehending and imprisoning individuals who have committed crimes, so that they cannot do us any further harm. If it required a rare skill or organizational talent to go into the heroin business, one might believe that somehow we could isolate enough of the suppliers to make a difference. Apparently, however, there is more than enough talent to go around, and for each heroin dealer arrested, there are usually several able to step into his place. Moreover, the failure of deterrence guarantees that the risk involved will not cause a shortage of those willing to try.

In theory, if an entire heroin organization were arrested, including the

---

66. *Narcotics Intelligence Estimate*, pp. 38–39.

67. Mark Moore believes that increased law enforcement may decrease the net rewards of heroin trafficking when nonmonetary rewards such as security are considered. See Moore, *Buy and Bust*, pp. 6, 10–12.

68. While not deterring addicts from dealing, law enforcement can influence them to sell only to known addicts by using the "buy and bust" technique. This effectively raises the price of heroin to neophyte users and, thus, discourages new consumers. See Mark H. Moore, "Policies to Achieve Discrimination on the Effective Price of Heroin," *American Economic Review* 63, no. 2 (May 1973): 270–77.

lieutenants and "Mr. Big" himself, it would be so disorganized that it could not recover. In practice, this does not happen very often since it is extremely difficult to put out of action all the members of any large organization at one time. Since there are usually enough members left with sufficient knowledge to carry on, damaged organizations have a way of rebuilding themselves quite quickly.

Even when a whole organization does go out of business, its demise may be barely noticeable. The market either brings about the expansion of other groups to fill the need or, after a time, calls a completely new organization into being. In 1955–56, the entire wholesale tier of the San Antonio heroin distribution chain was virtually eliminated as a result of Senate investigatory hearings. In a short time the dealers who had formerly been in the retail traffic replaced the wholesalers, and the market continued. There was some increase in price, either because the new smaller wholesalers could not buy in as large a quantity or because of a perceived increased risk of doing business, but essentially nothing changed.[69]

## Heroin in New and Old Areas

This is not to say that deterrence and isolation are completely ineffective against heroin trafficking. In areas where heroin has not gained a foothold, local police generally can prevent a retail market from developing. In fact, this is the major way in which law enforcement controls the pattern of heroin use in the United States.

The heroin-free areas tend to be populated by the middle class, and the police there usually have a level of resources comparatively high in relation to the criminal activity they must contend with. As a result, they are able to devote more attention to the relatively small number of heroin suppliers. Entirely apart from the police manpower available, sellers in these areas face a higher risk of detection, simply because there are fewer of them. They are unable to fade into any addict subculture; and in those areas where heroin appears but rarely, its presence often calls forth great public attention—both citizen cooperation and demands for police action by those who are used to voicing their desires effectively.

The availability of a greater range of alternatives to illegal conduct can increase the deterrent effect of the law upon potential heroin sellers. Being middle-class, the residents of these relatively heroin-free areas are likely to have other options open to them, apart from violating a criminal law which those about them take very seriously.

69. Lawrence J. Redlinger, *Dealing in Dope: Market Mechanisms and Distribution Patterns of Illicit Narcotics*, Ph.D dissertation (Ann Arbor, Mich.: University Microfilms, 1970), pp. 139–42.

Isolation is also comparatively effective as a means of dealing with those heroin sellers who are not deterred. Since there does not exist the same pool of those ready to replace them in the business, their imprisonment will actually constrict the availability of the drug in their areas. One might think, of course, that the unavailability of heroin in middle-class areas merely requires potential purchasers to travel to places where the drug is available. Although geographically the trip may be an easy one, the risks of predation and the difficulty of getting dealers to sell to a stranger who obviously does not belong in the neighborhood make the trip more risky and time-consuming than the great majority of would-be users will tolerate—at least as long as the police can suppress any open-air markets such as that which arose briefly in New York City.

As a result, if we are able to surmount the moral aspects of our reliance on predatory criminals to help us reduce heroin dealing, we may be able to take some satisfaction in the enforcement of the laws against heroin supply within the United States. Even though large amounts of heroin can be produced outside the United States, and it is almost impossible to interfere greatly with drug smuggling across our borders, heroin has long been practically unavailable to most people in most of the nation.

Not only is heroin rare in our large middle-class areas, but it seems to be far less available in some lower-class neighborhoods than in others. The statistics on drug emergency-room visits bear this out. Although, as a producer of drug emergencies requiring medical attention, heroin ranks third among drugs in the nation (after alcohol and tranquilizers), no other drug shows such a variation from one city to another. In San Francisco heroin ranks first; in Cleveland it ranks twentieth; in St. Louis and Philadelphia, nineteenth; and in Denver, eighteenth.[70] The most likely explanation is that in those areas where heroin does not have a foothold, law enforcement generally can make it relatively unavailable.

Finally, even in those areas where the drug is already well established, and law enforcement is relatively ineffective, the prohibition of heroin has important consequences. Everywhere it is available, the drug has been of high price and widely varying purity. This has lowered use, though as we will see, it has resulted in harmful consequences as well.

Despite its failures and costs, our heroin prohibition has had a major effect. After all, it is the criminal law within the United States that shapes the nature of the heroin market and the patterns of heroin use, making these so very different from those of other psychoactive drugs such as alcohol or tobacco.

70. Department of Justice, Drug Enforcement Administration, *Project DAWN Annual Report—1979* (Washington, D.C.: Government Printing Office, 1980), p. 26.

## The Criminal Justice System

On the other hand, various aspects of the heroin problem are a consequence of the fact that the peculiar pattern of heroin availability tends to perpetuate itself. In many areas inhabited by the urban lower class, heroin use is endemic. In these, a resident not only can easily discover who is selling heroin but can often find acquaintances to vouch for his reliability.

In the low-income, minority areas where most retail heroin dealing takes place, the police tend to be doubly handicapped. The high rate of other crime—often either more serious or more urgent than heroin trafficking—requires a great deal of the police manpower, and heroin use is already so high that huge police resources would be required to lessen it appreciably.[71] Furthermore, as the police increase their manpower, they become objects of resentment by the inhabitants, who regard the police presence as a reminder of the deprived position that they hold in society,[72] as well as an interference with many activities that they regard as legitimate. Nor is this view completely unrealistic. Of all crimes, the one where the percentage excess of blacks arrested over whites is greatest is gambling.[73]

To make isolation and deterrence work and thus make heroin unavailable we would have to do much more than increase police resources in areas of high heroin use. In the United States, resources are scarce at all stages of the criminal process, and this is especially the case in those areas where heroin is most available. In the cities and counties containing the neighborhoods where heroin use is endemic, the trial system is usually so overburdened that it lacks the resources to deploy against violent crime, let alone against the far higher number of burglaries and larcenies which swamp it. The courts, the prosecutors, and the public defenders can process their case loads only by offering concessions and otherwise pressuring defendants into pleading guilty in about 90 percent of cases.[74] The addition of more arrested heroin offenders would only further overcrowd the courts, requiring more tempting plea bargains to be offered to others awaiting trial.

Finally, what is called the corrections system is almost everywhere so

71. Gandossy et al., *Drug Use and Crime: A Survey and Analysis of the Literature*, pp. 24–26.

72. A vivid expression of such resentment is contained in James Baldwin, *Nobody Knows My Name* (New York: Dell, 1962), pp. 65–67.

73. *Sourcebook of Criminal Justice Statistics* (U.S. Department of Justice, Bureau of Justice Statistics, 1980), p. 345. Sixty-nine percent of those arrested for gambling offenses are black. Robbery is in second place with 58 percent of those arrested black.

74. John Kaplan and Jerome Skolnick, *Criminal Justice: Introductory Cases and Materials*, 3d ed. (Mineola, N.Y.: Foundation Press, 1981), pp. 444–72.

overcrowded that the term "corrections" has become somewhat of a joke—though to anyone who knows what life is like in our jails and prisons, it is, regrettably, a sick joke. The county jails, the state prisons, and other correctional institutions are forced to hold many prisoners under conditions which, if more of us knew about them, we would not tolerate any more than we would countenance cutting the hands off thieves, or blinding assaulters. And the probation and parole offices stagger under such a case load that they must ignore both the social needs and the subsequent criminality of those in their jurisdiction.[75]

## Improvements in the System

Of course, there may be some palliatives for all this. Numerous congressional investigations of drug enforcement have demanded that better coordination be achieved among police forces to choke off the supply of heroin before the drug reaches the areas of use. Indeed, this is probably the most common suggestion for solution of the heroin problem. It is true that law enforcement may suffer because of the multiplicity of agencies involved in drug investigation, and it is likely that improvements could be made in this activity. As one researcher has pointed out:[76]

> If Mr. X is a major drug importer the IRS may know that he has a large income, Customs may be aware that he travels frequently to drug producing countries, the Coast Guard may have registration information about his power boat (suitable for moving large shipments of drugs), the FBI may have file entries mentioning him peripherally as a "friend" of known organized crime figures, the Treasury Department may know that he conducts large cash transactions with his bank and the Drug Enforcement agency and the U. S. Attorney might still not realize that Mr. X should be seriously investigated.

It is hard to believe, however, that heroin traffickers would not soon respond to any law enforcement improvements by going to greater lengths—at some additional cost—to conceal their operations. Moreover, it is a commonplace among those who study drug control that illegal drugs corrupt all those who come in contact with them—police as well as dealers and users. As long as corruption and violations of citizen's rights are major problems in narcotics enforcement, there are good reasons to be careful of establishing too close a connection between the organiza-

75. Ibid., pp. 493–543.
76. Blaine Greenberg, "Federal Drug Enforcement in the Northern District of California: The Inside Dope," student paper, 30 November 1981, Stanford University.

tions charged with the suppression of drug trafficking and agencies with broader responsibilities.

Scholars, on the other hand, have long advocated decriminalization and legalization of various "nonvictim" crimes such as gambling, prostitution, and marijuana offenses, as a means of removing burdens from the criminal justice system.[77] It is true that many of the nonvictim (the better term is "consensual") crimes sop up law enforcement energy that could be better spent elsewhere. The chances are, however, that even this diversion of resources from less important crime would not free up enough means to reduce markedly the supply of heroin.

Liberals have also advocated that we save correctional resources by sharply lowering the number of the convicted who are actually incarcerated, and lessening the length of time served for those who are imprisoned. This would undeniably ease congestion in the jails and prisons and make such institutions more humane, but it would certainly not increase the deterrence or the isolation of the heroin suppliers.

From the other end of the political spectrum come quite different suggestions. It is proposed that we lighten the burdens on our courts by simplifying the legal rules and issues which add to court congestion and often allow the guilty to escape punishment. Such proposals, however, are rarely made in detail, and, when they are, they tend to focus on the exclusionary rule and the requirement of a unanimous jury verdict. Often these proposals come up against constitutional restrictions. Even when they do not they are likely to be perceived as unfair and as either lessening the accuracy of the trial process or jeopardizing other social values—such as our control over police misconduct.

Admittedly, if the police were spared the necessity of getting a warrant for a search or wiretap, they would be more efficient at catching heroin sellers. Not only could they save the bureaucratic work these documents require, but, they would not have to undertake the long and tedious task of gathering enough objective evidence to convince a magistrate that these intrusions were justified. In some nations, the police are given much more leeway; they may question someone they suspect, or even someone they do not, until they have answers that suit them. One might conceivably go even further and simply take the word of the police, convicting accused heroin sellers without demanding that objective evidence of guilt be presented to a court. This would in theory be a maximally efficient use of our law enforcement resources against heroin. The situation in the United States would have to get a great deal worse, however, before many Americans would be willing to revise their basic notions of fair play and engage in that sort of behavior. Besides, the rules preventing this type

77. Sanford Kadish, "The Crisis of Overcriminalization," 374 *Annals* 157 (1967).

of law enforcement are enshrined in the Constitution and are, as a practical matter, unchangeable.

It is often argued that some less fundamental legal rules (the right to bail, the exclusionary rule, and the Miranda requirements are most often named in this context), interfere with law enforcement more than they are worth and end up doing our society harm. To some extent this may be true. The problem is that even though these rules may not be fully enshrined in the Constitution and are vulnerable to relatively slight Supreme Court changes in viewpoint, they probably are only marginally important in the fight against heroin use. And the kinds of rules we would have to dispense with to have a major impact on heroin traffic are deeply engrained in our legal procedure.

Another suggestion, which at least raises no serious constitutional problem, is simply that we greatly increase the resources available to all stages of the criminal process. It is true that a sharp rise in the funding of each part of the criminal system might increase significantly the effect of the criminal law on various kinds of criminality—including trafficking in heroin. But resources must come from somewhere, and health, education, welfare, and housing, the competitors of the criminal justice system for funds, may in the long run be equally important in lowering crime.

Moreover, even if the criminal law were provided with new resources, it could be argued that these could be better spent than upon the enforcement of heroin prohibition. Rather, we might prefer to spend them to improve the fairness of our trials and the humanity of our correctional system; to extend the coverage of the criminal law to more modern crimes—such as the white collar crimes of pollution, safety violations, and consumer fraud, which are all but ignored today; or to get tougher with violent crime.

## Longer Sentences

A variation of the demand for more resources applied throughout the criminal process argues that we can purchase both deterrence and isolation without having to catch and process more criminals, simply by raising the penalties for those we have caught. Interestingly, heroin dealing has been the target of the greatest number of such proposals. On a number of occasions, one state or another has attempted to solve the heroin problem by enacting a mandatory minimum sentence law, often complete with attempted restrictions on plea bargaining to prevent either prosecutors or judges from extending leniency to those accused.[78]

78. National Council on Crime and Delinquency, *Criminal Justice Newsletter* 6. no. 17 (1 September 1975): 2.

In theory, much higher sentences should be somewhat more deterring to heroin dealers, and at the very least, heavier sentences remove sellers from circulation for longer periods. Unfortunately, deterrence seems to be more affected by the likelihood of apprehension than by the penalty if apprehended, and it is probable that the present sentences would be sufficient if those in the business thought their chances of being caught were substantial. Moreover, as we have seen, isolation is not a particularly effective way of coping with the sellers we catch. Their skills are not rare, and typically someone will be waiting to move into the vacancy they leave in the marketing system.

Moreover, the criminal justice system is overloaded at all its stages, not merely at the police apprehension stage. Though a mandatory sentence system does not appear to require additional police work in arresting heroin traffickers, it does put a considerably greater strain on the trial system. Restrictions on plea bargaining and on judicial leniency prevent precisely those activities which permit the courts to cope with their overload. Most people forget that the major effect of mandatory sentences and restrictions on plea bargaining is to induce a higher percentage of defendants to take their chances with going to trial, thus further overburdening the courts.

This effect can rather easily overtax our resources. If the percentage of defendants pleading guilty drops from 90 to 80 percent, the trial calendars must double, and twice as many courtrooms, judges, jurors, court officials, prosecutors, and defense attorneys will be necessary. And, if the percentage of guilty pleas drops to 70 percent—still a figure most citizens would consider unacceptably high—our trial resources would have to be tripled.[79]

Longer sentences for heroin sellers, whether mandatory or not, tend to have another effect. The number of heroin offenders confined gradually increases (though the police partially compensate for this by arresting fewer offenders so as to prevent the clogging of the prisons or the imposition of what they regard as too high a penalty for one who may be only a minor criminal). It is not obvious that this should happen; one might hope that no additional prison space would have to be allotted to heroin offenders, because the higher sentences deterred enough potential traffickers to balance the longer terms of those convicted. This would leave constant or even reduce the total number of person-years spent in prison on heroin offenses. Unfortunately, the increased deterrence caused by the contingent threat of longer sentences is simply not noticeable, and as the number of person-years spent in prison on heroin offenses increases, we are confronted by two choices: either other

79. For a general discussion, see Kaplan and Skolnick, *Criminal Justice*, pp. 444–91.

criminals, perhaps even more deserving of imprisonment than heroin traffickers, will have to be released from our already overcrowded institutions, or we will have to spend more money building and maintaining additional correctional facilities. The problem with the latter solution is that each new space in a medium security institution costs upward of $100,000 today; and the yearly cost per prisoner averages around $15,000.[80] It is by no means unreasonable for most legislators, albeit reluctantly, to decide that they can do better with their tax revenues.

All of this is hardly empty speculation. It gets proved and reproved every few years. The operation of New York's famous Rockefeller Drug Law, which provided high mandatory minimum sentences for heroin sellers and restricted plea bargaining, was studied quite carefully.[81] So far as we can tell, it caused essentially no decrease in heroin activity, but did lead to a drop in the number of heroin offenders arrested and convicted, a considerable increase in the court and correctional resources necessary to process those apprehended, and a significant increase in the overcrowding of the state's prison system.

## THE COSTS OF HEROIN PROHIBITION

Although there are some reasons for satisfaction with our efforts to prevent heroin supply, there are also many reasons for displeasure with the rather stable equilibrium we have reached. Our exertions have lowered the availability of heroin everywhere and made it satisfactorily unavailable in large areas of the nation; yet we must pay a sizable price for this achievement.

The social costs of our efforts to make heroin unavailable are not difficult to catalog. We have already seen some of the costs of enforcement outside the United States and at the borders. To appreciate the price of heroin enforcement within the United States, we must look somewhat more closely at the varying police tactics aimed at heroin suppliers.

At the very lowest level of street dealing, the beat patrolman will interrupt suspicious transactions he sees, questioning and searching those whom he thinks are involved. The drug squad is more likely to proceed by arresting potential informants—usually addict retailers. After inducing their cooperation by threatening them with long prison sentences, the officers will set their informants up with microphones and marked money,

---

80. Bob Bodian, "The Cost of Incarceration in California," student paper, 29 May 1980, Stanford University. Douglas McDonald, *The Price of Punishment: Public Spending for Corrections in New York* (Boulder, Colo.: Westview Press, 1980), p. 13.

81. See Department of Justice, National Institute of Law Enforcement and Criminal Justice, Law Enforcement Assistance Administration, *The Nation's Toughest Drug Law: Evaluating the New York Experience* (Washington, D.C.: Government Printing Office, 1978).

and send them to make purchases from their suppliers. If this technique is successful at catching a supplier, police may proceed to higher and higher levels of the distribution chain—until sòmeone becomes suspicious or the game is given away by mistake or treachery.[82]

At higher levels of heroin distribution, where addicts are quite uncommon, the drug squad may use undercover officers posing as purchasers to win the confidence of a narcotics dealer so that they can later testify as to his sales. It is important, for the strategy to succeed at this level, that the dealer be used to doing business with nonaddicted purchasers. At lower levels the police masquerade can more easily be unmasked by a suspicious dealer who simply insists that the would-be purchaser "shoot up" before his purchase. Narcotics agents, however dedicated, draw the line at this.

Occasionally—though this is quite rare—undercover agents may be able to penetrate the higher echelons of narcotic-dealing organizations. In that case they will be able to testify in large-scale prosecutions, aided by the usual panoply of conspiracy charges, surveillance, and wiretapping.

At all levels of heroin distribution, the police will be interested in the seizure of as much heroin as possible. Large quantities of the drug are the best evidence upon which to build criminal cases against heroin traffickers. Even if the higher-ups cannot be connected with a particular quantity, each seizure at least prevents that much heroin from reaching the ultimate consumer, and at the same time increases the overall financial risks of dealing. Typically, seizure of large quantities of heroin will require that drug raids be mounted with speed and force sufficient to prevent the evidence from being destroyed or spirited away.[83]

## Violation of Rights

The catalog of these methods of enforcement should be enough to highlight several of the major costs of our efforts to restrict the supply of heroin. Those against whom the police techniques are directed are entitled to the constitutional rights of citizens, and the violation of their rights must remain a matter of considerable concern in a society based upon law. This is not merely a matter of abstract principle. As we have learned from the numerous narcotic raids upon people who turned out to be completely innocent of any drug involvement, police methods in this area are an ever present threat to the rights of the innocent as well as the guilty.[84]

82. Moore, *Buy and Bust*. pp. 130–32, 161–62.
83. Ibid., pp. 140–47.
84. Perhaps the most notorious of these raids was the one in Collinsville, Illinois, in 1972. See Peter Goldberg, "The Federal Government's Response to Illicit Drugs," in Drug Abuse Council, *The Facts about "Drug Abuse"* (New York: The Free Press, 1980), p. 43.

Many of the techniques used to enforce the heroin laws do end up violating the constitutional rights of the individual. The stopping and questioning of a suspected street-level pusher by a beat patrollman easily becomes an arrest and search without the probable cause required by the Fourth Amendment. Wiretapping and police raids to seize narcotics without—and sometimes even with—a search warrant often transcend constitutional limits; and the use of undercover narcotics officers to purchase heroin from suppliers may amount to illegal entrapment.

Even when within constitutional limitations, street questioning of suspects, searches made pursuant to a search warrant, and wiretapping are nonetheless intrusive methods of investigation. And even when the pressure placed upon informants is legal, such tactics foster police habits that compromise the dignity of the individual and raise serious problems as to the role of the police in a free society.[85]

Legal or not, such tactics are much resented by those against whom they are used. Those who are caught on a minor charge and pressured into working as police informants feel the degradation of being forced into turning in their friends and associates—heroin suppliers though they may be. It is not only the guilty who suffer from these tactice. The use of informants undermines trust in personal relations; the giving of leniency in exchange for "work" compromises the idea of just punishment for the informant's original crime; and police treatment of heroin offenders, who are in no position to complain about being abused, develops in the police habits of casualness toward the rights of all who cross their path.[86]

Even more corrosive of the rule of law are police efforts to evade the exclusionary rule, whereby courts refuse to admit as evidence material unconstitutionally seized from a criminal defendant. The attempts of the police to prevent the exclusion of such evidence in order to make their cases stand up at trial are a notorious source of perjury in our courts.

Probably the most dramatic illustration of this widespread practice is the reaction reaction of the New York police to *Mapp v. Ohio*.[87] In 1960, the Supreme Court held in *Mapp* that the exclusionary rule must apply to prosecutions by the state as well as by the federal government. Since New York had not followed that rule prior to *Mapp*, its police discovered rather suddenly that evidence they had unconstitutionally seized could not be used against criminal defendants. A study of the six-month periods in New York City before and after the *Mapp* decision showed something

85. J. Dean Heller, "A Conflict of Laws: The Drug Possession Offense and the Fourth Amendment," in *Drug Use in America*, app., vol. 3, pp. 870–72.

86. A police burglary unit may overlook the drug offenses of its informants, while the narcotics unit overlooks the burglaries committed by its informants. See Jerome H. Skolnick, *Justice without Trial*, 2d ed. (New York: John Wiley & Sons, 1975), pp. 127–31.

87. *Mapp v. Ohio*, 367 U.S. 643 (1961).

quite remarkable. In the period after *Mapp,* according to officers' testimony, the number of suspects who threw their drugs to the ground (making seizure legal) increased dramatically—leading to one of two conclusions: either the suspects, knowledgeable of the requirements of *Mapp,* had acted to make their arrests and the seizure of their heroin legal; or else the police in numerous cases had simply perjured themselves so that their searches would be upheld.[88]

## Police Corruption

Widespread perjury is not the only police crime which should be accounted as a cost of enforcing the heroin laws. Both the large profits derived from dealing in heroin and the way the heroin laws are enforced—through informers and undercover agents—have led to staggering levels of police corruption.

Police departments have reacted to this by a whole series of rules such as those requiring police supervisors to be present when large seizures of heroin or of the proceeds of heroin sales are to be made. The object of such regulations, of course, is to make it more difficult for any officer or small group of officers to form partnerships with drug dealers and suppliers. Often, however, an officer may unexpectedly seize a sizable amount of heroin and then go, as it were, into business with his informant. On other occasions, one or a group of officers will simply accept bribes for not making certain seizures or arrests, or for providing information which will enable dealers to escape apprehension.[89]

The full extent of corruption in heroin enforcement is not known. Many of those who have looked at the problem estimate that it affects more than one-third of narcotics officers. For instance, about half of the federal narcotics agents in New York were indicted or fired for corruption around 1970, and the Knapp commission investigation into the New York City police indicated that corruption in the narcotics squad of that department was even more pervasive.[90]

This is not to say that the corruption in heroin enforcement is a major factor in the maintenance of the overall supply of the drug and, hence, that we could suppress heroin completely if only we could assure that all

---

88. Note, "Effect of *Mapp v. Ohio* on Police Search and Seizure Practices in Narcotics Cases," *Columbia Journal of Law and Social Problems* 4, no. 1 (March 1968): 94–95.

89. For a review of anticorruption strategies in the New York City Police Department, see Alan Kornblum, *The Moral Hazards* (Lexington, Mass.: D.C. Heath and Co., 1976).

90. New York City, Knapp Commission, *The Knapp Commission Report on Police Corruption* (New York: George Braziller, 1973), pp. 94–115. Testimony of Andrew C. Tartaglino, Chief Inspector, Drug Enforcement Administration, in *Federal Drug Enforcement*, Hearings, pp. 140–43.

police narcotics agents were completely honest. Even if the police always tried their very best, the other difficulties they face would seem to assure that there would be no gross changes in the availability of heroin on the street. However, as long as the profits in heroin dealing remain so high, and the means of law enforcment do not change, there will continue to be no way to guarantee the honesty of the officers enforcing the heroin laws.

On the other hand, the efforts of higher police authorities to keep their officers honest does interfere with narcotics enforcement. Many police departments insist on transferring their narcotics officers out of that specialty after two years to prevent the buildup of contacts leading to corruption. One result of this is that a great deal of expertise and information becomes unavailable to law enforcement.[91]

The police hierarchy has attempted to induce narcotics agents to share their informants and to write down information they receive, so that these valuable aids to enforcement will not be lost. Unfortunately, the tradition in narcotics enforcement is strongly to the contrary. Both the competition among agents for the best sources of information, and their need to encourage their informants by offering protection against identification, either by leaks from other officers or through court subpoena of police records, tends to make agents resist the bureaucratization of their employment,[92] despite any gains in increased efficiency and reduction of corruption. Interestingly, it has been noted that those narcotics officers guilty of bribery have tended to be among the largest producers of criminal cases and heroin seizures.[93] The possibilities of corruption may act as some kind of incentive for them to enforce the law—or else, being more active than their colleagues, they may work more closely with informants and come across more tempting opportunities to advance their own financial interests.

Of course, the interference with narcotics enforcement caused by corruption and the efforts to prevent it is not the most serious cost of this kind of police misconduct. When widespread bribery surfaces from newspaper reports of periodic scandals or simply from knowledge "on the street," the effect on public attitudes toward the police is devastating.

## The Price of Heroin

The last complex of social costs attributable to the policy of heroin prohibition arises from the high price of the drug and is a consequence of enforcement in other nations, at the borders, and within the United

---

91. Moore, *Buy and Bust*, p. 156.

92. Ibid.

93. John E. Ingersoll, former director Bureau of Narcotics and Dangerous Drugs, letter of 20 August 1981 to author.

States. We have already seen two of the disadvantages of the high price of heroin—the generous compensation for the risk that heroin suppliers run and the fuel for police corruption. What is perhaps the most serious cost of heroin enforcement—the production of property criminality—is also a direct result of the high price of the drug.

Obviously, the high price of heroin is caused by the drug's very scarcity. What Professor Herbert Packer has called the "crime tariff" is the inevitable economic consequence of attempting, with anything less than perfect success, to decrease the supply of heroin without correspondingly decreasing the demand. Moreover, the maintenance of the high price in many ways helps implement our heroin policy. It discourages experimentation by would-be users, retards the movement from experimentation to regular use, and makes it more difficult to move from regular use to addiction. Indeed, these very effects are intended consequences of any prohibition policy.[94]

Less intended, but equally real, is the social cost of forcing the addict to pay such a high price for his heroin. To be sure, addict criminality is far more than an automatic response to the necessity of coming up with the money to pay for a fixed, continuous, and implacable heroin need. Nonetheless, as we have seen, it does look as if the cost of heroin is a major factor in the number of crimes many addicts commit.

Heroin today sells at retail for approximately two dollars a milligram. This is in the neighborhood of two hundred times what the drug would cost if supply and demand—uninfluenced by legal restrictions—were permitted to take their course.[95] Some fraction of this increase boomerangs upon us in the form of additional addict crimes. The old saw in the police folklore is that the narcotics squad makes extra work for the burglary squad and, as we have seen, to a considerable extent this is true.

Moreover, even if addicts did not have to raise money by criminality, the high price of heroin would remain a constant drain on their resources, forcing them to compromise their health and welfare in ways which are good neither for them nor for society at large. The wide variations from day to day in the availability and purity of heroin add to this problem. This effect of law enforcement not only further undermines the addict's health, but makes it much more difficult for him to lead a productive life. So long as the addict is unable to stabilize his dosage on variable street heroin, he will not be able to avoid alternating between nodding euphoria and incipient withdrawal and, hence, will find it difficult to hold down any

94. Domestic Council Drug Abuse Task Force, *White Paper on Drug Abuse*, A Report to the President, September 1975 (Washington, D.C.: Government Printing Office, 1975), pp. 2–4.

95. Mark A. Deininger, "The Economics of Heroin: Key to Optimizing the Legal Response," *Georgia Law Review* 10, no. 2 (Winter 1976): 583.

honest employment. Finally, even though addicts for various reasons find it easier to obtain heroin than do the great majority of Americans, the task of making sure of their sources is a difficult and time-consuming one, which further complicates any effort to earn an honest living.[96]

## CONCLUSION

We have now looked in some detail at the costs and benefits of the policy of heroin prohibition. Other factors affecting this balance will come out in the subsequent discussions. For the present, we have seen enough to convince most people that the policy of heroin prohibition is by no means completely satisfactory. The question that we must ask, therefore, is, "Isn't there another policy which is better?" That will be the subject of the remainder of this book.

96. Domestic Council, *White Paper on Drug Abuse*, pp. 3–4.

# 3 ■■■
# FREE AVAILABILITY

*L*et us first examine the most radical change we might make in our heroin policy. Could we not lower the total social costs of heroin use and the governmental response to it by allowing the drug to be freely and cheaply available in liquor stores, or as an over-the-counter drug? We apply this type of legal treatment to some other abusable drugs, such as tobacco and alcohol, and a respectable body of opinion is espousing it for the control of marijuana.[1]

Application of such an arrangement to heroin would avoid virtually all the costs we have ascribed to our present prohibition. The drain on law enforcement resources presumably would decrease by as much, proportionally, as did that attributable to alcohol control when we repealed Prohibition. The police corruption and violations of civil liberties caused by attempts to enforce our present heroin laws would be similarly reduced.

A large heroin habit, if heroin were freely available, would be no more expensive and difficult to maintain than a cigarette habit is now. The proceeds of an honest living could easily supply all the heroin an addict required. In that case the time and energy presently needed to "score" heroin and to avoid detection would be freed for productive work, and the connection, however weak or strong, between addiction and crime would be attenuated.

1. John Kaplan, *Marijuana—The New Prohibition* (New York and Cleveland: World Publishing Co., 1970), pp. 311–52.

The question, of course, is whether the cure of free availability would be worse than the disease of heroin prohibition—though one could equally well phrase the question from the opposite perspective and ask whether the cure of heroin prohibition is worse than the disease of free availability.

## CONSISTENCY

In addition to the pragmatic costs and benefits we will be discussing, we must note a number of related jurisprudential and philosophical arguments for making heroin freely available. Although they will ultimately be rejected here, they are an important issue in the debate over the prohibition of any substance.

The first of these arguments relies on consistency and contends that, regardless of the tradition in other societies, ours is nonpaternalistic and does not rely on government to protect people from their own indiscretions. It is true that there are exceptions where we act to prevent people from giving in to their baser desires. The gambling, prostitution, and pornography laws all attempt to do this. But for the most part these prohibitions against what are called "nonvictim" crimes are not in very good repute, and arguably are fading away. According to this argument, the heroin laws themselves are probably the major exception to our general acknowledgment of the freedom of the individual to "choose his own poison," to eat and drink what he wants, and to enjoy himself in ways that may be bad for his physical or mental health.

One problem with the argument based upon consistency is that neither our past practices nor our present trends are that clear. Our statute books are laden with efforts by the government to prevent people from harming themselves—and most of these attempts are not even very controversial.[2]

Whenever the law goes beyond requiring full disclosure of the dangers of a product and attempts instead to prevent a transaction between a willing buyer and a willing seller, it is protecting the buyer of goods or services from himself. We are familiar with such attempts in the food and drug laws; the flammable fabrics act; the building codes; the provisions preventing the practice of law, medicine, or plumbing without a license; and volumes of other laws. Though usually the law acts directly upon the purveyor of the "dangerous" goods and services and not upon the consumer, its purpose is to protect the consumer from his own indiscretion.

Even those who most often decry prohibitions against victimless crimes in general may demand that we do more "to protect the consumer." Over the past five decades we have seen a vast increase in the number of

2. John Kaplan, "The Role of the Law in Drug Control," *Duke Law Journal* 1971, no. 6 (February 1971): 1076–77.

governmental regulations designed to protect the buyer of goods by requiring this or that safety device, even though its price or inconvenience would prevent it from gaining the consumer's loyalty in the marketplace. Such protections range from bans on food additives that cause cancer in animals to requirements that automobile manufacturers install seat belts, collapsible steering columns, and the like.

The minimum wage laws, too, are efforts to protect people from themselves, though we usually regard them as protecting the worker from an exploitative employer. We protect the worker from having to accept below-minimum wages on the theory that "necessitous men are not free men." However, the worker driven by economic necessity to work for less than the minimum wage seems no more driven than the compulsive gambler or the drug addict. Although he is willing to accept, and his employer is willing to pay, a low wage, our laws attempt to prevent this bargain, just as they seek to prevent the bargain reached between a heroin seller and his customer.

The list could be expanded almost endlessly. Restrictions on unsafe or ineffective therapeutic drugs; the modern no-fault laws, which require drivers to insure themselves against automobile accidents; the social security laws, which enforce a contribution from an employee to provide for his old age; even laws which prohibit swimming at public beaches while no lifeguard is on duty—all are cases where the government uses the force of the law to protect people from improvidently harming themselves in one way or another. The fact that under our present practice government does often interfere with the citizen's freedom in order to protect him from his own indiscretions forces us to abandon any argument based on consistency. If we wish to support the free availability of heroin, we must place our reliance either upon principle or upon practicality.

## MILL'S PRINCIPLE

Many people speak of the individual's right to do what he wishes with his own body, his right to harm himself, or his right to eat, drink, or otherwise ingest what he pleases. The problem with such "rights" is that they are merely assertions. They do not carry any argument with them. Perhaps all citizens should have such rights, and perhaps we would have a better and more moral society if we recognized them as absolutes—but perhaps not.

The classic statement of the absolute rights position is that of John Stuart Mill: "The only purpose for which power can be rightfully exercised over any member of a civilized community, against his will, is to prevent harm to others. His own good, either physical or moral, is not a sufficient warrant. He cannot rightfully be compelled to do or forebear because it will be better for him to do, because it will make him happier, because, in the opinions of others, to do so would be wise, or even right."[3] Mill's principle is aimed not only at controls which bear directly on the individual who is to be protected, but also at efforts to accomplish the same effect indirectly by restricting his access to harmful substances. Mill opposed laws against the sale of liquor or of poisons on the ground that "these interferences are objectionable not as infringements upon the liberty of the producer or seller but on that of the buyer."[4]

## The Protection of Youth

Mill himself placed two qualifications on his principle, either of which provides an argument that even he would not have supported the free availability of heroin. First of all, Mill excepted youth from his principle. "It is, perhaps, hardly necessary to say that this doctrine is meant to apply only to human beings in the maturity of their faculties. We are not speaking of children, or of young persons below the age which the law may fix as that of manhood or womanhood. Those who are still in a state to require being taken care of by others, must be protected against their own actions as well as against external injury."[5] In fact, Mill thought that a major reason why society should be denied the right to regulate the self-harming conduct of adults was that "Society has had absolute power over them during all the early portion of their existence; it has had the whole period of childhood and non-age in which to try whether it could make them capable of rational conduct in life."[6]

Certainly Mill would have had no objection to a law prohibiting the young from using heroin. The problem is whether he would have countenanced a law making the drug unavailable to all on the ground that this was the only way of protecting youth.

There is no doubt that, in a society such as ours, making heroin freely available to adults would render completely unenforceable any effort to prevent the young from having access to the drug. The median age for first heroin use is currently less than nineteen,[7] and it is quite likely that giving adults freer access to the drug would considerably increase the number of users younger than this. That at least would be the natural conclusion we might derive from our experience with alcohol and tobacco, where our laws attempting to keep these drugs from the young have been rendered notoriously ineffective by their complete availability to adults.

3. John Stuart Mill, *On Liberty*, ed. Currin V. Shields (Indianapolis: Bobbs-Merrill Co., 1956), p. 13.

4. Ibid., p. 116.

5. Ibid., p. 13.

6. Ibid., p. 100.

7. Waldorf and Biernacki, "The Natural Recovery from Opiate Addiction: Some Preliminary Findings," p. 64.

In all probability, Mill would have regarded this kind of reasoning as allowing the tail to wag the dog. It would seem that at the very least Mill would require that the benefits of protecting youth by prohibiting all access to heroin be balanced against the interference this would cause to the legitimate freedom of adults. In reaching such a balance, we would have to weigh the freedom for one group against the protection of the other, a matter which would force us to decide difficult empirical questions about the effects of heroin and its regulation upon different groups. This kind of inquiry, however, seems to remove the issue from the realm of principle and place it in that of practicality—a matter we will come to shortly. Finally, reliance on Mill's exception for the young is unpersuasive for another reason. While it is true we are interested in protecting the young, we wish to protect adults as well. Entirely apart from any effect upon youth, we are by no means prepared to acknowledge any right of adults to use heroin.

The Slavery Exception

The other of Mill's exceptions to his principle that might permit the government to prohibit heroin is a much less obvious one. The state, according to Mill, does retain the right to prevent an individual from selling himself into slavery.

> The ground for thus limiting [the individual's] power of voluntarily disposing of his own lot in life, is apparent, and is very clearly seen in this extreme case. The reason for not interfering unless for the sake of others, with a person's voluntary acts, is consideration for his liberty. But by selling himself for a slave, he abdicates his liberty; he foregoes any future use of it, beyond that single act. He therefore defeats, in his own case, the very purpose which is the justification of allowing him to dispose of himself. He is no longer free; but is thenceforth in a position which has no longer the presumption in its favor, that would be afforded by his voluntarily remaining in it. The principle of freedom cannot require that he should be free not to be free. It is not freedom, to be allowed to alienate his freedom. These reasons, the force of which is so conspicuous in this peculiar case, are evidently of far wider application.[8]

One may ask whether the use of heroin is within this "far wider application." At least some heroin users seem to us to be incapable of stopping their use, despite what appears to be their sincerely expressed desires. For them, the metaphor of slavery, in the sense of foreclosing future liberty, is not so farfetched. Of course, if the myths about the inevitability and permanence of addiction were correct, and everyone

8. Mill, *On Liberty*, p. 125.

who used heroin gave up his freedom not to use the drug thereafter, it would be considerably easier to bring heroin use within Mill's exception. As we have seen in our discussion of the once-an-addict-always-an-addict myth, the issue is not that simple.

Since Mill was dealing with the all-or-nothing act of selling oneself into slavery, he did not discuss whether society could prevent acts which merely involved some risk of "slavery." Perhaps he would have argued that any restriction on access to addicting drugs is too great an interference with the freedom of moderate users, despite society's right to protect those who would become lasting addicts.

Alternatively, Mill might have felt that interference with the freedom of the moderate or controlled user was necessary in order to accomplish the greater good of protecting others from drug slavery. Perhaps he would have regarded it as important that we are unable to predict who, among those with access to the drug, will become addicted. So long as this is the case, we can protect some people from "slavery" only by overprotecting others.

One can argue that it is not very significant whether heroin did or did not fall within the slavery exception to Mill's principle. If it did not, perhaps Mill would have erected a new exception to cover a situation he had not contemplated. If it did fall within his exception, Mill might not have fully appreciated how much of the game he had given away, and might have narrowed that exception to prevent any state interference with what he regarded as the liberty of the individual.

## QUESTIONING THE PRINCIPLE ITSELF

The examination of Mill's exceptions to his principle is not only inconclusive; it is probably unnecessary. The real problem is that the great majority of us do not agree with Mill's principle to begin with. Indeed, no modern state (or, so far as is known, any premodern state) has ever followed Mill's principle with respect to all activities.

It almost seems to be the nature of man to regard some types of predominantly self-harming conduct as, for one reason or another, the proper subject of official prohibition. Mill's principle may be regarded as a very wise admonition to caution and restraint in an exceedingly complex and emotion-laden area; but if it is to be taken literally (as he apparently intended), it may well be unwise.

Even if Mill's principle were correct for early Victorian England, we live in a society committed, more or less, to assuring to all a minimum standard of welfare and health care. Certain activities, which Mill demanded we permit, would now result in our being obligated to support and care for people who have harmed themselves. Justice does not require that they be permitted to place this burden upon us through their improvident actions; and while it may often be the wisest course to tolerate self-harming behaviors, there is no obvious reason in principle why society should not have the right to limit its expenses by preventing the harmful conduct.

## The Helmetless Motorcyclist

Take, for example, one of the starkest and most discussed confrontations between Mill's principle and our nation's actions, the laws in about half our states requiring that motorcyclists wear protective helmets.[9] Even though the helmetless cyclist does not place others in any appreciable physical danger, he does expose the rest of us to a financial risk. If he injures himself, we will have to make good on our commitments and undertake expensive measures to prevent him from dying. In Professor Robert Bartels's apt phrase, the helmetless cyclist exposes others to "public ward" harm—the danger of having to treat him should he not be killed outright.[10]

The issue, then, is whether society, because of the obligation it has assumed, should have the right to demand that the helmetless cyclist do his share to protect himself. It could be argued that if the cyclist's loss of freedom is the price of our benevolence, we should keep our charity and leave him alone.

This course would entail grave problems, however. First of all, most of us would feel that the penalty of allowing the cyclist to die would be shockingly out of proportion to his improvidence. Moreover, the problems of administration, if not humanity, would doom any such solution. Hospital authorities would in many cases have no way of determining whether an accident victim had been wearing his helmet before the accident, and it would be grossly impractical to set up a procedure for finding out before treatment.[11]

The right of society to protect against public ward harm is not the only reason for rejecting Mill's principle. The helmetless cyclist, by failing to guard against his own injury, may make himself unable to meet his legal responsibilities to others, such as his children. Even if society were not prepared to meet these obligations in the event of his default, it would still have the right to ensure that he meet his responsibilities and use minimal prudence to keep himself able to do so. One cannot avoid this issue by claiming that it is all society's fault for not letting him die in the street at minimal cost. His responsibilities must still be fulfilled.

9. Chris Barnet, "Fewer Buy, More Die," *Parade*, 13 May 1979, pp. 19–21.
10. Robert Bartels, "Better Living through Legislation: The Control of Mind-Altering Drugs," *Kansas Law Review* 21, no. 4 (Summer 1973): 460–61.
11. Kaplan, "Role of the Law in Drug Control," pp. 1065–67.

As an emotional matter, nonsupport justifications for laws which attempt to prevent self-harming conduct often command considerably more power than do public ward justifications. One of the most moving Prohibitionist posters showed a workingman drinking at the bar of a saloon ignoring his poorly dressed little daughter who stood in the doorway repeating, "Father, Father, please come home. Mother needs you." The same public interest which underlies nonsupport laws, then, can also justify helmetless cyclist laws—at least in the case of those who owe someone a support obligation. Mill himself had an answer for this argument:

> If, for example, a man, through intemperance or extravagance, becomes unable to pay his debts, or, having undertaken the moral responsibility of family, becomes from the same cause incapable of supporting or educating them, he is deservedly reprobated, and might be justly punished; but it is for the breach of duty to his family or creditors, not for the extravagance. If the resources which ought to have been devoted to them, had been diverted from them for the most prudent investment, the moral culpability would have been the same.[12]

Although Mill recognized that society might punish someone who had rendered himself unable to meet his obligations, Mill denied government the right to use foresight to prevent the harm before it was done. Usually, of course, it will prove wise not to anticipate harm, in order to avoid taking precautions that are too costly in terms of both resources and freedom. But there is no reason in principle why we must be bound by someone's decision as to the risks he is willing to take with the livelihood of those whom he must support.

## The Rejection of Mill's Principle

Most important, many people regard it as unnecessary to find any indirect harm to others before attempting to prevent an individual from harming himself. In other words, they flatly reject Mill's principle. One can philosophically justify the prohibition of self-harming conduct by relying upon Rawl's notion of a "just society." To do so, it is necessary to make convincing the view that a hypothetical individual, about to be born into a society and not knowing his own tastes and limitations, would prefer being born into a group which accepted responsibility for making reasonable efforts to prevent his weakness from causing him great damage. Rawls's view would be that if the hypothetical individual would so prefer,

12. Mill, *On Liberty*, p. 99.

society to be just should impose this type of restriction on its members, so long as this is practicable.[13]

One does not need such refined reasoning to reject Mill's principle, however. One may prefer to side with John Donne's view that "no man is an island." If one believes that we are all brothers, one may morally attempt to keep others from likely harm even though they themselves are foolish enough to take the risk. After all, Mill's view that all adults must be assumed to know their own best interests is certainly contrary to fact, as most of us see it.

On the other hand, if Mill's principle is regarded as a bit of practical advice rather than as a moral precept, it may make good sense. Our society might well be better off if it always acted on Mill's principle. Our experience with alcohol prohibition and many examples of overregulation show that when a law designed to protect people from themselves proves unenforceable or unduly burdensome, it may do a great deal of social harm.

Nonetheless, even people who think that, on the whole, the entire class of such laws has done more harm than good often believe that laws prohibiting some types of self-harming conduct are worthwhile. If this view is correct, and a law prohibiting self-harming conduct can reduce the total misery in our society, Mill to the contrary, it should be enacted.

## PRACTICALITY AS A GUIDE

Once we renounce Mill's absolutist principle, it becomes impossible to resolve the arguments for and against prohibition of a particular self-harming conduct on any but practical grounds. No one argues that just because, on principle, society has the right to prevent people from harming themselves, it should always make the attempt. We do not seriously try to prevent people from overeating, smoking, drinking, or doing many other things that we feel are not good for them—for eminently practical rather than moral or jurisprudential reasons.

In other words, to decide whether allowing heroin to be freely and legally available would be preferable to our present prohibition, we must determine the likely social cost of free availability, as compared to our present policy. To do this, we must imagine, as best we can, the hypothetical state of our society were heroin essentially freely available— say, sold in liquor stores or without prescription in drugstores—and compare this with our state under the present prohibitionist heroin policy.

Remember that we must look carefully at the likely results of free

13. John Rawls, *A Theory of Justice* (Cambridge: Belknap Press of Harvard University Press, 1971), pp. 208–9, 248–50.

availability as well as at those of our present policy. There is a considerable temptation to conclude without any such examination that our
present policy is so costly that free availability just *has* to be better.

## THE ANALOGY TO ALCOHOL PROHIBITION

One way of predicting the costs and benefits of substituting free availability for our present heroin prohibition is to examine what happened when
Prohibition was repealed in 1933. At that time, the nation took a similar
step with another widely abused drug, alcohol.

Of course, there are differences between heroin prohibition today and
alcohol prohibition before repeal. The addict criminality caused by the
high price of heroin seems to have had no counterpart in the case of
alcohol, and the difficulty of maintaining a heroin supply today is far
greater than that experienced by the drinker under Prohibition. Despite
the differences, however, the repeal of Prohibition brought benefits that
suggest analogies to our present heroin problems.

At any given level of consumption, the danger to the alcohol user's
health was lessened after repeal. Legal whiskey was far less likely than
the bootleg product to contain the methyl alcohol and other poisons which
had been a significant cause of blindness and death during Prohibition.[14]
In addition, the enormous inflow of profits to organized crime and the
large-scale corruption of public officials caused by the illegal alcohol
traffic dropped sharply with the repeal. And the large number of civil
liberties violations by Prohibition agents ceased as well.[15]

On the other hand, it should be remembered that the repeal of
Prohibition also produced adverse effects. The per capita consumption of
alcohol did not remain constant; rather, it increased substantially, bringing with it one of our major public health problems, alcoholism. According to the latest estimates, alcoholism results in somewhere between
50,000 and 200,000 deaths per year. In addition, its yearly cost to the
nation is estimated at about 45 billion dollars—in the neighborhood of four
times the costs attributed to heroin today.[16]

Comparing our experience under Prohibition with our alcohol problems

14. Andrew Sinclair, *Prohibition: The Era of Excess* (Boston: Little, Brown and Co.,
1962), p. 201.

15. Ibid., pp. 229–30, 415. Raymond B. Fosdick and Albert L. Scott, *Toward Liquor
Control* (New York: Harper & Brothers, 1933), p. 15.

16. Department of Health and Human Services, Fourth Special Report to the United
States Congress on Alcohol and Health, *Alcohol and Health*, ed. John R. DeLuca
(Rockville, Md.: National Institute on Alcohol Abuse and Alcoholism, 1981), pp. 15, 93.
Institute of Medicine, *Report of a Study—Alcoholism, Alcohol Abuse, and Related
Problems: Opportunities for Research* (Washington, D.C.: National Academy Press, 1980),
pp. 4–5.

today, most of us would probably agree that repeal was correct, and that our nation's overall relationship to alcohol is now a healthier one. This, of course, is no guarantee that the same would be true of heroin. Even though they have more in common than most people have believed, alcohol and heroin are different drugs. Moreover, even if the two drugs were much more similar than they are, there might still be other reasons to treat them by different legal arrangements. Pharmacological symmetry is by no means the most important factor shaping a rational drug-control law. The social costs and benefits of a drug control policy depend also on the technology of production and distribution, the number of users, the patterns of use, the means of administration, the most common sets and settings of use, the reasons for use, and even the kinds of people who use the drug.

## THE PROBLEM OF PREDICTION

Each of the variables is affected by the drug policy adopted, whether free availability, prohibition, or some other control arrangement. As a result, to estimate the advantages and disadvantages of a change in drug control policy, we must make predictions as to the effect of the new arrangement on all these complex variables.

In the cases of some drugs and some new drug control policies, these predictions are relatively easy ones. When the government moved from free availability to prohibition of cyclamates, it surprised no one that the drug disappeared with no major social effects.[17] So far as the free availability of heroin is concerned, however, the predictions are quite uncertain and difficult. Indeed, this in itself is a major difference between the alcohol and heroin situations.

Prohibition lasted only thirteen years, and, at the time we abandoned it, our society still remembered a great deal of its long experience with alcohol. As expected, it turned out that while drinking patterns had changed during the "noble experiment," they were not drastically different before and after that period.[18]

It is true, of course, that, for some time before the Harrison Act, opiates had been freely available and widely used in the United States. But that was over sixty-five years ago and things were very different then. Opiates, then, were generally taken orally, as "medicine," rather than for pleasure, and there was no subculture based on the enjoyment of opiate use. As we have noted before, it can be argued that we would have been better off had the Harrison Act, which helped change all this, not been

17. Kaplan, "Role of the Law in Drug Control," pp. 1086–87, 1094–95.
18. M. H. Tillet, *The Price of Prohibition* (New York: Harcourt, Brace & Co., 1932), pp. 35–36. *Alcohol and Health*, p. 15.

passed—and the argument is even stronger that when the act was passed, some provision should have been made to allow physicians to maintain addicts with opiates.

Although the problem would be far simpler if we could guarantee that opiates would be used as they were before the Harrison Act, there is no turning back the clock. If we made heroin available today, it would be made available under very different conditions, with social variables such as the purpose and meaning of use and the availability of group support all very much changed. Even the drug would be different. Before the Harrison Act, the problem was opium or morphine drunk in tonics and medicines. Today it is injectable heroin.

It is not only drug use patterns that have altered in the sixty-five years since the passage of the Harrison Act. The changes in America itself dwarf those which occurred during the thirteen years Prohibition was in force. The very lapse of time should make us far more hesitant to extrapolate from our past experience in a predominantly rural, relatively crime-free, free-enterprise society to our present urban, crime-ridden, partially-welfare state.

Despite the difficulty, however, there is no way around the problem. To decide the wisdom of a free availability policy for heroin, we must attempt to predict what our society would look like if such a policy were adopted. Here we will focus on the two most relevant social variables: how many people would use the drug in various use patterns, and how harmful would their use be for them and for society? It turns out that with our present knowledge, the uncertainties in each prediction are enormous.

## AVAILABILITY AND USE

Not only are we unable to make any confident predictions as to how many people would use or become addicted to heroin, if freely available, but we do not know enough to make even a rough estimate. One might even argue that if heroin were freely available, the number of its users would drop. If users desire the drug because of the thrill of enjoying "forbidden fruit" or because they wish to defy society's laws, they might lose interest in freely available heroin. There is good reason not to count on this, however. Regardless of what the law says, it is likely that for some time to come, heroin use will be stigmatized in most of society. Heroin will still have the power to evoke emotion, and the disapproval by parents and authority figures may prove as much of an inducement to some as does the illegality of the drug today.

More persuasive is the possibility that heroin, although difficult to obtain for most of the population today, is not so difficult to obtain for the only kinds of people who are willing to use the drug. If so, the number of users under free availability would not be significantly higher than it is today. Unfortunately, there is good reason to discount this possibility, too. The common statement that opiate availability is a major determinant of use means much more than the truism that when opiates are unavailable, no one uses them. It means that, within wide limits, the more available opiates are, the higher the rate of use—and of addiction.[19]

This principle is generally illustrated with two examples: First, in Vietnam, where heroin was cheaply and easily available, some 14 percent of American ground troops became addicted to the drug and considerably more were nonaddicted users.[20] Second, the medical profession, which has greater access to opiates than does the rest of us, also has a rate of addiction estimated to be about twenty times that of the general population.[21]

It is, of course, possible that our experiences in Vietnam and with the medical profession might lead to an overestimate of the likely heroin use under conditions of free availability. After all, the use in Vietnam took place under conditions not duplicated in the United States. The level of boredom and alienation that existed among American troops in Vietnam is probably unapproached anywhere in the United States—with the possible exception of those areas which already have high heroin use. And members of the medical profession are exposed to strains that are not shared by most of the population; indeed, they typically use opiates more for relief of stress than for euphoria.[22]

Nonetheless, there are other reasons to think that both analogies would lead to an underestimate of the heroin use which would occur, were the drug freely available in the United States. The use of heroin by American troops in Vietnam became established over a very short period of time and had by no means reached a steady state when the large-scale urinalysis and troop withdrawal ended the epidemic. It might well be that had the troops remained longer, opiate use would have become more respectable and the already large numbers of opiate users would have induced more and more nonusers to try the drug, increasing overall use considerably.

Moreover, if use in Vietnam had continued much longer, the percentage of users becoming addicted might also have risen, pushing the overall

19. Eric J. Meyers, "American Heroin Policy: Some Alternatives," in *The Facts about "Drug Abuse"*, pp. 197–204.

20. Robins, Helzer, and Davis, "Narcotic Use in Southeast Asia and Afterward, pp. 955–61.

21. Ralph B. Little, "Hazards of Drug Dependency among Physicians," *Journal of the American Medical Association* 218, no. 10 (6 December 1971): 1533.

22. Charles Winick, "A Theory of Drug Dependence Based on Role, Access to, and Attitudes Toward Drugs," in *Theories on Drug Abuse*, ed. Jan J. Lettieri, Mollie Sayers, and Helen W. Pearson, National Institute on Drug Abuse, Research Monograph Series, no. 30 (Washington, D.C.: Government Printing Office, 1980, pp. 229–31.

addiction rate far above the 14 percent reported. Indeed, by the time of the troop withdrawal, units had already been reported where heroin addiction ran to around one-third of the enlisted men.[23]

Nor does the extent of opiate use among members of the medical profession provide a ceiling on the use to be expected under free availability. First of all, the physician's most frequent drug of addiction is meperidine (Demerol), which is generally considered less enticing than either morphine or heroin. Moreover, although physicians have far greater access to opiates than does the population at large, they by no means have free access. Law enforcement and licensing authorities try strenuously to make it difficult for them to divert opiates from hospital supplies, from their own legitimate possession, or from their prescriptions. And the severe sanctions which medical societies impose upon addicted physicians also may help control their opiate use.[24] Finally, physicians as a class would not seem an especially addiction-prone group. Though they must cope with considerable stress in their professional lives, one would think that their education with respect to the dangers of drug use, their general future-orientation, and their opportunities for other satisfactions would make them among the less likely candidates for addiction.

Access to Heroin

Another way of approaching the problem is to ask several interrelated questions: How many more people in the United States would have access to heroin were the drug freely and legally available? How many of those with access to the drug would use it? And, of those who used heroin, how many would become addicted to it?

The answer to the first question depends, of course, on the meaning of "access to heroin." It is likely that almost any young person can gain access to the drug today if he is willing to spend enough time and energy on the project. Certainly in most of the nation, if he succeeds in getting himself arrested and jailed, he will find himself in contact with heroin users and sellers.

Nonetheless, if the term "access" means the casual, unplanned exposures to the opportunity to use heroin that result in most first use of the drug, it is clear that the majority of our youth do not have this kind of access to heroin. According to a recent study, some 16 percent of high

23. Morgan F. Murphy and Robert H. Steele, *The World Heroin Problem: Report of a Special Study Mission* (Washington D.C.: Government Printing Office, 1971), pp. 1, 9.

24. Solomon Garb, "Drug Addiction in Physicians," *Anesthesia and Analgesia* 48, no. 1 (January–February 1969): 129–33. Gary Thatcher, "The Respectable Pushers," *Drug Enforcement* 4, no. 1 (February 1977): 26–35.

school seniors report that they have "easy access" to the drug.[25] For the most part, they are in our black and Spanish-speaking ghettos and in a few lower-class white neighborhoods. Obviously, were heroin as available as alcohol or tobacco, this percentage would be raised from less than one-fifth to almost the entire population.

## Heroin Use

Having access to heroin, however, is not the same as using it. In some areas of Turkey, Pakistan, and India, opiates are widely available but seem to be used by a very small percentage of the population.[26] It is possible, theoretically, that almost everyone who would be willing to try heroin if it were freely available already tries it despite our present prohibition. This would be the case if a predisposition to use heroin existed only among residents of those areas where heroin happens to be widely available.

As we have seen, our experiences with Vietnam and the medical profession do not encourage this belief. Nor is the example of tobacco a comforting one for those who would rely on the good sense of people residing outside the deprived areas of our central cities. Considering the adverse information we have on the health dangers of tobacco, an alarming percentage of young people do try (and, indeed, continue to smoke) cigarettes.[27] Obviously reliance on their caution and prudence is misplaced.

It is not at all clear that the dangers of heroin could be so realistically brought home to young people that the great majority of them would be unwilling to try that drug were it freely and continuously available. At least on first thought it would seem that the ailments brought on by tobacco use—lung cancer, emphysema, strokes, and heart attacks—can be as frighteningly and vividly brought home to young prospective users as could the dangers of addiction—especially remembering that under our postulated policy of free availability, addiction would be far less debilitating than it is today.

The fact is that young people in many ways tend to be heedless of their health and welfare if the rewards in peer approval, thrill, or pleasure are sufficient. Nor is it merely that the damage from cigarettes occurs too far

25. Lloyd D. Johnson, Jerald G. Bachman, and Patrick M. O'Malley, *Drug Use among American High School Students 1975–1977*, National Institute on Drug Abuse, DWEH Pub. No. (ADM) 78-619 (Washington, D.C.: Government Printing Office, 1977), pp. 180–82.

26. Alaeddin Akcasu, "A Survey on the Factors Preventing Opium Use by Poppy-growing Peasants in Turkey," United Nations *Bulletin on Narcotics* 28, no. 2 (April-nJune 1976): 13–17.

27. *Smoking and Health*, pp. 17-5–17-9.

in the future to be noticeable to the foreshortened vision of the young. Despite the genuinely horrible and immediate consequences which can flow from motorcycle accidents, large numbers of young people continue to ride those dangerous vehicles.

Perhaps we could take more comfort if heroin could only be used intravenously, since there does seem to be a psychological barrier against the use of a hypodermic needle upon oneself. The problem is partly that heroin injection, unlike sky-diving, is one of those activities that can be approached gradually—and, hence, more easily. When plentiful, the drug can either be smoked in cigarettes or snorted. Indeed, in Vietnam, where heroin was abundant, most users began by smoking or sniffing the drug. Of this number a good percentage then went on to skin popping and then to intravenous use. Moreover, the psychological barrier against intravenous injection does not seem to be *that* high. Many young people today take their first heroin intravenously, sustained apparently by peer encouragement and the promise of euphoria.[28]

## Changes in Culture

Even if we could be confident that the great majority of our youth would avoid the drug if it suddenly became freely available, we could not be sure that the cultural constraints on use would long endure. Although we do not have any clear understanding of how culture changes, we do know that dramatic changes in drug use have taken place in a relatively short time—without significant changes in availability.

Sometimes these changes have been in the direction of sobriety. For instance, in what anthropologists have called "the great Jewish drink mystery," the Jews, somewhere between 500 and 300 B.C., changed from a people well known for their drunkenness to one equally celebrated for their moderation in the use of alcohol.[29] On the other hand, a number of American Indian tribes are known which used alcohol for two generations with no social disruption—and then began to drink excessively.[30]

Moreover, youth culture seems to be subject to especially dramatic fluctuations. The rapid changes in styles of dress, hair, music, entertainment, and other fads among the young have baffled their elders for generations; and the appearace of a charismatic proselytizer for heroin, as Timothy Leary was for LSD and marijuana, could change their attitude toward that drug entirely.

28. Zinberg, "Rehabilitation of Drug Users in Vietnam," pp. 264, 269.

29. Mark Keller, "The Great Jewish Drink Mystery," *British Journal of Addiction* 64, no. 3/4 (January 1970): 290–94.

30. Craig MacAndrew and Robert B. Edgerton, *Drunken Comportment: A Social Explanation* (Chicago: Aldine, 1969), pp. 111–23.

Even if no one person exerted a dramatic influence on heroin use, new cultural practices and meanings might grow up around heroin as they have around alcohol. The use of alcohol is considerably increased by its association with sexuality; the stereotype of the amusing drunk; and the social institutions of the singles bar, the "happy hour," and the cocktail party. If analogues of these grew up around heroin, they might overcome even strong inhibitions against the use of the drug. It is possible, even, that heroin use might piggyback upon that of alcohol. There are many alcoholic drinks that could disguise the bitter taste of heroin, and the painkilling, anxiety-reducing power of the opiates might be an attractive supplement to the depressant effect of alcohol. This seems to have been the case in some areas of eighteenth-century England, where a popular drink was beer laced with opium.[31]

In addition, the very act of making heroin legally accessible might change the cultural message we convey about the dangers of the drug and indicate to many that it was safe enough to try. The broadcast of such a message is, of course, a disadvantage inherent in the repeal of any drug prohibition, including, for instance, that of marijuana. As applied to heroin, however, we perhaps have more to lose by blunting our present message. Not only is the popular view as to the dangers of use probably truer of heroin than of marijuana, but the cultural barriers to marijuana use have already been greatly weakened by our widespread experience with that drug.

A somewhat similar consequence of free availability would be to accustom the population to moderate users, thus eroding the incorrect, but perhaps functional, belief that heroin use almost invariably leads to addiction and serious social and health problems. Ironically, if heroin use always led to such consequences, we might better rely on the innate good sense of American youth—however weak a reed that might be—to avoid use. Similarly, of course, if we could be confident that heroin would only rarely lead to addiction, we might regard its use with more equanimity. It might, however, be that moderate use would be common enough to help erode our cultural constraints against trying heroin—and yet so difficult for users to maintain that it would leave us with an unacceptable level of addiction.

## THE LIKELIHOOD OF INCREASED ADDICTION

This brings us, of course, to the next question: To what extent would increased use of heroin bring increased addiction? It is, after all, possible that though more people would try heroin, no more would become

31. Virginia Berridge, "Fenland Opium-eating in the Nineteenth Century," *British Journal of Addiction* 72, no. 3 (September 1977): 275.

addicted. If so, there would be little cause for concern since one-time or even occasional use of heroin—so long as it remained occasional—would probably not cause us any serious problems.

The difficulty is that one can make no such prediction. We do not yet understand the factors which permit one heroin user to avoid addiction while another becomes addicted—any more than we can know in advance which alcohol users will have trouble with that drug. As a result, without a great background of experience with the whole population, we cannot estimate how widespread the predisposition to—or against—addiction is.

We have already seen that we cannot rely on the theoretical possibility that willingness to try heroin is concentrated in the relatively small number of areas where the drug is already available. Nonetheless, vulnerability to addiction might be so restricted if, for instance, those who became addicted today had an abnormal liking for heroin and most normal people would not find the drug enjoyable enough to continue use until they were addicted.

## The Effect of Heroin on "Normal" People

Some authorities have argued that even if a substantial percentage of the population tried heroin once or twice, the great majority would not become even moderate users, let alone addicts. The reason, they assert, is that most "normal" people would not enjoy heroin use enough to continue.

A number of studies do support the view that a sizable percentage of the population would not find opiate use enjoyable. One, for instance, reported a double-blind test on twenty "normal" volunteers, none of whom, presumably, had used an opiate for other than medical purposes. Less than half of the subjects found heroin or morphine euphoric, and fully half actively disliked both drugs. Indeed, the average "pleasure score" of those who were given heroin or morphine was lower than the score of those who were given a placebo and a great deal lower than that of the subjects given an amphetamine.[32]

Other medical authorities, too, have asserted that "only in rare instances, if at all, does anyone except the emotionally unstable—the psychopath or the neurotic—experience positive pleasure from morphine," and that the great majority of medical students "have found it difficult to understand why anyone would ever become addicted."[33]

32. Henry K. Beecher, *Measurement of Subjective Responses: Quantitative Effects of Drugs* (New York: Oxford University Press, 1959), pp. 321–41.

33. Louis Lasagna, John M. von Felsinger, and Henry K. Beecher, "Drug Induced Mood Changes in Man: 1. Observations on Healthy Subjects, Chronically Ill Patients, and 'Postaddicts,'" *Journal of the American Medical Association* 157, no. 12 (19 March 1955): 1017.

Although hospital patients differ from the general population, studies of their reactions to opiates tend to support this view. One study of 386 doses of morphine administered to 150 patients after operations found that on only 14 occasions did the patients suggest any reaction that might be called euphoric—and, in 11 of these, the euphoria seemed simply to be a relief from postoperative pain.[34]

If we could be confident as to the implications of these results, we could face the prospect of free access to heroin with correspondingly greater equanimity. There is, however, reason to be hesitant in accepting such a conclusion. First of all, there is no reason to think that the residents of the areas which produce our present heroin addicts are less "normal" than the volunteers and patients who were studied. If the poor and the ethnic minorities did differ from the rest of the population in some biochemical factor which affects enjoyment of a drug, it would be quite remarkable.

Perhaps all that has happened is that the effects of set and setting in the experimental studies and medical reports overwhelmed the "pharmacological" effect of the drug. Even if opiate use would otherwise have been pleasant for those in the double-blind study, the use of the drug in an austere hospital or laboratory environment, as part of a scientific experiment involving drugs which were primarily regarded as medicine, might well have dissipated any euphoric feelings. Use in a relaxed situation among one's friends who were plainly enjoying their drug would be expected to make a considerable difference to many users.

The studies of heroin use by "normals" may point to an unrealistically low addiction rate for another reason. Reliance on these studies implicitly assumes that those who do not enjoy heroin will therefore not continue to use it. In fact, this is often not the case. Many of those who continued heroin use until they became addicted have later reported that they did not find their initial use of heroin pleasant.[35] There are two explanations for this phenomenon. First, tolerance may develop quickly to the unpleasant effects of heroin. This is probably the case with tobacco as well, since many users of that drug report that their first smoke was unpleasant, but that they soon came to enjoy smoking. Second, heroin, like most drugs, has many effects, and the user soon learns to select and enjoy a very few as the objectives of his use. Initial opiate use typically produces both euphoria and nausea, but the user who continues soon labels the former as the drug's effect and ignores the latter. Addicts often report that after a heroin injection they became sick and vomited—but that it was a "good sick."[36]

Nor would it be very comforting if we accepted the implications of the

34. Ibid.
35. McAuliffe, "Second Look at First Effects," p. 383.
36. Ibid., pp. 382–84.

double-blind experiment and concluded that only 50 percent of those who tried heroin would enjoy its effects enough to continue use. The 50 percent figure is so high that we would have to place much confidence in other barriers to addiction before we could predict that the percentage of addicts in the population would be tolerable.

## Vulnerability to Addiction

Even if the rest of the population would find heroin use as enjoyable as did the inner-city residents, this would not necessarily mean that the number of addicts would be far higher under free availability. Residence in a violent, depressing, or aimless atmosphere, together with a lack of employment opportunity, might somehow inhibit the individual and social controls necessary to avoid addiction. If so, susceptibility to addiction would be confined primarily to just those areas of social disorganization where heroin is currently most available.[37]

Two conclusions could be drawn from such a view. First, in the rest of the nation outside these susceptible areas, free availability of heroin would not result in much addiction; and, second, in the vulnerable areas where heroin is already available, free availability would cause little increase in the addiction rate. Unfortunately, both predictions are probably incorrect.

## Free Availability in "New" Areas

There is probably some sense in the prediction that, holding availability constant, heroin addiction would be less common in middle-class America than in the areas inhabited by poorer members of ethnic minorities. It would be surprising if different groups in the population did not differ significantly in their vulnerability to addiction, just as they vary in a host of other factors, from their percentage attending college to their rates of alcoholism and mental disease. Nor is it unreasonable to believe that whatever characteristics predispose one to heroin addiction are to be found more often in those areas where heroin is now available.

The problem comes with believing that these variables, which we hardly begin to understand, are *sufficiently* localized in those areas. Though we cannot disprove it, it taxes credulity. The rate of alcoholism and schizophrenia, for instance, is higher in these areas than in most others—but it is not *that* much higher.[38] Even if vulnerability to addiction

37. This is the theory implicit in James H. McHearn, "Radical and Racial Perspective on the Heroin Problem," in *Heroin in Perspective*, pp. 119–20.

38. William W. Eaton, "Residence, Social Class and Schizophrenia," *Journal of Health and Social Behavior* 15, no. 4 (December 1974) 289-n97. Donald Cahalan and Robin Room, *Problem Drinking Among American Men*, Rutgers Center of Alcohol Studies, Monograph No. 7 (New Brunswick, N.J., 1974), pp. 83–86.

were five times as high in the enclaves where heroin is now available, the rest of the nation is so much more populous that it would still end up contributing the bulk of the addicts under free availability. And the fivefold figure grossly exaggerates the differences on what may be the most relevant indicator—alcoholism—where a difference of merely 30 percent would be more accurate.

Moreover, we have so often seen the rapid spread of heroin addiction to areas where it was formerly unknown that we have become wary in drawing conclusions as to the invulnerability of particular regions. There was always a temptation to conclude that the absence of an addiction problem in an area could be attributed to stable psychological and social variables, rather than to the lack of availability. Those who believed that heroin addiction was caused by a rare and localized vulnerability would, in the past, have picked out many "invulnerable" areas only to find again and again that they had been wrong.[39]

Moreover, even if an area were somehow invulnerable today, it might not remain so. Unless we find in the heroin-free areas some widespread biochemical or genetic factor which prevents a large segment of the population from becoming addicted—a discovery that now seems extremely unlikely—we can have no confidence that the situation could not change drastically. New use patterns, a change in public consciousness as to the meaning of heroin use, or some other unforeseen factor might undermine existing social controls and sharply raise the likelihood that those who tried the drug would thereafter become addicted.

## Animal Experiments

Animal experiments, though perhaps not entitled to great weight, seem to support the view that vulnerability to opiate addiction is not a rare trait. At one time it was believed that monkeys would use opiates regularly only if they had already become addicted through involuntary administration. Over the past two decades, however, self-administration equipment has been improved, and it is now clear that, if permitted, virtually all monkeys will continue injecting themselves with opiates until they become addicted. Experiments also show that even nonaddicted animals will perform considerable amounts of work to "earn" their injections—though the addicted monkey, like the addicted human, will work even harder to keep up his use.[40]

Interestingly, the opiates lie somewhere between alcohol and cocaine in their reinforcing power. Alcohol seems much less attractive. It is quite

39. Vincent P. Dole, "Addictive Behavior," *Scientific American* 243, no. 6 (December 1980): 140.

40. Gerald A. Deneau, Tomoji Yanagita, and M. H. Seevers, "Self-administration of Psychoactive Substances by the Monkey: A Measure of Psychological Dependence," *Psychopharmacologia (Berl.)* 16, no. 1 (3 November 1969): 37.

difficult to get most animals to drink alcohol; and, unless they are already addicted, monkeys and many strains of other animals will go to some length to avoid ingesting that drug.[41] Cocaine, on the other hand, proves to be even more reinforcing than heroin. Even though cocaine is not usually classed as addicting, animals will do enormous amounts of work to earn their cocaine shots—more even than monkeys addicted to heroin.[42]

## Studies from Other Cultures

It is true that we do not have a great deal of information on human use of opiates under conditions of free availability. Nonetheless, the available information is not encouraging. The examples of the medical profession and the American soldiers in Vietnam are confirmed by the only other study which seems directly pertinent. William McGlothlin and his associates studied two villages in the midst of an opium-growing region in Pakistan. In both, the drug was, for all practical purposes, freely available; but in one the addiction rate among males was 5 percent while in the other it was over 50 percent. Subjects from the low-using village were far more likely to report that they used opium for the self-treatment of pain, coughs, dysentery, etc., and to be better able to work or function. In the village with high opium use, the largest number of addicts reported that they initially used the drug for pleasure, euphoria, or peace; and that they had begun their use because of social interaction and curiosity.[43]

Any prediction of the likely extent of opiate addiction under free availability must take account of this problem. If the rate of addiction is not dependent upon stable biological factors but rather is the result of labile cultural variables such as purpose of use, we can take even less comfort in any promises of a low addiction rate where heroin is freely available. Moreover, even if we are not impressed with this argument, we should note at least that in the "low-using" village the addiction rate was over ten times that of the United States today.

## THE CONSTANCY OF DRUG ABUSE

Nor can we derive any more reassurance from the related view espoused by some authorities that the total number of serious drug abusers in any

41. John L. Falk and Herman H. Samson, "Schedule-induced Physical Dependence on Ethanol," *Pharmacological Reviews* 27, no. 4 (December 1975): 449.

42. Travis Thompson and Roy Pickens, "Stimulant Self-administration by Animals: Some Comparisons with Opiate Self-administration," *Federation Proceedings* 29, no. 1 (January-February 1970): 6–12.

43. William H. McGlothlin et al., "Opium Use in Two Communities of Pakistan—A Preliminary Comparison of Rural and Urban Patterns," United Nations. *Bulletin on Narcotics* 30, no. 4 (October-nDecember 1978): 1–15.

society is relatively constant. This would imply that even if heroin addiction did greatly increase under free availability, new addicts would primarily be drawn from the ranks of those who would otherwise abuse drugs such as alcohol. If this were so, the social cost of their drug use might drop rather than rise.

The problem with this assertion is that there is no reason to believe it. We know of many cases where alcoholism increased greatly in a short period without any compensating drop in any other form of drug abuse or, indeed, without a reduction in any other harmful behavior.[44]

The example of cigarettes also may be instructive. Between 1910 and 1970, per capita consumption of cigarettes in the United States increased by a factor of approximately 15, without any apparent decline in any other drug use—aside from that of other tobacco products such as snuff and chewing tobacco, which did not nearly balance the increase in cigarette use. Indeed, smoking increased with great rapidity during the 1930s when Prohibition was repealed and alcohol consumption increased as well.[45]

It is true that we do not, today, classify cigarettes along with mind-altering substances such as heroin or alcohol. This may be a consequence of its social acceptability, however. For several hundred years after tobacco was introduced into Western society, it was regarded as a powerful mind-altering drug, and certainly the percentage of tobacco users who become dependent upon their drug exceeds that with respect to any of the other legal—and probably most of the illegal—drugs.[46]

If the analogy to cigarettes seems farfetched, data involving opium itself refutes the idea that increases in one kind of drug dependence will be balanced by decreases in another. In the McClothlin study of two villages in Pakistan, the village with the lower addiction rate did have slightly more users of other drugs, primarily alcohol and marijuana, but this difference—68 percent versus 58 percent—by no means balanced the difference in opium addiction.[47]

## HEROIN USE IN "OLD" AREAS

Even if one conceded that sizable increases in addiction might result from the extension of heroin availability to those areas where the drug is not now available, it could still be argued that at least where heroin is available already, free availability would do little harm. The fallacy in this argument is that even in these areas, heroin is not currently *that* available.

One study strongly indicates that even in the areas of relatively high heroin availability, our present policy still depresses the addiction rate

44. See below, "The Gin Epidemic," "The Indian Experience," and "South African Bantus."

45. Schuman, "Patterns of Smoking Behavior," pp. 40–41.

46. Brecher, *Licit and Illicit Drugs*, pp. 209–13.

47. McGlothlin et al., "Opium Use in Pakistan," p. 7.

considerably. Robert Schasre interviewed a sample of 40 former heroin users who had used and enjoyed heroin for a while, but had terminated their use before becoming addicted.[48] Of these, 18 had made a specific decision to stop using the drug, while 22 had ceased for what might be called external reasons.

Of the 18 sample members who made a specific decision to stop heroin use, 6 did so because they or their friends had run afoul of the narcotics laws—presumably in situations which would not have occurred had the drug been freely available. Nine others decided to stop because they had experienced the beginning of physical addiction. Perhaps they would have ceased anyway, even if the ready availability of heroin had made addiction much easier to manage. It is undeniable, however, that their incentives to avoid addiction would be far less under a policy of free availability.

Of the 22 sample members who made no particular decision to cease use, 13 had stopped because they no longer had easy access to a supply, due to the arrest or departure of their connection; and 9 stopped when they moved out of the neighborhood or town. It is possible that these 9 former users stopped because they were separated from their drug-using friends rather than because they were separated from access to the drug itself, but it is also quite likely that one reason they stopped was the inconvenience in obtaining the new connection.

Schasre's data, at the least, force us to consider the possibility that between one-half and nine-tenths of those in the areas of high heroin use who at one time seemed headed for addiction but stopped short would have become addicted had heroin been freely available. Moreover, these figures may still underestimate the increase in addiction which free availability would produce in areas of already high heroin use. Many heroin experimenters in the same neighborhood had tried the drug only once or twice and, hence, never even made it into Schasre's category of those users who seemed headed for addiction. The failure of some of these one or two time users to continue may also have been a consequence of our restrictions on free availability.

In addition, both the one or two time users and those in Schasre's sample who had used heroin for a longer time had experience with only relatively small amounts of diluted heroin. It is likely that with a purer drug the rewards in euphoria would have been greater and, hence, more would have continued use. Finally, since drug use is only one of the competitors for the money of the young—along with clothes, automobiles, dates, and other forms of entertainment—sharp decreases in the price of heroin could only stimulate consumption.

48. Robert Schasre, "Cessation Patterns Among Neophyte Heroin Users," *International Journal of the Addictions* 1, no. 2 (June 1966): 23–32.

## THE PROLONGATION OF ADDICTION

Entirely apart from its effect in increasing addiction, free availability would probably act to make that condition longer-lasting and more difficult to cure. Even in our areas of relatively high heroin use, a major reason why many addicts give up the drug—either temporarily or permanently—is the unavailability of heroin at a price they can afford. This is not only true of those who enroll "voluntarily" in our treatment programs, almost all of whom complain that heroin addiction has become too much of a "hassle" for them; it is also true of the many addicts who stay out of treatment but go through withdrawal and either temporarily give up the drug or permanently "mature out."

The most important reasons why addicts give up heroin, according to virtually every study, are the trouble and expense of maintaining a large habit; fear of involvement with the legal system because of the demands of their habits; and the inability to "score" enough good heroin.[49] Since none of these reasons would apply were heroin freely and cheaply available, it is likely that free availability would further lower the remission and cure rates among addicts.

We see a similar phenomenon with respect to tobacco. As many cigarette smokers have found out, the ready availability of that drug has two major effects. First, it increases the amount they use at those times when they happen to want to smoke; and, second, the fact that they can always start again easily, even after they have stopped use, increases their difficulty in giving up the drug completely.[50]

As a result, even if we did believe that the determinants of heroin use or addiction were concentrated overwhelmingly in our black and ethnic minority areas, we would still have to acknowledge that free availability might considerably increase addiction there. It is true that the inhabitants of these areas bear a great part of the total costs of heroin prohibition today, but a very sizable increase in their addiction rate might prove even more costly to them, and add to rather than decrease their social problems.

Moreover, although we can only speculate about the matter, there may be a "tipping point" in a community where the social consequences of addiction change when the percentage of addicts in an area reaches a certain level. Even a neighborhood of considerable social disorganization can change greatly for the worse, and it is certainly possible that a further rise in the rate of heroin addiction could exhaust the already limited community services, set a more dangerous example of drug abuse for the children of the area, and deplete their working manpower. Worse yet, all

49. Waldorf and Biernacki, "Natural Recovery from Opiate Addiction: Some Preliminary Findings," pp. 65–67.
50. Jaffe, "Drug Addiction and Drug Abuse," p. 543.

these effects might reinforce each other to lower drastically the quality of life for all.

Even if we decided that the overall cost to the nation of heroin addiction would be lowered by free availability because the increased addiction in our ghettos would be overbalanced by the lessened costs of enforcement and addict crime in other areas, we would still face a major problem. The symbolic effect of tolerating, indeed making easy, widespread heroin addiction among the poor, the black, and the Hispanics might have long-term costs for our society which we should weigh very carefully. At the very least, in moral terms, we should worry about adding to the burdens of those groups in our society which most need help.

## THE CONSEQUENCES OF ADDICTION

Up to now, we have discussed the effect of the free availability of heroin upon addiction as if addiction consisted merely of a physical need for regular doses of an opiate. This is the model of heroin addiction held by many advocates of free availability, and if one grants their premise that heroin addiction has no effects other than creating a need for that drug, the policy implications are clear.

The creation of a need for a drug, even in a sizable proportion of the population, would not be very costly in social terms so long as the drug was cheap, easily available, and not harmful. Free availability, then, would remove most of the adverse effects upon the addict and upon our society which we presently attribute to heroin—leaving only three worries about widespread addiction, none of which compares in magnitude to our present concerns.

First, we could be unhappy about what would be a considerable expenditure on heroin of money which we, as nonusers, might think could be better spent in other ways. However, as a society, we spend great amounts on cosmetics, showy automobiles, and many other things which those of us who do not have those particular tastes tend to deplore—all without considering this a major social problem. And, although cigarette smoking is a major public health problem, the siphoning off of a portion of the gross national product to buy cigarettes does not seem to be one of our concerns.

Second, the heroin addict's tolerance to opiates might prove a problem to him in surgery or in any other medical situation where the unblunted effects of opiates were needed. Although this could make things inconvenient on occasion, it would prove no more of a problem than do dozens of other habits or behaviors which we tolerate without even considering the medical problems they produce.

Finally, even a policy of free availability would not preclude the possibility of an interruption in the opiate supply. For instance, a strike in the producing or distribution industry, damage to the poppy crop by some as yet unknown blight or insect attack, or a manipulated shortage caused by a cartel of producing nations might prove quite awkward. The prospect of a major fraction of the population all going into full-blown withdrawal is awesome to contemplate—but we risk a similar fate with cigarette smokers and solve the matter quite nicely through individual and commercial stockpiling.

The problem, however, inheres in the premise that heroin addiction is a phenomenon no more complicated than a recurring need for that drug. The fact is that we know amazingly little about the consequences of addiction under conditions of easy access to heroin. Nonetheless, the possibility of a great increase in addiction under free availability requires us to look much more closely at the dangers inherent in addiction itself, which, though lower per addict, might affect far more people.

## The Physical Damage Caused by Heroin

In our discussion in chapter 1 of heroin myths, we might well have included the myth that there is something intrinsic in the drug that causes heroin addiction to be severely damaging to the addict's physical health—the myth arising, of course, from the damage addiction now causes the heroin addict.

To be sure, the impurity of the street drug and the wide variations in its potency cause many health complications. The high price of heroin may force the addict to compromise his nutrition and the conditions of sanitation under which he lives. And, by turning the addict into an outlaw, the law makes it harder for him to seek medical treatment for any ailment, whether or not caused by his addiction. These, however, are costs better attributed to our heroin prohibition than to addiction itself, and they are so great that they completely overshadow any harm heroin might do to the addict were the drug freely available.

Surprisingly, the best estimates of the physical damage heroin does to its user, when used under conditions of free availability, indicate that the drug is a relatively safe one, at least as compared to alcohol and tobacco. While the long-term, heavy use of these legal drugs may cause serious, indeed fatal, tissue damage, heroin produces no analogy to the cirrhosis, peripheral neuritis, gastritis, and central nervous system damage caused by long-term, heavy use of alcohol, or to the cardiovascular and lung impairment caused by tobacco use.[51]

Indeed, perhaps because the body treats opiates more as a substance

51. John C. Ball and John C. Urbaitis, "Absence of Major Medical Complications among Chronic Opiate Addicts," in *The Epidemiology of Opiate Addiction in the United States*, pp. 301–6.

which occurs naturally in the bloodstream, heroin may cause no long-term physical problems at all. A standard medical text reports that "there is no evidence that the opiates produce organic central nervous system damage or other pathology, even after decades of continuous use. An 84 year-old physician who was a morphine addict was found to exhibit no evidence of mental or physical deterioration after continuous use for sixty years."[52] Studies of the rare middle-class heroin and morphine addicts who, either legally or illegally, had been maintained on opiates confirm this. They indicate that such addicts suffer from no health problems that are not shared by the general population.[53]

Intravenous Injection

One major question, however, involves the relation between heroin use and intravenous injection. Even if heroin use by other routes of administration created no major health problems, use of the drug intravenously might still be a considerable cause for concern. Of course, to some extent intravenous injection may itself be a consequence of the heroin prohibition, which has made it too expensive to take the drug by other routes. Once heroin became cheap, it might be that users would revert to other simpler and less dangerous means of administration.

It is true that before the Harrison Act, when opiates were cheap and plentiful, they were very rarely injected. Moreover, injection is rare in those Asian countries where opiates are inexpensive and easily available. For instance, in Hong Kong until recently, heroin, though illegal, was cheap and relatively available, and the drug was inhaled in smoke rather than injected. In the last few years, however, law enforcement has been able to exert pressure on the supply of the drug, raising its price considerably and resulting in a significant increase in the use of injection.[54]

Despite this, predictions that free availability of heroin would mean the end of intravenous injection are probably based on too simple a view of drug use. It may be a great deal harder for a society to abandon injection than it would have been to discourage it in the first place. Culture often determines the method of drug administration, and American addicts now use heroin primarily through intravenous injection. They have developed

52. Gregory G. Dimijian, "Contemporary Drug Abuse," in *Medical Pharmacology: Principles and Concepts*, 9th ed., ed. Andres Goth (St. Louis: C. V. Mosby Co., 1978), p. 299.

53. David F. Musto and Manuel F. Ramos, "A Follow-up Study of the New Haven Morphine Maintenance Clinic of 1920," *New England Journal of Medicine* 308, no. 18 (30 April 1981): 1075–76.

54. Shoesmith, "Chasing the Dragon, 39. *South China Morning Post*, 26 April 1978, p. 8.

a whole system of beliefs as to why this is the best and most pleasurable way to use the drug—including an almost religious exaltation of the rush. One would think that so long as these attitudes and beliefs persist, addicts will continue to be socialized into intravenous injection.

This view seems to have been borne out by our experience in Vietnam. Although intravenous use rose sharply among addicts there when law enforcement began to make heroin less available, there had been a notable tendency even earlier for addicts to move from smoked heroin to intravenous injection. The move took place often as addicts' tolerance to the drug built up and they began to regard themselves as heroin users.[55]

Even if intravenous injection did not cease under free availability, there seems no doubt that the health problems associated with that means of administration would abate considerably. Injection of a material subject to no quality control and often containing adulterants is a major cause of vein problems. And the necessity for avoiding detection helps promote the sharing of needles, which aids the spread of hepatitis.[56]

Nonetheless, an examination of British addicts who injected legally prescribed heroin reveals health problems that are a consequence of intravenous injection itself, despite the purity of the heroin used. The vein damage and embolisms suffered by intravenous injectors of heroin arise in part simply from the number of injections—three or four a day plus a certain number of misses. The often drawn analogy to the diabetic who must inject insulin is not apt since that drug is injected subcutaneously—a much simpler and safer process.

Nor is the use of unsterile needles, which spread infections and hepatitis, purely a consequence of heroin prohibition. Experience with British addicts indicates that as long as heroin addicts inject their drug in groups, they will probably share needles, either as a gesture of solidarity and trust or simply because—as cigarette smokers share matches and cigarettes—it is more convenient.[57]

## Overdose Deaths

Although intravenous injection can be connected with many serious health problems, its relation to the most dramatic of the health consequences of heroin use—the death by overdose—is quite obscure. Indeed, though heroin overdose is a serious medical problem, accounting in one

55. Zinberg, "Rehabilitation of Drug Users in Vietnam," p. 264.

56. Jan Howard and Philip Borges, "Needle Sharing in the Haight: Some Social and Psychological Functions," in *Heroin in Perspective*, p. 128.

57. Thomas H. Bewley, Oved Ben-Arie, and Vincent Marks, "Morbidity and Mortality from Heroin Dependence, 3: Relation of Hepatitis to Self-injection Techniques," *British Medical Journal* 23 (March 1968): 730–32.

recent year for the largest number of deaths in the 16-to-25-year-old age bracket in New York City, little is understood about the phenomenon.[58]

The "overdose" is to some extent a result of injecting street drugs, which vary widely and unpredictably in potency. One pharmacological effect of heroin is the production of respiratory depression, and occasionally an unexpectedly large dose will exceed an addict's tolerance and precipitate his respiratory collapse.[59] This, of course, is primarily a consequence of the illegal system for marketing heroin, just as occasional sales of wood alcohol and the resulting poisoning were a result of the marketing of bootleg liquor under Prohibition. The same is true of accidental poisoning due to one of the materials with which the heroin is "cut," and perhaps even of the deliberate murders with "hot shots," since heroin users, by the nature of the lives they lead, often become liabilities to others.[60]

Other "overdose" deaths do not seem to be a consequence of our heroin prohibition. These include the deaths resulting from the use of heroin in combination with alcohol or barbiturates, presumably in ignorance of the fact that the depressants and opiates increase each other's effects.[61]

Finally, there are some deaths we cannot account for. We know of cases where several experienced addicts have divided up their heroin supply into equal dosages and shot up, only to have one go into respiratory collapse and die. Even more baffling are the situations where an addict has divided his day's supply of heroin in thirds and, after having no problem with the first dose, tried the second four hours later and immmediately suffered an "overdose."[62]

Indeed, the contribution of heroin use itself to the death rate of addicts is not at all understood. Perhaps it is understandable that the rate among American addicts should be extremely high for their age group. It is more difficult to explain why British addicts, who had legal heroin dispensed to them by physicians, suffered from an equally high mortality rate.[63]

We must recognize the nagging possibility that the long-term health consequences of heroin use may be much more severe than we had

58. Brecher, *Licit and Illicit Drugs*, p. 102.

59. Jaffe and Martin, "Opioid Analgesics," p. 502.

60. Moore, *Buy and Bust*, p. 149.

61. Brecher, *Licit and Illicit Drugs*, pp. 111–14.

62. Such impressionistic reports notwithstanding, many physicians conclude that these deaths are indeed overdoses. Mark H. Greene, James L. Luke, and Robert L. DuPont, "Opiate 'Overdose' Deaths in the District of Columbia 1: Heroin-Related Fatalities," *Medical Annals of the District of Columbia* 43, no. 4 (April 1974): 175–81. It is likely that variables related to conditioning make the difference.

63. O'Donnell, *Narcotic Addicts in Kentucky*, pp. 23–30. Thomas H. Bewley, Oved Ben-Arie, and Ian Pierce James, "Morbidity and Mortality from Heroin Dependence, 1: Survey of Heroin Addicts Known to the Home Office," *British Medical Journal*, 23 March 1968, 725–26.

thought. Our evidence of harmlessness is so weak that we cannot be sure that the health effects of heroin use under free availability would not constitute a major public health problem. In this respect heroin may be compared to tobacco. Although tobacco use is seen today as an important cause of sickness and death, it was not shown to be harmful until our investigations became far more probing than those to which chronic use of heroin has been subjected.

Despite all this, the health problems of heroin addicts are not a serious reason to oppose free availability. There is no doubt that our present prohibition makes the health of those addicted much worse, so that on this count we could probably regard the likelihood of more widespread, but also more benign, heroin addiction with equanimity. Considering what we know about cigarette and alcohol use, it does not look as if heroin, under conditions of legal availability, would be a much greater threat to health—and it would probably be a lesser one.

Indeed, it might be relatively easy to rationalize the matter as we do with cigarettes and say that those dying from heroin use have brought it upon themselves and that our duty is to inform the potential user as best we can; to offer him help if he sincerely wishes to break his habit; and perhaps to discourage his use in relatively subtle ways—well short of invoking the criminal law.

## SOCIAL PRODUCTIVITY AS A GOAL

It is a very different danger of heroin use on quite another dimension, which seems more worrisome than the health effects of the drug. Probably the major reason for discouraging heroin use is the view that the social productivity of the addict is destroyed or greatly damaged by his addiction.

Advocating the prohibition of heroin on the grounds that we must preserve the social productivity of the citizenry raises both practical and moral questions. Indeed, the issues in such an argument involve even more fundamental questions as to the relation between the individual and the state than does the debate over prohibition of purely self-harming conduct.

One might ask whether it is an appropriate function of government to inquire into the social productivity of its citizens and attempt to force them to be what it regards as useful members of society. Most of us take the view that in a free society the government should be able to insist only that we do not harm others; that we perform certain civic duties, such as paying our taxes or, if called, serving in the military; and perhaps that, despite John Stuart Mill, we do not harm ourselves—at least in certain ways. We do not usually think that the government should require us to be productive, too. First of all, definitions of what is productive labor incorporate so many value judgments—many of which are dubious at best—that they are quite unworkable. Though some nations punish as "parasites" those who, without excuse, do not work at paying jobs, we take pride that we do no such thing.

However, one need not uphold the punishment of "parasites" in order to assert that a government may appropriately prevent the use of substances which would deprive large numbers of its citizens of their social productivity—defined perhaps as the ability to hold some gainful and legal employment. In other words, there is no logical inconsistency between saying that a government should not punish laziness and saying that it may use its law to prevent access to things that make people lazy— or even aid in their being lazy.

It is true that most attempts to prevent things that cause laziness or help people to be lazy—just like attempts to prevent people from harming themselves—are absurdities. We would not try to pass most such laws, if only because it is so obvious that we could not enforce them—at least in our kind of society. There are, to be sure, other inducements to laziness, such as television watching, which, if the political consensus were obtainable, might easily be restricted simply by cutting broadcasting hours—indeed, many countries do just this. Their reasoning is not so unlike that of Edward III of England, who decreed that bowling was to be made illegal, not because there was anything intrinsically wrong with the activity, but because it distracted England's yeomen from an activity of national importance—practicing their archery.[64]

As to most of our diversions, however, the majority of nations, like ours, seem to have concluded that the benefits in pleasure to those who do not "abuse" the activity outweigh the social damage caused by those who do. Moreover, there are some kinds of inducements to a lack of productivity which our society is particularly committed to tolerating. Subverting exhortations such as Timothy Leary's "turn on, tune in, and drop out," are protected by the First Amendment freedoms to speak and to publish.

Nonetheless, merely because we would wish—or are compelled—to allow some encouragements to a lack of social productivity, does not mean we must allow all. It is, after all, possible that the lowering of productivity caused by the use of a freely available substance would impose even greater social costs on us than would our efforts to suppress it. And, even if we gave what we thought was appropriate weight to the personal pleasure caused by the substance use and to the human freedom to be unproductive, we might still feel suppression was appropriate.

It might be that a distinction should be drawn between two cases—the

64. Alec R. Myers, *England in the Late Middle Ages*, The Pelican History of England (Harmondsworth, England: Penguin Books, 1952), p. 139.

first where the sole social effect of the drug use would be to lower the user's occupational level, in prestige or income; the second where the use of the substance produced the gross difference between employability and unemployability. In the first situation, one might argue that the only reason for using the criminal law to prevent inducements toward less productive labor is an unworthy greed for a greater gross national product. In the second, different considerations may come into play; there is a considerable difference between a substance which induces people not to work as hard as they can and one which induces them not to work at all.

It may be that, in the latter case, government intervention could be justified in any society committed to pay some kind of welfare to those unable to hold employment. Part of the welfare problem is that we are unable to draw a hard and fast distinction between those who cannot and those who will not work. We have already seen another facet of this difficulty in attempting to determine the appropriateness of the disease model with respect to the "addictive disorders." For instance, if we take the position that the heroin addict cannot work because he has the "disease of addiction" we will be paying a high price for our use of the medical model. The free availability of heroin, then, may not only cost us a considerable amount in welfare payments but may also undermine the moral basis of the welfare laws. On the other hand, if we say the addict simply will not work, and deny him welfare, we may still remain committed on humanitarian grounds to preventing his starvation. Moreover, even if we were willing to let the heroin addict starve, the chances are he would turn to crime first—thus making addiction almost as good a predictor of criminality as it is today—except that free availability might then saddle us with a far higher number of addicts.

Though this issue deserves a considerably greater discussion than it has received, virtually all governments have taken the view that they do have the right to interfere in the distribution of drugs which might produce widespread unwillingness or inability to work.[65] Here, as in the related area of self-harming conduct, the only debate seems to be whether the exercise of this right in a particular instance is worth what it costs.

## HEROIN ADDICTION AND SOCIAL PRODUCTIVITY

It is one thing to decide the abstract jurisprudential question of whether the government has the right to forbid the free availability of a drug which causes a widespread loss of social productivity; it is quite another thing to determine the relevance of this discussion to any particular drug—

---

65. Caplovitz, *The Working Addict*, pp. 7–8.

specifically heroin. In answering this question, the nature of the society in question will be at least as important as the nature of the drug. We have already seen how societies differ in various ways—such as their ability to enforce their criminal laws—which help determine the balance between the costs and benefits of an attempted prohibition. Here the relevant difference involves the ability of the society to tolerate drug-caused impairment.

Societies will show considerable variation in the availability of employment for those who are impaired by drug use. In a rural subsistence society, a drug which lowered the ability to do industrial or clerical labor might not be seen to cause a significant social problem.

At first thought it would seem that the nature of our society as one of the world's richest would militate against suppressing a drug. After all, we can afford a degree of deviance and pursuit of pleasure which poorer societies cannot. On the other hand, poorer societies tend to lack the welfare and "hustling" opportunities which might be essential for the survival of the drug abuser, while the United States is still, in that respect, a land of opportunity.

Similarly, in a society such as ours, with large-scale structural unemployment, one might think that drug impairment among those unable to obtain jobs anyway would not be a matter for great societal concern—at least as compared with the unemployment itself. Unfortunately, there is no reason to think that addiction would be confined to those without hope of employment; and if it is not so confined, our already large unemployment could be swelled considerably by a growth in the number of addicts.

## ADDICTION AND WORK

The real problems, then, are the factual ones of determining whether heroin addiction, under free availability, would impair the addict's productivity or ability to hold employment—and if so, by how much. The answer, remarkably, is that we do not know. Under our present heroin prohibition, the addict suffers such an obvious loss of productivity that his situation is no guide to the likely effects of heroin addiction under free availability.

Up to now, we have used the concept of addiction as a shorthand for the kind of seriously damaging opiate use which is often called in other contexts, drug abuse. True, it is unlikely that anyone who used heroin abusively—in the sense that it caused serious interference with his health or adjustment in society—could long avoid addiction. The converse, however, is not true. It is possible that someone could be addicted and yet so stabilize his dosage that his drug use did not interfere significantly with his employability. Indeed, even today we come across previously undiscovered heroin addicts who have held employment for long periods, despite the distractions caused by our heroin prohibition.[66]

Nonetheless, there are reasons to believe that for many people addiction would be incompatible with productive work. To be sure, one popular stereotype of heroin addiction—that the addict, in his quest for a high, uses more and more of the drug so that he maintains a virtually constant state of euphoria, nodding dreamily and unable to perform any useful work—is, of course, inaccurate as a picture of today's addict. The demands of obtaining and affording sufficient heroin today are such that only a very small fraction of addicts can do this, even for short periods. Whether or not opiates act on receptors in the brain which affect drive reduction, as seems to be the case, many addicts do credit the drug with the power to solve all their problems, temporarily. Regardless of whether they might be in need of food, sex, or recreation, they feel they need take no other action than heroin use, except, of course, action directed toward securing the drug.[67]

One should not rely too heavily on the counterexample of today's working addicts. Though we know that some addicts do manage to hold steady, legitimate employment today, we do not know what proportion of the addicted population they constitute, and they almost certainly are a minority. In addition, free availability might worsen rather than improve their adjustment. The high price of heroin under heroin prohibition now lowers the amount they use and often allows them to afford only enough heroin to stave off withdrawal, rather than to achieve any states of euphoria.[68] The easy availability of cheap heroin might permit them to use the drug more abusively. This is certainly the case with other "addictive" behaviors such as overeating, smoking, and heavy drinking. All are harder to prevent when the abused substance is more available, more widely used, and lower in price. It is not unreasonable to conclude that under free availability many working addicts would find enough satisfaction simply through use of increased quantities of heroin, rather than through the more conventional rewards of employment and social life.

That is not to deny that free availability might well improve the productivity of others—perhaps much higher numbers—of those already addicted. Their inability to work today is more properly attributed to the demands heroin prohibition places on the maintenance of a habit than it is to the disabilities caused directly by heroin use. Under conditions of free availability, it is likely that some who are now addicted could hold employment. The possibility which must concern us, however, is that any increase in the overall productivity of today's addicts would be swamped

66. Dan Waldorf, *Careers in Dope* pp. 37, 40.
67. McAuliffe and Gordon, "A Test of Lindesmith's Theory of Addiction," pp. 262–64.
68. Brecher, *Licit and Illicit Drugs*, pp. 33–39.

by the greatly lowered productivity of large numbers of new addicts, whose heroin use is due to free availability. For large numbers of these new addicts the popular picture of the addict's lack of interest in employment might become accurate.

## EMINENT ADDICTS

It is true that we know of quite eminent persons who were addicted to opiates for many years and yet led extremely productive lives. Some had become addicted before the Harrison Act and were thereafter maintained by physicians acting compassionately but illegally. Others have been physicians themselves whose access to opiates insulated them from the worst effects of the prohibition.[69]

There are dangers, however, in drawing conclusions about heroin addiction from stories about a few persons who have enjoyed a kind of free availability. For instance, let us look more closely at the case of the most famous of these "productive addicts," Dr. William Stewart Halsted. Halsted is famous in medical circles as one of the great founders of the Johns Hopkins Medical School and a pioneer in American surgery, even though throughout most of his adult life, until his death in 1922, he was a morphine addict.

It is often asserted that Halsted's addiction raised no problems and went unnoticed by his colleagues. Since the release of the papers of Fredrick William Osler, another of the giants of Johns Hopkins in that era, a quite different picture has begun to emerge. It is quite likely that Halsted's colleagues did a considerable amount of covering up for him, since his addiction was by no means without problems.[70]

Often he would disappear for several days at a time and on a few occasions was inexplicably absent for several weeks. Sometimes, without notice, he would not receive guests, students, or patients. It is also perhaps noteworthy that at Columbia, before his opiate use began, Halsted had been regarded as a superb classroom teacher—while throughout his period of addiction at Johns Hopkins he was celebrated as a brilliant surgeon but has been described as a genuinely dreadful lecturer.

Moreover, even if Halsted had managed his addiction without its affecting his life at all, the career of one remarkable individual can no more prove the harmlessness of opiate addiction than the life of Winston Churchill, or of some other prodigious drinker, could prove the harmlessness of alcohol.

69. Peter D. Olch, "William Halsted and Local Anesthesia: Contributions and Complications," *Anesthesiology* 42, no. 4 (April 1975): 479–86.

70. Gerry V. Stimson, "Treatment or Control? Dilemmas for Staff in Drug Dependency Clinics," paper presented at the Cropwood Conference on Problems of Drug Abuse in Britain, 9–11 December 1977, at King's College, Cambridge. Mimeographed.

Finally, the productivity of addicts such as Halsted is more relevant to heroin maintenance (a matter to be covered in Chapter 4) than to free availability. We now know that Halsted's morphine supply was carefully monitored by his colleague, Osler. Similarly, most of the addicts whose ability to hold employment is cited in favor of free availability had their intake controlled by their physicians, who usually stabilized their dosage at the lowest effective level.

The same, indeed, is true of British addicts maintained on heroin under the "British system." Although their behavior has often been cited to show that heroin addiction under free availability is not incompatible with productivity, it proves no such thing. The British system was not free availability but a maintenance system where the amount of heroin the addicts received, though large by American standards, was subject to careful control by a physician, and was often determined through hard bargaining between doctor and patient.[71]

## CONTROLLED ADDICTION

Knowing something about the enormous range of individual variability in reactions to drugs, it would make sense to predict that some people could remain addicted to heroin and yet be productive, while others would abuse the drug, in the sense that they would disable themselves through drug use. What we need is some way of forecasting the likelihood of abusive use of heroin by addicts under conditions of free access. Unfortunately we do not have the remotest idea how to make such an estimate.

The percentage of heroin addicts who could stabilize their dosage and function effectively might be below 10 percent or above 90 percent, and even this broad range is basically a guess. As little as we know about controlled heroin use short of addiction, we know even less about controlled addiction. There is, however, some reason to believe that heroin might be used by a sizable portion of addicts in ways which would impair their social productivity, prevent their employment, and cause them to become a drain upon the rest of us.

In the study of the two villages in rural Pakistan by McGlothlin and others, the researchers asked the opium users what effect the drug had on them. In the town with the high addiction rate, where the great majority of addicts were not "medical" addicts, the users reported that their use had an adverse effect on their health (82 percent); and upon their work (75 percent). Most said that their drug use also adversely affected their family and social relations and that it caused weakness. Not only did they state that they would like to stop their use, but, as if to guarantee their

71. McGlothlin et al., "Opium Use in Pakistan," pp. 7–8, 10.

sincerity, around 90 percent said that they were willing to spend two weeks in a hospital if they could be cured.[72] It is true that these results took place in a non-Western culture where the differences in set, setting, and the alternatives open to addicts are too great for comparison. Nonetheless, if the information is worth anything, the picture is not encouraging.

Other indications, also marred by differences in set, setting, and the range of available alternatives, have come out of the laboratory experiments which permit addicts as much heroin as they desire. Although these, too, are hardly decisive, they raise similar worries about addiction under free availability. Typical of these is the work of Vincent Dole, which led to the concept of methadone maintenance. Dole had tried to maintain two addicts on morphine in a hospital setting. During the month the effort lasted, their drug consumption increased fourfold. As their tolerance developed to each increase in their dosage, they tended to sleep badly and to become depressed and irritable until Dole raised again the amount of morphine they received. More significantly—presumably because of the uneven development of tolerance—both addicts grew increasingly listless and showed more nodding after each injection.[73]

Dole's initial experience with methadone, moreover, tends to question the importance of the setting of the opiate use—even though it can be argued that experimental wards of hospitals are usually such boring places that both morphine use and nodding are reasonable responses to the experimental situation. Having decided that his attempt to stabilize the addicts on morphine had failed, Dole began to detoxify them, using the longer-acting methadone. In about two weeks he noted such a dramatic improvement in their behavior that he began to experiment with methadone itself as a maintenance drug. His notes, sixteen days after the first methodone dose, state: "Patient A is back in good spirits, working on a painting. If this feeling could be maintained on the outside . . . he would probably not seek supplementary heroin."[74]

Although Dole's experience with morphine is not comforting, it is possible that in a setting more natural than a hospital many addicts might be sufficiently motivated to stabilize their dosages of heroin and, hence, to function normally. Some animal experiments even support this view. Those monkeys who self-inject morphine until they become addicted generally increase their dosage until, at a relatively high level, they stabilize their use and then will perform work to earn food or other

72. David Zimmerman, "Narcotic Maintenance Has Been Tried in U.S.," *U.S. Journal of Drug and Alcohol Dependence* 1, no. 8 (September 1977): 1, 3, 5.

73. Ibid., p. 5.

74. Deneau et al., "Self-administration of Psychoactive Substances by the Monkey," pp. 39–41.

rewards. Interestingly, when cocaine is used instead of morphine, the monkeys continue to work to inject more and more of that drug, neglecting food or any other bodily need until either their cocaine supply is cut off or they die from debilitation.[75]

## CULTURAL CONTROLS ON HEROIN ADDICTION

The percentage of addicts who could stabilize their dosage and perform productive work under free availability may also depend on the cultural and psychological reasons for using heroin—matters about which we understand very little. From anecdotal evidence, it seems that those who become addicted through using opiates for relief of pain can more easily stabilize their dosage than those who use the drug for euphoria. We know of many cases where physicians prescribe opiates for patients suffering chronic pain, where, above a certain dosage, tolerance to the painkilling effect no longer develops. Such patients, though addicted, continue to use opiates, usually morphine or Demerol, with no discernable ill effects, physical or social.

There is reason to believe that "medical" addicts would be more likely than other addicts to remain productive under conditions of free availability. As we will see, our social rules are not at all clear or strong on how addicts should take opiates to minimize the disruption such drugs cause in their lives. However, medical addicts may follow the simple rule that they neither desire nor expect pleasure from their drug use but use it solely to relieve their pain.

The relative job success of British addicts maintained on heroin may be related in part to the difference between medical and other opiate addicts. The British addicts, as we will see, are much more likely to be medical addicts—culturally quite different from those Americans who are addicted today, or who probably would be addicted under free availability.

Cultural Norms

Probably the most important unknown with respect to the effects of heroin use and addiction is the nature and strength of the cultural norms that will develop to control use. We have already alluded to the importance of cultural controls in discussing controlled nonaddictive use and have also noted that in some areas of the world, even though opiates are cheap and available, social controls still keep addiction low and not too socially damaging. Conversely, as the experience of the United States indicates, opiates may be very expensive and available only with some

---

75. Cahalan and Room, *Problem Drinking among American Men*, pp. 96–101.

inconvenience, but addiction nonetheless may be relatively high and extremely damaging.

We have long known that the rate of alcoholism varies enormously among different societies and among social groups in the same society. A major reason for this is the variation in the number and strength of the rules with respect to the consumption of alcohol shared by the group. In some cultures, such as the Italian—and, until fairly recently, the Jewish— virtually all drinking was done at meals, and drunkenness, except on very special ritualized occasions, was regarded as shameful behavior. Alcoholism, as a result, was extremely rare.[76]

Most people in the United States today observe many cultural rules that govern their alcohol use. We typically do not drink in the morning, do not drink alone, do not drink to get drunk; and, at least in the case of hard liquor or wine, we do not drink from the bottle. Not only that, but we look askance at those who do. Moreover, although alcohol abuse is a very serious and costly problem in America, the drug is moderately well controlled by the great majority of users. We have approximately 100 million alcohol users in our population, more than 90 percent of whom use the drug without significant damage to their health or adjustment in society.[77]

It is in the groups with markedly different rules—or without rules—that alcoholism rates are very much higher than the norm. Among Americans, the children of abstainers, once they drink at all, have among the highest alcoholism rates. Those who are brought up in families which not only do not drink but frown upon the practice are very good candidates for complete abstention. However, they have incorporated no rules for moderate drinking, and, as a result, once they start to drink, they are much more likely to experience problems with alcohol than are the children of moderate drinkers.[78]

The fact that different cultures use drugs differently does not give us much of a basis for any predictions about the way our society would use heroin were it freely available. The absence of widespread cultural rules for moderate or controlled heroin use is ominous, however.

## THE GIN EPIDEMIC

One dramatic example of the damage a "new" drug can cause is what has been called the "gin epidemic" of eighteenth-century England.[79] Until the end of the seventeenth century, the English generally consumed their

76. *Alcohol and Health*, pp. 15, 18.

77. Cahalan and Room, *Problem Drinking among American Men*, p. 116.

78. T. G. Coffey, "Beer Street, Gin Lane: Some Views of 18th-Century Drinking," *Quarterly Journal of Studies on Alcohol* 27, no. 4 (December 1966): 669–92.

79. MacAndrew and Edgerton, *Drunken Comportment*, pp. 109–10, 149–52.

alcohol in the form of beer or wine. Brandy, a distilled liquor, was known but was not used recreationally and was considered more of a medicine.

Around the middle of the seventeenth century, the Dutch learned how to distill grain alcohol in the presence of juniper berries (called *junever* in Dutch). This new drink, "gin," was introduced into England by soldiers returning from their campaigns in the Netherlands. There they had drunk it to give themselves "Dutch courage."

After the Glorious Revolution of 1688 had brought the Dutch prince, William of Orange, to the English throne, gin consumption escalated rapidly. In England, consumption went from 527,000 gallons in 1685 to 11 million gallons in 1750, a twentyfold increase. In London, per capita gin consumption in 1750 exceeded 16 gallons (in the United States today consumption is less than one-third of this); and the estimate was that over 200,000 Londoners, about one-quarter of the population, maintained a pint-a-day gin habit.

If gin had been the only alcoholic drink, the situation might not have been quite so catastrophic, but the English merely superimposed gin upon their previous drinking patterns and continued to drink great amounts of beer. Indeed, the per capita consumption of beer in England was almost twice that of gin—though, of course, since gin was of much higher "proof," it accounted for more of the total alcohol consumed.

According to one commentator, the gin epidemic produced a "perfect pandemonium of drunkenness" in which the greater part of the population of the metropolis seems to have participated. Not only were there six or seven thousand regular dram shops in London and Westminster, but cheap gin was given by masters to their employees instead of wages, hawked about the streets in barrels, and sold at every market stall. The death rate in London reached 5 percent per year, a sizable increase from that of a hundred years earlier. Indeed, only a sharp increase in immigration into the city maintained London's population.

Probably the most compelling commentator on the gin epidemic used pictures rather than words. Hogarth, in his famous engraving *Gin Lane*, shows the pawnbroker, the undertaker, and the distiller prospering among the complete degradation of the population. In the center foreground is a drunken woman, her exposed breasts swollen with dropsy—one common consequence of alcohol abuse—and her legs covered with infected sores. She ignores her naked and neglected child falling from the step, while in the left foreground an inscription on the archway above the inn reads, "Drunk for a penny, dead drunk for two pennies. Clean straw for nothing." Above that, an old man fights with a dog for a bone. Further above, the pawnbroker is doing a thriving business, while elsewhere a man hangs himself in his attic; a drunken woman is pushed along in a wheelbarrow as an attendant pours gin down her throat; and a crazed man hobbles down Gin Lane with a child spitted on his crutch.

The names of the brands of gin available indicated the uses to which the drug was put. One was called Royal Poverty (because "when beggars drink they are as great as kings"); another, Strip Me Naked (because gin addicts were known to pawn their clothes for the price of a drink). Names like Cuckold's Comfort and The Last Shaft require no explanation.

In 1720 and again in 1736, Parliament tried to impose high taxes on gin to discourage consumption, but both times the law was met by such rioting and civil disobedience that it had to be repealed.

Gradually, however, the gin epidemic burned out. One reason was the rise of Methodism; from 1748 on, John Wesley and his followers preached temperance throughout England. Moreover, a new drug came on the scene; by 1765 an estimated nine-tenths of English families drank tea twice a day—though not without causing raised eyebrows—and one moralist was provoked to remark that "the vast consumption and injurious effects of tea seem to threaten the lives of the common people equally with gin." It has also been noted that the British pub began to take shape at about this time. Perhaps to some extent it helped substitute good fellowship and conversation, along with a lesser intake of alcohol, for the previous drunkenness. In addition, Parliament, in 1751, finally adopted a taxation policy which made the less abused and abusable beer cheaper than gin.

Probably most important, however, an awareness of the consequences of overindulgence, and an acceptance of cultural rules to prevent them, developed in the population, causing moderate drinking to replace drunkenness. All these reasons, perhaps together with others we have not noted, caused the gin epidemic to recede after two generations of carnage, and by 1780 gin consumption in England had dropped to less than one-fifth of its previous maximum.


## THE INDIAN EXPERIENCE

Another example of the importance of social controls—or of their absence—in the assimilation of a new drug is the experience of the American Indian with alcohol. Although certain tribes in the Southwest brewed a kind of beer, the great majority of North American Indians had no experience whatsoever with alcohol until the white man introduced them to hard liquor in the eighteenth and nineteenth centuries.

The effect was dramatic. There is a dispute as to whether the violence triggered by drunkenness among the Indians was a pharmacologic effect of alcohol or was the consequence of considerably more complicated cultural factors, including the cultural expectation that one was not "responsible" for his actions while drunk.[80] It is clear, however, that the introduction of alcohol bowled over one tribe after another.

80. Norman H. Clark, *The Dry Years: Prohibition and Social Change in Washington* (Seattle: University of Washington Press, 1965), pp. 3–6.

Whole tribes were described as being wildly drunk, and the outbreaks of violence which accompanied these orgies were graphically recounted by many observers. The Indians of the Northwest provide probably the best studied example of the coming of alcohol to the Indian culture. According to one summary,

When Captain Meriwether Lewis reached the mouth of the Columbia River in 1805, he found the natives there to be a "mild and inoffensive" people who "uniformly behaved to us with great friendship." They lived in houses, provided well for their children, their women, and their old people. They enjoyed a benign, harmonious society "scarcely ever interrupted by disputes." The remarkable tranquility of their private lives, their aversion to violence and warfare, Lewis thought, had been secured by their "ignorance of spiritous liquors, the earliest and most dreadful present which civilization had given to the other natives of the continent. . . ."

By 1824, Sir George Simpson [of Hudson's Bay Company] wrote, that these Indians were "getting as much addicted to Drunkenness as the tribes of the East side of the Mountain."

Sir George thus witnessed a massive breakdown of group morality and a major step in sociocultural disintegration. . . . In their sorrow, in their social disorientation, and in their moral confusion, the Indians finally reached for the bottle of rum which the fur traders had for years been offering them. In the white man's liquor they found a source of ecstasy and a release from their grief that their native culture had neither provided nor demanded. . . .

Drunkenness probably became in part the evidence of status which allowed the Indians to identify themselves in some degree with the power and the prestige of the whites, and when the Indian turned to whiskey, he turned all the way. "One of the outstanding characteristics of Indian drinking in the coast areas from early times to the present," [one commentator] writes, "has been the very rapid consumption of liquor"—that is to say, drinking until the supply is gone or the drinkers fall. And drinking was always a group activity, never a solitary one, with entire adult populations, sometimes, given to excess.

Most significantly for whites, these massive losses of self-control released the aggressive tendencies which the social values of the native culture had so successfully restrained. . . . Thus it was that the Indians, who had shunned violence before they knew whites, began to take up the techniques of bloodshed in orgies of terror. In the late 1820's, for example, the brig *William and Ann* struck a spit at the mouth of the Columbia River, and her captain and crew of twenty-six landed in small boats at Clatsop Point. The natives, whom Meriwether Lewis had found "mild and inoffensive" people, butchered the twenty-six to the last man.[81]

---

81. Charles S. Lieber, "Metabolism of Ethanol and Alcoholism: Racial and Acquired Factors," *Annals of Internal Medicine* 76 no. 2 (February 1972): 326–27.

It is true that there are additional explanations for the devastating effect of alcohol upon the Indian culture, apart from the absence of developed social controls on drinking. First of all, there is some evidence that Indians metabolize alcohol differently from Causasians—though probably not so differently as to account for their very different use of the drug.[82] In addition, many of the Indian tribes prized visions, hallucinations, and other magical experiences; and the fact that something similar to these could be achieved with a large intake of alcohol made drunkenness more acceptable—perhaps even desirable.

It is also important that the Indian culture was under serious attack and that its anchors and definitions of appropriate behavior were being swept away by contact with the white man. Because of this, the life of the individual Indian under cultural, economic, military, and political attack was in many cases so painful or drab that temporary escape into alcohol was perhaps a rational response.

Nonetheless, the absence of social controls appears to have been a major factor in the Indian experience with alcohol. In most tribes the alcohol problem, though still serious, has diminished with time. "The passage of the years has produced a remedy of sorts. For as generation after generation has become, as it were, domesticated on the reservation, the awesome mayhem that characterized their earlier drunkenness has greatly diminished."[83] Despite this, the proportion of Indians arrested for all alcohol-related crimes is not only higher than that of any other ethnic group in the United States, it is more than twelve times the national average.[84]

The Eskimos today seem to be reenacting much of the Indians' experience with alcohol. Entire Alaskan villages are known to pool their resources and purchase a planeload of liquor. When the cargo arrives, everything in the village stops, and the inhabitants drink not only until drunkenness but until all the liquor is consumed.[85]

Bantu tribes of South Africa similarly show the devastating effect a new drug can have on well-established and controlled drug-taking practices.

The traditional importance of beer and beer-drinking in Bantu culture is so familiar that it is unnecessary to make more than a general reference to it. Solitary drinking appears to have been extremely

---

82. MacAndrew and Edgerton, *Drunken Comportment*, p. 107.

83. Omer Stewart, "Questions Regarding American Indian Criminality," *Human Organization* 23, no. 1 (Spring 1964): 61–66.

84. Reginald G. Smart, "A Note on the Effects of Changes in Alcohol Control Policies in the Canadian North," *Journal of Studies on Alcohol* 40, no. 9 (September 1979): 913.

85. Bertram Hutchinson, "Alcohol as a Contributing Factor in Social Disorganization: The South African Bantu in the Nineteenth Century," *Revista de Antropologia* 9, no. 1 (June 1961): 2, 11.

rare, although group and ritual consumption of beer took place frequently. Indeed, the convivial beer-drink played a central part in the cementing of old and the creation of new friendships, and in reinforcing the ties which linked kinsmen together. The conduct of the beer-drink was strictly regulated. Although brewing was itself a woman's task, women were excluded from beer-drinks, or were permitted to take part only in such as were held separately from the men. The carrying of weapons was forbidden, and intoxication was not held to justify violent or offensive behavior, continued respect for age, status and authority being insisted upon. The beer-drink gave refinement to daily life, and a man anticipated with pleasure the opportunity which marriage would give him of offering this hospitality to his relatives and friends.

The coming of the Europeans to the area introduced hard liquor and wine, beverages for which there were no social controls.

The new liquors were therefore used as a means of personal indulgence, untrammelled by group or ritual associations, and decreasingly inhibited by values imparted in childhood. The conditions in which the liquors were obtained also did much to encourage their being looked upon as a matter of merely personal and individual concern. They were paid for from individual earnings, obtained through devious and often illegal means, and consumed either in isolation or in a group intent, not on conviviality, but on the personal enjoyment of its individual members; while the state of separation from tribal influences and of relative personal anonymity in which the urban Bantu lived left unchecked disorderly behavior which traditionally would not have been tolerated. Liquor, in becoming associated with unrestrained intoxication, followed by violence, theft and imprisonment, and with prostitution, became a significant and positive factor in social disorganization, and not merely its symptom.[86]

## THE PROSPECT OF CULTURAL CONTROLS ON HEROIN ADDICTION

It is, of course, hard to reason from another culture's experience with alcohol to the effect freely available heroin would have upon our own society. First of all, objective deprivation in most of our society is far from that in London during the early Industrial Revolution or in the Indian or Bantu societies after the white man had undermined their cultures.

It might well be that those who have regular employment, a family life, or perhaps just something else to do would be able to control their heroin

---

86. MacAndrew and Edgerton, *Drunken Comportment*, p. 139–49.

use or even their consumption once addicted, simply because they would have too much to lose if they did not. And their example might stiffen the social controls for the rest of the population.

On the other hand, Thoreau's observation that "most men lead lives of quiet desperation" may still be true today—indeed, perhaps more so than when he wrote it 150 years ago. And it may be true in the affluent suburbs as well as in the inner cities.

Moreover, even though the great majority of our employed population may have something they would rather do than center their lives on drug use, the same may not be true of many adolescents in our society. Drug use and gaining peer approval may at various times be the most important of their objects. This may be especially serious if the habits of drug use they acquire early are difficult to give up, or if their drug use in youth interferes with their development of those satisfactions which might later make abstinence or controlled use easier.

One parallel, moreover, may cause us particular concern. It has been pointed out that a major reason the Indians had such difficulty in controlling alcohol was that they were introduced to the drug by trappers and hunters, who themselves were among the segments of white society which most abused drink.[87] Unfortunately, one would expect those who already use heroin to become the most likely models for the use of that drug under free availability. Worse yet, among heroin users the addict is far more conspicuous than the controlled user. The cultural model for heroin use, then, might turn out to be the junkie.

This is not to say that social controls cannot develop over heroin use. In fact, studies of moderate users indicate to the contrary.[88] As a result, it is conceivable that if heroin were made freely available, the development of these controls would soon occur, making the problem considerably more manageable. If the time for this were of the same magnitude as in the Gin Epidemic, however—on the order of two generations—it might take too long. Modern communications might speed this process—though we have already seen, both in the case of alcohol and in the "soft drug" epidemic of the latter sixties, that the mass media may do much more to encourage drug use than to lower it.[89]

In short, one would have to be an incurable optimist to believe that heroin could be made freely available without a considerable degree of social dislocation. Whether this dislocation would be worse than that of our present heroin prohibition is for the reader to decide—though the

87. Norman E. Zinberg, "Nonaddictive Opiate Use," in *Handbook on Drug Abuse*, pp. 308–9.

88. Esther H. Kramer, "A Review of the Literature Relating to the Impact of Broadcast Media on Drug Use and Abuse," in *Drug Use in America*, app., vol. 2, *Social Responses to Drug Use*, pp. 586–611.

89. Brecher, *Licit and Illicit Drugs*, p. 242.

general human prediliction for preferring the evils we know to those we do not may act to encourage caution.

## VARIATIONS OF FREE AVAILABILITY

### Competitors to Heroin

Up to now we have spoken of free availability as if it were an all-or-nothing arrangement. Although, as a technical matter, availability is not free if it is restricted in any way, a number of possible legal arrangements short of the free availability of heroin are similar enough to it to be discussed under the same heading.

For instance, we might make some of the presently illegal opiates freely available without changing our legal treatment of heroin itself. True, it would be hard to argue for such an arrangement on purely philosophical grounds, since no abstract principle involving the right to harm onself would seem to differentiate between opium or methadone on the one hand, and heroin or morphine on the other. Nonetheless, insofar as we regard the decision as an essentially pragmatic one of balancing social costs and benefits, the differences in abusability and attractiveness among the presently illegal opiates may then become relevant. Considering the high abusability of heroin, especially if injected, we might be better off making some of its competitors—but not it—freely available.

There is an analogy for this in the alcohol control area. Though most forms of alcohol are legal and available, many states have prohibited the sale of the very strongest forms of that drug. In view of the ease with which the available forms of alcohol can be abused, the benefit to public health in the restriction does not seem very great. Nonetheless, there is some difference between the abusability of gin or scotch, and that of 180 proof rum—and often the law reflects this. Interestingly, some nations have tried a similar plan with respect to cigarettes. Sweden has not only made illegal the sale of the highest nicotine and tar cigarettes, it has promoted the sale of nicotine chewing gum as a less dangerous competitor to smoking.[90]

It is quite likely that the free availability of opiates other than heroin would have some benefits. Legal opium or methadone might win some regular users away from high-priced and illegal heroin and conceivably could allow addicts to treat their own withdrawal and, hence, to give up opiates more easily. Similarly, a noninjectable form of heroin, made up on the analogy to denatured alcohol, might prevent the most destructive—and persistent—form of heroin use.

90. James A. Inciardi, *Methadone Diversion: Experiences and Issues, National Institute on Drug Abuse*, Services Research Monograph Series (Washington, D.C.: Government Printing Office, 1977), p. 3.

As we will see later, our present policy occasionally accomplishes something like this though not, we are told, intentionally. Diversion to the illegal market of a noninjectable form of methadone, at considerably lower prices than heroin, aids addicts in managing their withdrawal without medical help.[91]

All these variants of free availability raise similar difficulties, however. The more the drug to be made available is like injectable heroin, the more it will be able to win users away from illegal heroin, hence, the more the arrangement will approximate the advantages of free availability of heroin in lowering the social costs of heroin prohibition. At the same time, the closer the freely available drug is to heroin, the more similar will be its public health and welfare costs to those of making heroin freely available. Contrariwise, the less the freely available drug is as able as heroin to meet the needs of addicts, the less able it will be to entice heroin users from their drug—which by hypothesis will still be prohibited. Free availability of such a substitute drug would not impose on us as great public health and welfare costs as would the free availability of heroin, but it would not do as much to alleviate the costs of heroin prohibition either.

Of course, the advantages and disadvantages of each arrangement would not necessarily balance each other exactly. It might be that if we made some presently illegal opiate freely available, we would win enough users away from heroin as to lower greatly the costs of our prohibition without at the same time contributing proportionately to a public health or welfare problem. The problem is that we simply have no confidence that this is possible, and even if we knew, somehow, that such a drug did exist, we simply would not know which one it was.

Moreover, we might make matters even worse. It is possible that by choosing badly we might make freely available a drug that turned out not to compete with illegal heroin while becoming widely abused itself. Unless one adopts the view discussed earlier that the number of individuals who will abuse a drug is fixed and that the only issue is which drug they will abuse, we must recognize the possibility that we might accidently start up a wholly new drug problem without decreasing our heroin problem significantly.

Another danger in attempting to make available a competitor to heroin is that our selection might be converted into more attractive and abusable form. This danger applies particularly to opium which is generally considered to be less abusable than heroin. Entirely apart from the balance between its attractiveness to heroin addicts and the effects of its

91. *Smoking and Health* pp. xiv, A-20–A-22. Stanley Schachter, "Pharmacological and Psychological Determinants of Smoking," *Annals of Internal Medicine* 88, no. 1 (January 1978): 104–14.

consumption by entirely new users, opium can easily be made to yield morphine and heroin in relatively pure, injectable form. It is true that doing this would be uneconomical for most individuals; and, hence, so long as opium were sold only in individual doses to the ultimate user, conversion would not be a serious problem. But a system of free availability implies the likelihood of diversion and theft, and of organizations capable of buying up large numbers of doses. This would make practicable the domestic manufacture of heroin on a large scale, and we might then find our opium competing not with the high-priced, impure, and diluted heroin now on the street but, rather, with a cheaper, purer, and stronger but still illegal heroin.

Moreover, there is a danger that even if the legally available competitor is not itself very likely to be abused or converted to more dangerous form, it may nonetheless act as an introducer to the use of more abusable drugs. This is not to revive the dubious stepping-stone theory whereby use of marijuana allegedly causes subsequent use of the very different drug, heroin. The use of one drug may act as an introduction to stronger drugs of the same type—especially when, as would be likely, the two drugs are cross-tolerant.

There have been suggestions that this kind of introduction mechanism has already happened with respect to cigarettes. The availability of low-nicotine, low-tar cigarettes seems to be one factor making it easier to begin a cigarette smoking habit today. In former times, when only relatively strong cigarettes were available, a good percentage of experimenters quickly stopped because they found the drug not to their liking. Today, a greater percentage may continue use with weaker cigarettes, and some of these, who might otherwise not have smoked more than experimentally, now build up enough tolerance to move on to stronger and presumably more dangerous brands.[92]

We have had a similar experience with opium in Vietnam. Many of the American soldiers who became heroin addicts in Vietnam smoked opium initially and, as they developed a tolerance to that drug, began to smoke and then to inject heroin.[93]

Nor is there much hope that a free but inconvenient availability would lower the potential costs of this arrangement. We have long known that relatively small differences in availability can result in sizable differences in consumption. Thus, opium consumption in England dropped sharply in 1868 when, though the drug continued to be legally available, its sales

92. Norman E. Zinberg, "Heroin Use in Vietnam and the United States," *Archives of General Psychiatry* 26, no. 5 (May 1972): 488.

93. Berridge, "Fenland Opium Eating," p. 282.

were restricted to pharmacies. A number of nations similarly have tightened their control over alcohol simply by lowering the number of retail outlets for the drug and by restricting the hours of sale. It is unlikely, however, that such weak restrictions could seriously diminish the demand as powerful as that to be expected for heroin.

Taxation Systems

Another common means of restricting consumption—taxation—has the great advantage that any money taken in relieves the demands upon the public fisc. Unfortunately, this method seems singularly ill-adapted to the control of legalized heroin.

It is true that since there is some elasticity in the demand for heroin, taxation could lower the amount legally sold by increasing the price of the drug. The problems with such an arrangement overwhelm the advantages, however. Any such system, to a greater extent than licensing the sale of a substitute drug, would undermine the cultural message of the dangers of heroin use. Moreover, though it is true that the lower the tax rate, the more likely freely available heroin would put the illegal marketeer out of business, it is also true that the lower the tax rate, the more we would be saddled with the public health and welfare problems of free availability. Conversely, the higher the tax rate, the more the system becomes like heroin prohibition; as the tax rises, so does the temptation for illegal marketeers to divert or import the drug for tax-free sale. A heavy enough tax could make legal heroin even more expensive than it would be on the illegal market. The situation, in that case, would be even worse than from our present heroin prohibition. Presumably, the majority of heroin addicts, who, as a class, do not seem particularly constrained by fear of the criminal law, would purchase their heroin from the cheaper, illegal source at prices approximating those under heroin prohibition. The illegal seller would continue in business, subject only to being called a tax evader rather than a narcotics violator, and the full costs of heroin prohibition would still be with us.

We must remember, however, that increases in taxation raise only the financial costs of purchasing heroin. Many nonaddicts would have far easier access to the drug than they do today, even if the financial price were very high indeed. In addition, any tax scheme would make the drug comparatively cheaper for the beginning user than for the addict, since, before the development of tolerance to the drug, the neophyte would use far less.

This kind of differential increase in access for the nonuser would be a complete reversal of our present philosophy—that the best way to avoid the problems of heroin addiction is to lower the access of nonusers to the drug. And it also forfeits the great advantage of any free availability system in that it does not make the price lower for the addict, who may have to steal to pay for his habit.

Perhaps the most we could hope for is that, within wide limits, changes in tax rate might simply substitute one kind of social cost for another without changing the total costs attributed to heroin in our society. If this were the case, the sum of the public health and welfare costs caused by greater use of legal opiates, the costs attributable to the generation of crime caused by the still high price of the drug, and the costs of enforcing the tax arrangement might be relatively constant. This might be the case even though each of the separate categories of cost would vary widely depending on the tax rate chosen. This view is probably much too optimistic, however. Even if we decided that free and cheap availability would be more socially costly than is our present heroin prohibition, any significant increase in the price of legally available heroin—short of the point where virtually no one could afford the drug—might still do more harm than good.

Finally, though it is perhaps an exercise in overkill to point this out, one disadvantage shared by all methods of control by taxation is that the optimum tax rate, if it exists, is likely to change over time in unpredictable ways. If the tax on alcohol was optimal in 1933 when Prohibition was repealed, it has now become wildly insufficient. The effect of the flat tax per gallon of alcohol has eroded as the value of the dollar has slipped; and as American disposable income has risen, the price of alcohol, as a fraction of the average American's income, has dropped even further. Small wonder then that we are becoming increasingly concerned with alcohol abuse.[94]

There is much more that could be said about the many varieties of free, somewhat free, and taxed availability. One particular means of making heroin available requires close examination. It is not free availability because, rather than treating all heroin consumers similarly, its essence is to make the drug legally and cheaply available only to addicts. Since this option—heroin maintenance—has received so much discussion, it is appropriate that we should consider it separately and at some length. This will be the object of the following chapter.

94. Merton H. Hyman et al., *Drinkers, Drinking, and Alcohol-Related Mortality and Hospitalizations: A Statistical Compendium* (New Brunswick, N.J.: Center on Alcohol Studies, Rutgers, 1980). Mark H. Moore and Dean R. Gerstein, eds., *The Alcohol Problem*, Report of the Panel on Alternative Policies Affecting the Prevention of Alcohol Abuse and Alcoholism, Committee on Substance Abuse and Habitual Behavior, Assembly of Behavioral and Social Sciences, National Research Council (Washington, D.C.: National Academy of Sciences, 1981), chapter 4, "Regulating the Supply of Alcoholic Beverages."

# 4 ▖▖▖
# *HEROIN MAINTENANCE*

*P*robably the most popular suggestion today for lowering the costs of heroin prohibition is that we should adopt what is thought to be the British system. We would then make heroin legally available to addicts at very low cost, while maintaining the prohibition for sales to anyone else.[1]

Obviously, if we could make such a system work, it would have many advantages. Unlike a policy which prohibited supply of heroin to anyone, a policy which allowed addicts easy and cheap access to the drug would free us from the costs which we all suffer by making their quest for it so difficult. However, unlike a free availability arrangement which exposes the entire citizenry to heroin, a policy of allowing only addicts easy and cheap access to the drug would not entail the unknown but, perhaps, huge public health and welfare costs that we fear would result from free availability.

## SEPARATING THE MARKETS

In economic terms, such an arrangement can be seen as an attempt to divide the demand for heroin into two separate markets. One would be for addicts and the other for those who might use heroin but who are not

---

1. See, for example, Milton G. Rector, "Heroin Maintenance: A Rational Approach," *Crime and Delinquency* 18, no. 3 (July 1972): 241–42. Three such proposals are detailed in Paul Danaceau, *What's Happening with Heroin Maintenance?* (Washington, D.C.: Drug Abuse Council, 1977), pp. 12–17.

addicted—the experimenters, occasional users, and nonaddicted regular users.[2]

In the heroin market for addicts, where the demand for heroin is far more urgent, presumably the price of the drug should be kept very low. If addicts respond to increases in price by paying more to feed their habits, it is not in our interest to compel them to raise more money than necessary for what they will buy anyway. We have already noted that a major disadvantage of our heroin prohibition is that it forces up the amount of money addicts must pay for their heroin supply to a level where they have to obtain at least part of that price by theft or other crime—or, at the very least, to compromise their own health and welfare.

On the other hand, we regard increases in price to nonaddicted users as a social benefit. For these users, heroin competes with all kinds of other activities, including the demands of everyday life. As the price of the drug increases, then, the nonaddict uses less or none at all; and, of course, the less heroin he uses, the less likely he is to become addicted and cause problems both to himself and to us.

To some extent, heroin prohibition already separates the addict from the nonaddict markets. As mentioned in chapter 2, the total cost to the user of heroin may be considerably higher than the dollar price he must pay for the drug. The true cost of a quantity of heroin to a user includes, in addition, the time and effort he must spend in finding someone who will sell it to him, his risk of detection, and the chance that he will be "burned" by having his money stolen or being sold a worthless powder.

These costs turn out to be considerably less, on the average, for the addict than for the nonaddicted user. Since addicts tend to reside in or near the heroin copping areas anyway, they do not need to waste much time traveling to where the sellers are; those in the addict subculture have more opportunities to find out who is selling, who can be trusted not to burn them, and where they can get the best price. Because they are more likely to be known to sellers, addicts need spend less time and energy convincing a "connection" that they can be relied on not to bring the police into the transaction, and they are better able to take action should they be cheated.

The nonaddict—except for the regular controlled user who usually has a reliable and convenient connection—may face formidable obstacles in his efforts to purchase heroin. He will be more likely to have difficulty in finding out who is selling heroin, becoming sufficiently inconspicuous while buying, convincing the seller he is not an undercover agent, and making sure he is not cheated.

The problem, then, with our heroin prohibition is not that it fails to

2. Moore, "Policies to Achieve Discrimination on the Effective Price of Heroin," pp. 270–77.

separate the addict from the nonaddict markets, but that it does not do a complete enough job. The overall price to the addict remains too high, while the price to the nonaddict is still too low—a problem compounded by an unfortunate pharmacological fact. Since tolerance to heroin develops quite rapidly, the cost to the addict is raised simply because he uses more of the drug.

As we will see, a heroin maintenance scheme can be conceived of simply as a means of separating further the two markets by reducing the price of heroin to addicts. It is here that we face the fundamental difficulty in any attempt to maintain widely different prices for the same product in two separate markets. The greater the difference in price between the two markets, the greater will be the leakage of the product from the low-priced to the high-priced market.

This is the classic problem faced in the economic texts by the price-discriminating monopolist. His efforts to gain a greater return by selling at different prices to different consumers are constantly frustrated by competition from his own low-priced customers, who resell his product in the high-priced market.

## THE BRITISH SYSTEM

Before we look more closely at the advantages and disadvantages of heroin maintenance, it will be helpful to describe what is often called the British system. Almost everyone knows that the British treat heroin as a medical, not a legal, problem; hence, they make heroin available to addicts under a prescription system. Unfortunately, like so much of what almost everyone knows, this is not true.[3]

At the time of the Harrison Act, the British law as to opiates was very much like that in most American states. Though in 1868 the right to sell opiates had been restricted to pharmacists, opiates were still freely available and were widely consumed in tonics and as home remedies. The drugs were used not only to cure ills and to make people feel better, but also to quiet children. In some areas, such as "the fens" around Cambridge, opiate addiction was quite common, but, though this was seen as a public health problem, it was not regarded as very important. As in the United States, it was the pressure resulting from the international opiate traffic that required that something be done about Britain's own legal treatment of opiates.[4]

3. For a good review of British practice, see Horace Freeland Judson, *Heroin Addiction in Britain: What Americans Can Learn from the English Experience* (New York and London: Harcourt Brace Jovanovich, 1974).

4. Virginia Berridge, "Opium and the Historical Perspective," *The Lancet*, 9 July 1977, pp. 78–80.

Like the Americans, the British acted. In 1920, Parliament passed the Dangerous Drugs Act, a law which, on paper, seems strikingly similar to the Harrison Act of six years earlier. Most opiates were prohibited from over-the-counter tonics, and it was made a serious criminal offense to buy or sell such drugs outside of medical channels.[5]

As in the Harrison Act, the issue of medical maintenance of addicts was unresolved, and even the language of the two statutes was parallel. The Harrison Act provided that opiates could be supplied by a physician only "if in the practice of his profession," while the British law allowed a physician to supply opiates "so far only as is necessary for the practice of his profession."

The crucial difference, however, came with the interpretation of these words. Unlike the American authorities, who successfully moved to prevent any maintenance on opiates, the British appointed a distinguished committee of physicians to look into the question. The commission held some twenty-three meetings, listened to over thirty witnesses, and submitted its report. It recommended that addiction should be treated simply as a medical complaint and that physicians should be allowed, under very general guidelines, to prescribe opiates for the maintenance of their addicted patients.

The committee agreed that, in general, physicians should attempt to cure what it regarded as the disease of addiction and to wean their patients away from opiates. It felt, however, that a physician should be free to prescribe opiates to maintain his patients if he thought that efforts to withdraw them would lead to serious symptoms or if, in his opinion, they were leading more normal and useful lives while addicted than they would if drug-free.

The authorities enforcing the law not only acquiesced in this view but, in practice, left the occasions of maintenance almost entirely up to the physicians. As a result, under the British approach, addiction became a matter between the addict and his physician. The doctor would prescribe morphine or heroin and the addict would obtain his supply from a pharmacy just as he would any other medicine.[6]

This situation endured essentially without change until the 1960s. By that time, many American authorities were clear that Britain had "the answer." And even those who disputed whether heroin maintenance would work in the United States tended to agree that Britain's system was working quite well in that country.[7]

---

5. Lindesmith, *The Addict and the Law*, pp. 10–11, 167–68.

6. Judson, *Heroin Addiction in Britain*, pp. 16–21.

7. Eric Josephson, "The British Response to Drug Abuse," in *Drug Use in America*, app., vol. 4, p. 176. H. B. Spear, "The British Experience," *John Marshall Journal of Practice and Procedure* 9, no. 1, (Fall 1975): 67–68.

There were only a few hundred addicts in the whole nation. These were overwhelmingly medical addicts, who had become addicted during a course of treatment with opiates—often for chronic pain. They did not use drugs for euphoria and did not seem particularly inclined toward crime. Probably most significant, they did not belong to any addict subculture; indeed, most addicts did not even know another addict.

Not only did the addicts themselves seem to adjust well to heroin maintenance, but there were societal benefits as well. Because of the low price of the drug, no addict had to steal or sell drugs to maintain his habit.

In addition, the heroin maintenance system was credited with having prevented the development of an illegal market. Since addicts could obtain heroin quite inexpensively from their private physicians, and then, after World War II, virtually without cost from the National Health Service, it was believed that no profit could be made from trafficking in the drug.

Of course the system was not foolproof. The addict could conceivably sell a part of his supply, if he wished to and could find a buyer. And the individual physician had to be trusted, for the benefit both of his patient and of society, to hold down the level of his opiate prescriptions to the amount needed to sustain the addict's habit. Nonetheless, by all accounts the system worked well until the early sixties. Then it began to break down.

## The Breakdown of the System

It has been said that the problem was caused by a few (sometimes the number is given as twenty-six) American-style addicts who came to Britain fleeing a new Canadian law which sharply increased the penalties for drug violations.[8] Others have argued that the social use of heroin was a cultural innovation imported from the United States, where, around the same time, recreational taking of drugs other than alcohol and tobacco became the thing to do among a sizable group of young people.

Perhaps the most important factor was the development of a youth culture which was, for the first time, large and affluent enough to develop certain folkways of its own in opposition to the dominant older culture. This style not only included clothing (Carnaby Street) and music (the Beatles), but the recreational taking of marijuana, "pills," and, to a limited extent, opiates.

In any event, it is now clear that a relatively small number of young men who centered their lives on opiate taking and dealing, aided by a

8. This thesis is refuted by H. B. Spear and M. M. Glatt, "The Influence of Canadian Addicts on Heroin Addiction in the United Kingdom," *British Journal of Addiction* 66, no. 2 (September 1971): 441–49.

considerable degree of naivete or simply profiteering on the part of a few British physicians, quickly destroyed the British system as it then existed.[9] The new-style addicts, it turned out, could often induce physicians into prescribing considerably more than needed to sustain their habits, and they were able to find ready purchasers for the surplus among their friends. Between 1961 and 1969 the number of British addicts increased more than fivefold, and, perhaps even more significant, the kind of addict changed dramatically.

The new addicts were younger and less stable and had values very different from those of the medical addicts who had previously been the grist for the system. While the total number of addicts in Britain still amounted to only about three thousand, a figure which could be matched in a five-block area of Harlem, the public became alarmed; a commission was convoked to look into the problem; and, in 1967, Parliament made major changes in the system.

The most important change made by the 1967 law was the withdrawal of the ordinary private physician's power to prescribe opiates for the maintenance of addicts. Only physicians specially licensed for the purpose could now do this. Moreover, though some general practitioners were in fact licensed to do so, the prescription of heroin or morphine to maintain addicts soon became restricted, as a practical matter, to a number of hospitals and clinics—of which the thirteen in London handled the great bulk of British addicts.

These clinics were staffed by physicians who quickly became specialists in heroin addiction and who tended to be considerably more suspicious of addicts' stated requirements than the individual practitioners had been. The clinic physicians recognized that their responsibility was not only to their patients but to society as well. They tried very hard to make sure that their patients used and did not sell the heroin they had prescribed, refrained from the use of other illegal drugs, and held steady, noncriminal, employment. The preference was still that the addict be weaned away from his drug, but it was understood that he would continue to receive his heroin if he made a tolerable adjustment.[10]

So far as we can tell, for the most part, the switch to the clinic system was successful.[11] The explosive growth of heroin addiction was halted,

9. Judson, *Heroin Addiction in Britain*, pp. 38-39. Charles W. Lidz, et al., "Heroin Maintenance and Heroin Control," *International Journal of the Addictions* 10, no. 1 (February 1975): 38–39.

10. Ian Pierce James, "The Changing Pattern of Narcotic Addiction in Britain—1959 to 1969," *International Journal of the Addictions* 6, no. 1 (March 1971): 119–23. Bruce D. Johnson, "Understanding British Addiction Statistics," United Nations *Bulletin on Narcotics* 27, no. 1 (January–March 1975): 54.

11. Josephson, "The British Response to Drug Abuse," pp. 185–88. Thomas H. Bewley et al., "Maintenance Treatment of Narcotic Addicts (not British nor a System, but Working Now)," *International Journal of the Addictions* 7, no. 4 (Winter 1977): 598–99.

and the success of the clinics at reducing diversion of prescribed heroin is shown by a doubling of the price of the drug on the illegal market in 1968 when the clinic system took hold.

In recent years, there has been yet another major alteration in the British system. Unlike the 1967 change, which was the result of a new statute amidst considerable publicity, this one has been the product of a gradual and almost unnoticed evolution.[12] The pressures toward greater social control over a new and more refractory kind of addict, together with a feeling that, by and large, oral methadone was a safer and more therapeutic maintenance drug than injectable heroin, have caused the clinics to maintain fewer and fewer addicts on heroin and to substitute methadone instead. For a while, a number of clinics maintained many of their addicts on injectable methadone, but, with time, more and more have tended to rely on oral methadone, very much as do the American programs, which we will discuss in chapter 5.

The extent to which this has occurred is quite surprising to those who still believe in the unique "British system." One study of two London clinics showed that only five of 2258 addicts under treatment were receiving heroin. Another clinic entirely discontinued prescribing heroin when the staff decided that the major reason they were still maintaining a few patients on that drug was to impress the visiting Americans.

Even the few clinics that still maintain any number of addicts on heroin or morphine do so under a kind of grandfather clause. Those patients who were started on such drugs when they originally were treated for addiction, and have made what their physicians regard as a good adjustment, may continue to receive those drugs.

New addicts, those who have returned to the clinic after temporarily dropping out of treatment, and those who have not adjusted in the sense that they have remained unemployed or been in trouble with the law, have been placed on oral methadone, often over their strenuous objections. In short, as a practical matter, the "British system" of prescribing heroin to maintain addicts is no more.

## The Relevance of the British Experience

Of course, the fact that Britain has abandoned heroin maintenance does not in itself mean other nations should not try it. It is possible, after all, that the British have simply made a mistake.

12. Bruce D. Johnson, "How Much Heroin Maintenance (Containment) in Britain," *International Journal of the Addictions* 12, nos. 2-3 (April–June 1977): 390–92. Martin Mitcheson and Richard Hartnoll, "Heroin Maintenance vs. Methadone Maintenance in Great Britain and Answers to Questions Concerning Heroin Maintenance There," in *Alternative Heroin Control Policies*, comp. and ed. Peter B. Bjorklund (Palo Alto, Cal.: Center for Planning and Research, 1979), vol. 3, app. H, pp. 57–58.

Alternatively, even if the British were quite correct in abandoning heroin maintenance, it might still be that this would be the best solution for the United States with its quite different problems. British physicians might have the luxury of deciding that the welfare of their individual patients was better served by prescriptions of oral methadone than of heroin, but the United States might not be able to afford such a decision. Because addiction is a far greater social problem in this country, we might have to look beyond our view of the addict's best interests and consider the total social cost of the system as opposed to its alternatives. It might be, then, that heroin maintenance, by attracting a higher percentage of addicts into treatment and out of criminality, would best lower the overall social cost that heroin now imposes on us.

On the other hand, the fact that the British long used heroin maintenance is not a very persuasive argument for this arrangement in the United States—even though while Britain maintained addicts on heroin, its heroin problem was far less serious than that of the United States. First of all, the British never had an opiate problem as great as that of the United States. Even before the Harrison Act, the percentage of opiate addicts in the American population was noticeably greater—a situation which has not changed since that time. Moreover, Britain has ceased heroin maintenance and it still has much less of a problem. The number of addicts in Britain stands at about 2 percent of the American total, and, even on a per addict basis, the social cost of addiction in Britain is far smaller than in the United States, primarily because British addicts tend to be much less involved in crime.

Nor can we attribute the difference between the social costs attributed to heroin in the United States and in Britain to Britain's on the whole successful experience with heroin maintenance. Other European countries, such as France and West Germany, for a long time had a heroin problem no greater than Britain's without having adopted any kind of opiate maintenance.[13]

Moreover, heroin addicts in Britain and America are very different kinds of people, and were even more so when the British system was most conspicuously successful.[14] A far higher percentage of British addicts were medically created, while many more American addicts initially used heroin for pleasure. Similarly, most American addicts had criminal records before their first use of heroin while this is true of a much smaller

13. It may be that for reasons we do not understand, some nations for a long while had very few people willing to use heroin and no groups which supported such use. As a result, private physicians may have been able to take care of their few addict patients without attracting official notice. Now that West Asian heroin has become available and certain groups have begun to use heroin, the problem has become quite alarming to a number of nations.

14. Judson, *Heroin Addiction in Britain*, pp. 47–49, 62–70.

percentage of British addicts. White youths are overrepresented among British addicts, while ethnic minorities are overrepresented among American addicts. Moreover, the differences between the two nations are not limited to the nature of their addicts. Britain and the United States are very different countries, with different kinds of social structures, values, and attitudes toward life and the law.

For instance, an often overlooked point is that medicine is practiced quite differently in the two nations. The relative discipline and small number of British physicians might be able to make a heroin maintenance program work better and more economically than would our much larger, more heterogeneous, and less disciplined medical profession.

The difference in the way medical care is structured in the two nations may be even more important. Heroin maintenance fits comparatively well into an organized system of health delivery such as the National Health Service. Our present anarchic medical system may have some advantages over socialized medicine, but a number of commentators on the British system have pointed out how much easier it is to care for heroin addicts in a clinic setting where a wide variety of other ailments are also treated, and in a system which also cares for the many health needs of addicts apart from their maintenance.[15]

Finally, the number of addicts in the United States today is so much larger than the number that British heroin maintenance has ever coped with that the changes in the scale of the problem might produce genuine differences in kind. After all, one man with a bucket might cope well with a small leak in a ship, while a leak one thousand times as large might pose insuperable problems for a thousand men, each with his own bucket.

In short, though the British experience with heroin maintenance provides us with a considerable amount of arguably relevant data, it is not very helpful in deciding whether the United States should attempt such a system. Perhaps the most reliable conclusion we can draw from observing the course of heroin maintenance in Britain is that our heroin problems would probably be fewer today had we begun some kind of opiate maintenance at the time we passed the Harrison Act. Turning back the clock and starting from that point a second time is obviously impossible, however, so we must consider the costs and benefits of heroin maintenance in today's world.

## VARIETIES OF HEROIN MAINTENANCE

Heroin maintenance is an extremely plastic concept. As the British experience indicates, relatively small changes in the method of implemen-

15. Ibid., p. 115.

tation—such as the shift from prescription by private physicians to that by specialized clinics—may result in very different consequences.

Let us look first at two quite different ways of maintaining addicts on heroin—the prescription system and the use-on-the-premises system. As we will see, each of these has its own problems. Afterward we will examine the more complex issue of whether some variation of one or both of the systems would produce a better balance of cost and benefits than does either of the "pure" arrangements.

## THE PRESCRIPTION SYSTEM

At the one extreme, we might follow the pre-1967 British system and simply allow any private physician to prescribe heroin for the maintenance of his addict patients. This measure would be unlikely to work, since it failed even in Britain. Rather than open ourselves to the charge of setting up a straw person, then, let us adopt, as our extreme, the model of heroin maintenance that the British used in 1969, in the early stages of the clinics.

Heroin clinics would prescribe heroin on the basis of the clinic physician's assessment of the addict's need, and the addict then would pick up his supply at a pharmacy of his choice. Such a system would probably have a strong appeal for the great majority of addicts. The amount of time and energy they would have to spend in getting their heroin would be vastly reduced, and they would be using a safer and far cheaper drug.

Many of the social costs of heroin prohibition would be lowered by such a system. A higher percentage of addicts would be able to stabilize their doses and become more productive citizens And even those who continued to steal would at least not have to meet the demands of an expensive heroin habit. Moreover, the system would not be very expensive to administer. The best recent estimate of the cost per addict is about $2,500, or about one-fifth more than a well-run methadone program costs today.[16]

16. Judson, *Heroin Addiction in Britain*, p. 135, estimated the cost of a heroin clinic operating in the U.S. in 1974 dollars at $2500 per patient per year. The Stanford Research Institute estimated the cost of an average outpatient methadone clinic at $2200 per client per year. Peter B. Bjorklund et al., *A Survey of Drug Abuse Treatment Costs*, Final Report prepared for the National Institute on Drug Abuse (Menlo Park, Calif.: Stanford Research Institute, November 1975), p. 5. Bjorklund, in May 1978, estimated the cost of a heroin maintenance clinic (weekly visits to clinic, daily pharmacy dispensing) at $4700 per client per year. Peter B. Bjorklund, "Estimates of Costs of Heroin Maintenance in California," in *Alternative Heroin Control Policies*, vol. 3, app. L, pp. 1–2.

## The Problem of Leakage

The prescription system, however, has one major and intractable disadvantage. Those addicts who pick up their supply of low-cost heroin will have a strong incentive to resell at least part of their supply, and the more they can sell, the more closely will the maintenance system then approximate free availability.

This problem of leakage is not a mere consequence of sloppy administration, which could be corrected by sufficient controls. It is inherent in any system that allows the addict to possess resellable heroin outside the confines of a guarded clinic, laboratory, or hospital.

Of course, the clinic staff will try to lower the amount of heroin the addict can sell by prescribing no more than he needs. Several factors, however, make their task extremely difficult. First, it is impossible to tell how much heroin an addict does need. Often he will be able to make a convincing case that his tolerance has increased his need—and, the more prescribed heroin he can sell, the greater will be his incentive to do this.

Moreover, the addict will always be able to strengthen his case by threatening to supplement his dosage with street heroin. Since the purpose of heroin maintenance is to prevent precisely this, the clinic physicians will be under some pressure to take the addict's word for his requirements. And because tolerance can escalate to extremely high levels, even a relatively small number of cases of undue credulity in prescribing can release considerable amounts of heroin onto the illegal market.[17]

To complicate the matter further, the refutation of the once-an-addict-always-an-addict myth must awaken us to the likelihood that even prescribing the "correct" dose for an addict will not be enough. Today's heroin addicts have learned how to get along on wildly fluctuating heroin dosages. Their intake varies enormously when times of heroin glut are succeeded by shortages, and even during periods of stable price and supply, when their income changes. If the addict wishes to earn money by selling part of his prescription, he can lower his use, either temporarily or permanently, and simply get along on less.

In addition, since methadone will probably remain available on the street, at a lower price than heroin, it is likely that the addict will be able to stave off withdrawal by using that drug. This would allow him to sell all of the heroin he receives from the maintenance system even while remaining addicted.

Interestingly, heroin addicts are not the only drug abusers who can swear off their drug temporarily when it suits them. One researcher, for

17. Such was the case in Britain before the 1967 law. See Judson, *Heroin Addiction in Britain*, pp. 41–42.

instance, found that even chronic alcoholics could refrain from drinking for a week if they were paid enough for their abstinence.[18]

## Law Enforcement and Illegal Sales

Unfortunately, we cannot rely on the threat of detection to prevent the addict from selling some of his heroin supply. Though the clinic can use urine tests to monitor whether he uses methadone or street heroin cut with various substances, it cannot determine whether he has used all the heroin that has been prescribed for him. As a result, urinalysis would be a deterrent only to the addict's selling all of his supply.[19] And, as we shall see in chapter 5, urinalysis is not foolproof even for this purpose.

Nor could the police do much either. The addicts in heroin maintenance would be far too numerous to watch; they would be legally in possession of their heroin; and could easily make their sales in private.

In fact, heroin trafficking through diversion from a prescription maintenance system would be much more difficult for the police to contain than is our present illegal heroin distribution system. Often law enforcement is best able to disrupt heroin distribution by intervening at the higher end of the chain. As we have seen, this is quite difficult, but if the police do manage to seize a large shipment of heroin, put a large ring out of business, or disrupt cultivation in a foreign country, there may be a sizable—if temporary— contraction in the heroin supply.

Where the addict sells the heroin prescribed for him, the maintenance system itself takes the place of the illegal manufacturer, importer, large-scale wholesaler, and small-scale wholesaler. The huge number of extremely short supply chains—each consisting of an addict in maintenance and his customers—would make the illegal market virtually invulnerable to law enforcement.

The prescription heroin maintenance system may create a wholly new and very large class of regular sellers who will make heroin more accessible as well as cheaper. Although virtually all street-level dealers are addicts today, the converse is not true. Most addicts may sell to accommodate a friend or if they suddenly gain access to more than they need, but they do not sell the drug regularly, often because they lack a low-cost connection. A maintenance system may become the low-cost connection they need. Even among the relatively noncriminal English addicts, one study showed that 11 percent regularly sold part of their

18. Miriam Cohen et al., "Alcoholism: Controlled Drinking and Incentives for Abstinence," *Psychological Reports* 28, no. 2 (April 1971): 575–80.

19. K. K. Kaith, "Guide to Urine Testing in Drug Abuse Prevention and Multi-Modality Treatment Programs," *Journal of Chromotography* 141, no. 2 (21 August 1977): 149–50.

heroin supply.[20] In the United States, one would expect the figure to be far higher.

We must be concerned with the purchasers as well as the sellers of prescribed heroin. If addicts in maintenance sold their supplies only to each other, it would not be a matter of serious concern. True, some would receive more than their physicians prescribed and others less, but though this might not be therapeutic, the social damage would not be too great. So long as the heroin would be sold at low cost, the major problem would be that those in charge of the programs would find it more difficult to stabilize their patients.

Nor would the social damage be great if those on maintenance also sold to addicts who stayed off the maintenance rolls. This would amount to a kind of unofficial maintenance system, not so therapeutic as being enrolled, but still providing heroin at much lower cost than does the present illegal market.

Moreover, so long as only those already addicted receive the diverted drug, the maintenance system would still fulfill its main function of separating the addict from the nonaddict market. Where one addict on maintenance merely buys some of the supply of another, we have a kind of "wash" transaction creating no new addicts—and producing less property crime than would transactions at higher prices.

The problem is that many of the customers for illegally sold heroin would be nonaddicts. This is the case today and there is no reason to think it will be less so if we adopt a heroin maintenance system. Indeed, there are reasons to think that more nonaddicts will be able to purchase heroin under a prescription maintenance system. The availability to many more addicts of enough heroin to sell will probably guarantee that many more will sell the drug. Equally important will be the greater social integration of the new class of sellers. Freeing addicts from the need to pursue their own heroin requirements makes it easier for them to integrate themselves into more areas of our society. Indeed, that is one of the purposes of heroin maintenance. The problem is that so many addicts have become more adept at illegal than legal methods of earning income. The likely prospect is that many of them would supplement their incomes by selling some of their prescribed heroin to their new, nonusing associates.

The effect of a prescription system, then, would be to expose a much

20. Mitcheson and Hartnoll, "Heroin Maintenance vs. Methadone Maintenance," p. H-49. Gerry V. Stimson and Alan C. Ogborne report that of a sample of London addicts receiving prescriptions of heroin, 37 percent admitted that on occasion they had sold or exchanged or loaned some of their prescribed drugs. "A Survey of a Representative Sample of Addicts Prescribed Heroin at London Clinics," United Nations *Bulletin on Narcotics* 22, no. 4 (October–December 1970): 17.

larger segment of the population to access to heroin. It would not only
lower the financial cost of the drug to large numbers of people, it would
greatly lower the nonfinancial costs as well—the difficulty, inconvenience, and danger of obtaining heroin.


## The Enrollment of Nonaddicts

Nonaddicts might even be able to obtain heroin through the prescription
system directly rather than indirectly from those addicts in maintenance.
It has been alleged that the almost automatic provision of welfare
payments to those enrolled in certain methadone programs has acted as a
significant inducement to nonaddicted heroin users, and even some
nonusers, to pass themselves off as addicts and enter maintenance.[21]

Similarly, the opportunity to profit from the sale of prescribed heroin
can act as an incentive to both addicts and nonaddicts to enter the
maintenance system. The income from heroin sales would presumably be
considerably greater than that from welfare payments today, and would
provide a more exciting and, in some circles, a more respectable way of
earning a living. Unfortunately this income would be gained at considerable social cost. It would increase the number of heroin sellers, increase
the costs of the maintenance system by adding extra clients, and be a far
more explosive issue politically than welfare is today.

It is true that if a heroin maintenance program were run with considerable care, it could avoid taking most nonaddicts onto its rolls. It turns out,
however, that this is not so easy as might appear.

We saw in chapter 1 that, although we tend to use the term "addiction"
as if it were a precise, either/or condition, the fact is that it is a very
imprecise term. Often the question of addiction will turn out to be one of
degree—and even then dependent upon the expectations of the user.

Admittedly, injection of an opiate antagonist will throw into withdrawal
someone with a relatively low degree of physical dependence, while it will
not affect a mere user. There are disadvantages in this somewhat drastic
screening method, however. First of all, it is likely to make signing up for
the maintenance program considerably less attractive to those who are
addicted. More important, it requires a considerable degree of care and
skill—characteristics which may not always be in great supply if heroin
maintenance proliferates.

As we will see, one of the great problems with methadone maintenance
is that the programs are very rarely as well run as, in some ideal sense,

21. Blake Fleetwood, "Psst . . . Kid, Wanna Be a Junkie? Try Methadone!" *New York
Magazine* 17 October 1977, p. 81.

they should be.[22] Indeed, this is true of the criminal law—and just about every other social institution one might name. Bureaucratic problems always develop; empire building by individuals within the organization seems to require that component parts try to expand and negate the restraints upon their growth, often until their budgets are cut; whereupon they economize where they can least afford it.

Even on the individual level, people are not always as intelligent, well-motivated, hardworking, and honest as we would like. There is certainly no reason to believe that heroin maintenance programs would be exceptions to these iron laws.

As a result, we must be careful to do more than merely consider how heroin maintenance would work in a perfect world. After all, in a perfect world we would probably not have heroin addiction to begin with. Rather, we must consider how heroin maintenance would work with the imperfect human beings and institutions that would, in fact, run it.

Even where the nonaddict wishing to join a maintenance system cannot convincingly feign addiction, the staff may be too busy or burdened to notice the imposture. Worse yet, our experience with methadone programs gives us reason to expect that patients and staff will sometimes collude.[23] Prospective patients counterfeit addiction for various reasons. The staff members ignore the safeguards meant to bar nonaddicts, both because the support for such clinics is based on a per patient payment and because they are sympathetic with the reasons the nonaddict wants to join. This, as we will see, has been a problem with maintenance systems using methadone, a much less troublesome and less attractive drug than heroin. We would have to expect that considerably more would go wrong with any system making use of heroin itself. Finally, a prescription maintenance system exaggerates the problems of heroin maintenance because it adds to the allure of the drug and the welfare payments, as well as the additional opportunity of earning extra income by selling some or all of the prescribed drug.

## THE EFFECT ON HEROIN DEMAND

Some advocates of prescription heroin maintenance have recognized that such a system would greatly lower our controls over heroin supply. They

22. The creators of methadone maintenance blame many of the shortcomings on excessive government interference in physicians' practice. Vincent P. Dole and Marie E. Nyswander, "Methadone Maintenance Treatment: A Ten-Year Perspective," *Journal of the American Medical Association* 235, no. 19 (10 May 1976): 2117–19. Edward J. Epstein, "Methadone: The Forlorn Hope," *Public Interest* 36 (Summer 1974): 3-24, blames the physicians and the very concept of methadone maintenance.

23. Fleetwood, "Psst . . . Kid, Wanna Be a Junkie," strongly implies that the monetary rewards of running methadone clinics discourage tight screening procedures.

have argued, however, that this disadvantage would be offset by the effect of heroin maintenance upon the demand for illegal heroin. The assertion is that it does not matter whether heroin can be diverted from the maintenance system so long as no one will buy the drug. The argument, in other words, proceeds on the apparently self-evident view that no one would buy heroin at a high price when it would be available to him at much lower price through the maintenance system.

There are three fallacies in such reasoning, however. These advocates of prescription heroin maintenance assume that all addicts would be in the maintenance system at any one time; that all their heroin would be provided by the system; and, finally, that addicts would be the only users of heroin. In fact, none of these is likely to be the case.

The assumption that all addicts will be within the heroin maintenance system is dubious at best. The British experience gives us reason to believe that even the most permissive programs may still be unattractive to many addicts.

Even when heroin was prescribed by the clinics, there were, at any one time, a considerable number of relatively new addicts who, for one reason or another, had not acknowledged their condition or persuaded themselves to take the important step of appearing for maintenance. In addition, some long-term addicts did not register because they did not wish to be "tamed" by the system. Though the number of these in Britain was rather small, it would probably be much larger in the United States.[24]

The self-image as an outlaw, a "righteous dope-fiend" or a "stand-up guy" may be one of the satisfactions of the American addict's life, and those who value this may find many reasons not to accept our treatment. If the alternative is to accept the label of "sick"—as the medical model of heroin maintenance implies—many would not come forward willingly, even if maintenance seemed to their practical advantage.

Moreover, no matter what legal arrangements we make, the addict in maintenance will be socially stigmatized. If he is already known as an addict, his former associates—or some number of them—will say he has "sold out." If he has kept his addiction secret, perhaps at some cost to himself, he is unlikely to register officially in a maintenance program and risk disclosure to the rest of a society, which will still denigrate and presumably discriminate against him.

The second assumption—that an addict receiving cheap, pure heroin would not be in a market for additional quantities of the drug at a higher price—seems perfectly reasonable, but probably is wrong, too. Many of those within the heroin maintenance system would probably continue to live the addict's life style because of its other satisfactions, and it is

24. Spear, "The British Experience," p. 88.

certainly possible that this will continue to include the use of extra, illegal heroin.

Entirely apart from any social forces impelling the addict in maintenance to use additional heroin, there is the pharmacological fact that many addicts seek euphoric doses of the drug. Although some addicts would probably be content with regular and fixed allotments of heroin, there would be others who, as their tolerance develops, would want more and more in order to continue receiving the feelings they desire. Such addicts do not take well to stabilization on fixed dosages of heroin. Ominously, the British experience would indicate that the easiest patients to stabilize are those who are regularly employed.[25] The majority of American addicts, however, are characterized by a gross instability in employment.

Our experience with methadone supports the likelihood that it will be hard to stabilize. A number of addicts in methadone maintenance programs nonetheless buy more of that drug. Presumably they feel they are not getting enough. A black market has therefore developed, where both the buyer and the seller are in maintenance programs.[26] It would seem that heroin maintenance, involving a much more desired drug, would be the subject of a more extensive black market. Moreover, the efforts of physicians to avoid overprescribing can be expected to contribute to the problem. While in certain cases they will guess wrong and prescribe too much, there will be other cases where they will prescribe too little. Since they will have no way to be sure, it is likely they will make many errors—and it is important to realize that errors of underprescribing will contribute to the demand just as the errors of overprescribing will contribute to the supply.

As we have already noted, no very serious problems will result directly if addicts in or out of the maintenance system are the sole customers for heroin diverted from the system. It is true that the possibility of such dealing encourages the seller to obtain an illegal income from selling his supply; makes it more difficult for the system to stabilize the doses of both the buyer and the seller; and imposes upon the buyer the requirement of coming up with the price of illegal heroin—but compared to the analogous burdens of our present system, none of these problems is serious.

The real problem with this type of market is that it is a market, and that once such a market exists, it can serve customers other than addicts. This is why it is important that the third part of the maintenance argument—that only addicts will purchase heroin—is also false.

25. Stimson and Ogborne, "A Survey of a Representative Sample of Addicts Prescribed Heroin at London Clinics," pp. 19, 21.
26. Inciardi, *Methadone Diversion*, pp. 12–16.

## The Nonaddict Market

Indeed, this is the crucial fallacy in the whole argument that no one will buy illegal heroin if legal heroin is available at lower cost. Heroin maintenance, unlike a free availability system, does not purport to make heroin available to everyone. Rather, it purports to restrict availability to addicts.

Addicts, however, are not the only heroin users today; nor would they be under heroin maintenance. The nonaddicted customers for diverted heroin would include those who today are controlled moderate heroin users; experimenters; nonaddicted users on their way to addiction; and former addicts who risk readdiction by using the drug occasionally. Most important, the nonaddict customers for heroin diverted from the maintenance system would include all those who had never used the drug but would be willing to try it if it were cheaper and more easily available to them.

This is not to deny that, at least temporarily, heroin maintenance would probably provide enough legal heroin to decrease the total demand for the illegally sold drug. Though it is likely that addicts are a minority of users, their *per person* use is such that they account for most of the heroin presently consumed. Simple economics, then, tells us that if the maintenance system enrolled any sizable number of addicts, the amount demanded on the illegal market at current prices would drop. All other things being equal, this would lead to a lowering of price, a drop in the profits of illegal dealing in smuggled heroin, and, assuming no decrease in law enforcement pressure, an overall constriction in the supply of this commodity. Of course, this says nothing about the total amount of heroin consumed—the legally prescribed, the illegally diverted plus the smuggled. Presumably, that would rise considerably because the amount legally prescribed to an addict would be greater than that available to him on the street.

Whether the illegally supplied heroin—the sum of that smuggled and that diverted—would be more or less than is now illegally supplied (all of which today is smuggled), is not so clear. It might be less if maintenance were so attractive that a high proportion of those who became addicts thereafter quickly entered the system. Such a decrease, however, might occur only because at any one time the number of addicts using illegal heroin would be relatively small. The total number of addicts might rise to unacceptable levels as a constant stream of new addicts piled up in the maintenance system.

Moreover, the amount of the drug illegally sold to those addicted might actually increase rather than decrease. This would be the case if the stream of new nonaddicted users, and hence new addicts, caused by diversion from the prescription heroin maintenance system, became so large that, despite the relatively prompt removal of addicts onto the maintenance rolls, the users of diverted heroin consumed a greater amount than users of smuggled heroin consume today.

Actually, the amount of heroin consumed illegally is not nearly so important as the number of new addicts produced—even if they are promptly taken into the maintenance system. Taking the new addicts into maintenance does not solve the problem. It costs something to maintain them; their own social and economic stability may be compromised; and, perhaps most important, the larger the number of addicts in maintenance, the more prescribed heroin they can divert to produce more new addicts.

## The Disappearance of the Pusher

Presumably, the more comforting view that heroin maintenance would lower the number of new addicts is premised on the pusher mythology rejected in chapter 1. It is true that if traffickers actively attempted to create addicts, hoping to profit from their later trade when they were addicted and had to buy heroin, the availability of the drug, cheaply and legally, to all who became addicts would discourage such activities.

As we have seen, however, the street-level seller is not a major spreader of addiction—except in the sense that he makes heroin available to the peer groups through which heroin use spreads. A prescription heroin maintenance system, by replacing the street seller of imported heroin with the seller of diverted heroin, could provide at least an equivalent supply.

Nor can we place any confidence in the prediction that a heroin maintenance system would remove so many of the customers for illegal heroin that there would be insufficient volume to justify the costs and risks of the present illegal distribution system—and therefore that it would disappear.[27] There are several reasons to discount this view. One is that the economies of scale in heroin supply are not that great. The removal from the illegal market of a substantial percentage of addict customers, as already noted, would depress the price of heroin, which in turn would depress the profits of traffickers and the amount of the drug sold. There is no reason to believe, however, that profits would reach such a low level that the traffickers would have an insufficient incentive to service whatever market remained.

This prediction, moreover, is directed at the supply side of the heroin market rather than at the demand for the drug. In fact, of course, there very likely would be a destruction of the present supply system—but not because of a contraction in demand. What would probably put the present

27. Deininger, "The Economics of Heroin," pp. 608–9.

system out of business would be the competition from resales of pre-scribed heroin. This offers no comfort for we would merely be replacing one distribution system by another—with the newer system able to deliver the drug more cheaply and easily than the present one.

## THE PRICE OF DIVERTED HEROIN

Exactly how much more cheaply a prescription maintenance system could deliver illegal heroin is an interesting question. As we have seen, such a system would lower the street price of heroin in two major ways. First, by removing many addicts from the market, it would depress the demand for the illegal drug; second, increases in the number of addicts on maintenance would increase the number of sellers of diverted heroin, thus raising both the supply and the competition among suppliers.

One would expect that two counterbalancing factors would then arise to prevent the price of heroin from sinking too low. As the price of heroin falls, it becomes less attractive for addicts to enter the maintenance system. The greater the number of users and addicts outside the mainte-nance system, the more they will bid up the price of the drug. Moreover, the smaller the number of addicts in maintenance, the fewer there will be to sell their prescriptions.

Of course, we do not know where the equilibrium will lie under a prescription heroin maintenance system. Although the number of addicts would probably not be so great as under free availability, the likely drop in prices, as well as in the lowered difficulty and danger of purchasing heroin, might result in an unacceptably high addiction rate—even consid-ering what would probably be the lowered social cost of theft per addict.

## THE PRESCRIPTION SYSTEM VERSUS FREE AVAILABILITY

A prescription heroin maintenance system, as we have seen, has some of the advantages and some of the disadvantages of free availability. Although the heroin maintenance system would probably lead to a much lower level of addiction than would free availability, it would entail a significant administrative cost. First of all, on purely therapeutic grounds, it would entail expenses for monitoring and prescribing for the addicts. In addition, we would need to establish careful controls to prevent the wholesale embezzlement of heroin. We would have to invest a consider-able amount in auditing the practices of clinics to prevent prescription fraud and other corruption—though, of course, our efforts could never be completely successful. Similarly, the pharmacies that filled the prescrip-tions would have to be protected from robbery as well as embezzlement.

Finally, the social cost of a prescription maintenance system includes not only the resources expended on it and the increases in addiction it might bring, but also the results of the inevitable police efforts to stem the tide of diversion. The greater these efforts, the more the overall system takes on the disadvantages of heroin prohibition in the consumption of law enforcement resources, fostering of police corruption, and violations of civil liberties. Alternatively, the less effort law enforcement puts into this task, the more the prescription heroin maintenance system approximates free availability itself.

## THE ON-THE-PREMISES SYSTEM

The intractable problem of diversion from a prescription maintenance system forces one to examine more carefully the other major type of heroin maintenance: the on-the-premises system. Here, diversion would be minimized by not allowing the addict to possess heroin, except inside a secure clinic. If the addict were required to shoot his heroin on the premises, relatively little supervision would be needed to prevent the massive diversion entailed in a prescription system. The on-the-premises system, however, raises other difficulties, most of which stem from the brute pharmacological fact that heroin is a short-acting drug. Since its effects last for only about four to six hours, the addict in maintenance would be forced to appear for his shot three or four times a day. The interruptions required by such a schedule would make a normal working life difficult, if not impossible, and the inconvenience of so many trips to the clinic might well make this kind of heroin maintenance no more attractive to most addicts than are their present alternatives: abstinence, methadone maintenance, or continuing life on the street.[28]

Moreover, unless we vastly increase the number of clinics, the addict's problem of going for his heroin four times a day would be more than a nuisance—it would be a practical impossibility. Addicts often do not have access to automobiles, and public transportation where many of them live is usually bad. A fair estimate of the average traveling time for addicts to the nearest methadone clinic today is about three-quarters of an hour. It is hard to believe that if their clinic required them to inject heroin on the premises, their total business there could be done in less than half an hour. Three trips daily to the clinic would then require that the addict in such maintenance spend about six hours a day getting his heroin supply. The great majority of heroin addicts probably do not want our legal, cheap heroin *that* much.

Obviously, to make an on-the-premises heroin maintenance system work, we would have to lower the addict's traveling time considerably.

28. Mary Jeanne Kreek, "Methadone in Treatment: Physiological and Pharmacological Issues," in *Handbook on Drug Abuse*, ed. Robert L. DuPont, Avram Goldstein, and John O'Donnell (Washington, D.C.: Government Printing Office, 1979), p. 59.

We would need far more clinics to dispense heroin than presently dispense methadone. There are several serious costs in doing this, however.

## Diversion from an On-the-Premises System

Not only would the clinics, the central heroin warehouses, and the vehicles delivering the drug from one place to another all be targets for robbery and theft, but the greater the number of clinics, the greater the security problems of preventing diversion by employees corrupted by the profits to be made in selling heroin. Although diversion by addicts of their allotments could be made very difficult by an on-the-premises system, the same cannot be said concerning the employees of the system.

Sale of heroin legitimately coming into police possession has been a nagging problem of heroin enforcement; dealers arrested for selling heroin have been given back the drug supply seized from them and permitted to continue their business—with policemen as senior partners. And we know even of cases where confiscated heroin has found its way from guarded police property-rooms onto the street.[29] There is certainly no reason to think that the profits of heroin dealing would prove less tempting to those working for the maintenance system; and the problems of designing a security system would be far greater. The police, at least, are not expected to distribute heroin at all. Once one allows distribution on any scale, diversion becomes much easier. It becomes possible to keep nonexistent addicts on the rolls, diverting their allotment of heroin to the illegal market, or to shortweigh the dosage addicts receive and sell the difference. And, of course, "unexplained" inventory shrinkages can result from simple, crude theft.

It is no doubt possible to design methods of combating each of these problems. The difficulty is that as the number of clinics goes up, so do—more than proportionally—the costs of supervision, the likelihood of corruption somewhere in the system, and the difficulty of simply keeping track of both heroin and addicts. That is not to say that the amount of diversion from on-the-premises maintenance system would be comparable to the hemorrhaging to be expected from a prescription system. It would probably be much less. As a result, the price of the illegal drug, both in money and in terms of the difficulty and danger in securing a supply is likely to be higher.

## The Attractiveness of the On-the-Premises System

On the other hand, the on-the-premises system is less likely to disrupt the present patterns of heroin trafficking. Such a system would be much less

---

29. Nicholas Pileggi, "Further Developments in the 'French Connection' Case," *New York* 6, no. 39 (24 September 1973), pp. 42–48.

attractive to the addict than a prescription system. He would have to contend with all the inconvenience of traveling and waiting around for the inevitable bureaucratic procedures within the clinic. He could not shoot up in his home surroundings or, presumably, with his friends, and it is hard to believe that the institutional setting of a heroin maintenance clinic would be a pleasant, attractive place for him. Finally, the time and energy that treatment in such a clinic requires would prevent the addict from enjoying many of the exciting satisfactions of his former life style.

It is likely, therefore, that a substantial percentage of addicts would not sign up for this kind of heroin maintenance. To the extent that the price of heroin remained high, but more addicts remained on the street, the situation would resemble our present heroin prohibition. The fact that some addicts would be attracted into the system might lower the social costs they impose upon us—but only at the price of adding other costs.

## The Location of the Clinics

Any sizable increase in the number of maintenance clinics would not only be more expensive financially, it would cause major political problems. The location of methadone clinics has caused considerable opposition from the surrounding neighborhoods, and heroin clinics would be likely to generate much stronger resentment.[30] The amount of traffic per addict generated by a heroin clinic would be much greater because of the larger number of visits necessary, and the short time between injections would tend to induce those addicts who had nothing else to do to congregate in the area, either nodding from their last shot or waiting around for the next.

This would raise community objections on a host of grounds; many would protest on the ground that the congregation of addicts near the clinic might become a magnet to the youth of the area or the focus for a local drug culture. In addition, if past experience is any guide, the areas where the addicts gathered would soon become prolific sources of both petty crime and unsightly litter.

Moreover, the small area served by each heroin clinic would make it impossible to locate all outside of residential areas. Many would have to be located within the ghetto rather than on its edges, thus increasing the political opposition to the clinics and exacerbating their abrasions of the surrounding community.

These are not merely public relations difficulties. The opposition of the clinics' neighbors would most likely be based on a genuine lowering of the quality of their lives—and one which would be differentially imposed on those least able to afford it.

30. Meyers, "American Heroin Policy: Some Alternatives," pp. 212–13.

The Problem of the Automobile

As if this were not enough, we must consider the problem of the automobile. Although, in the most crowded inner cities, it is likely that most addicts do not drive cars, there are many, perhaps a majority, in places such as California, who do.

The difficulty here is that many addicts on heroin are not in good enough condition to drive safely.[31] Heroin, in this respect, is quite unlike methadone, where, as we will see, the longer-acting nature of the drug and the fact that it is taken orally make its onset far more gentle.

Even those addicts who are taking stable doses of heroin will not be in good enough condition to drive just after their injection, and should they be delayed in traffic on the way to the clinic, the beginnings of withdrawal may make them a danger then. Entirely apart from any legal liability the clinic may incur, there is the moral problem of creating a risk to those on the streets, and this danger will be most concentrated nearest the clinic.

The more one thinks about this problem, the more intractable it becomes. The clinic, in theory, could bar its patients from coming by car—but this would be unenforceable, since they could simply park nearby and lie about their transportation. Moreover, as a practical matter, driving a car might be the only way the addicts could arrive.

There is, to be sure, a way of solving a number of the transportation problems caused by on-the-premises heroin maintenance—though it smacks somewhat of Swift's modest proposal. We might simply make our system a mobile one. A large armored car would then cruise around the areas of heroin use. In the car would be technicians, injection devices, and a supply of heroin, together with identification systems which could recognize a card—and perhaps even a fingerprint pattern—of a certified addict. As the car moved slowly through the ghetto, the addict would walk along close beside it, put his arm into a hole in the side of the car for a moment, have his identity and dosage checked, and receive a heroin injection (more likely intramuscular rather than intravenous but enough to be satisfying to him). Then he would simply go about his business as best he could until the next time the "Kaplan Wagon" went by.

The advantage of such an arrangement over the immobile on-the-premises system are obvious—but those who would argue that there are only a few public relations problems to be ironed out may, unfortunately, be wildly optimistic.

Short of such a method, we might be able to make an on-the-premises system work only by providing convenient transportation for addicts and

31. See, generally, Gregory A. Austin et al., eds., *Drug Users and Driving Behavior*, National Institute on Drug Abuse, Research Issues 20 (Washington, D.C.: Government Printing Office, 1977).

by locating large numbers of clinics throughout our areas of heroin addiction. The costs of this kind of service, however, may simply price the whole program out of the market.

## The Cost of the System

Indeed, the financial cost of the program would probably raise the most serious obstacle to an on-the-premises heroin maintenance system. For a host of reasons, including the fact that it must be staffed day and night, an on-the-premises heroin maintenance system is considerably more expensive than a prescription heroin scheme or one using methadone. It is likely that an on-the-premises heroin maintenance system would cost some $15,000 per addict per year.[32]

Arguably this expenditure would still be worthwhile, since the yearly social cost imposed by many addicts under heroin prohibition is well above $15,000. The wisdom of such expenditures is by no means clear, however, for several reasons. Those addicts who would stay in this kind of treatment would probably tend to be the less criminal and more stable addicts, who impose less than $15,000 a year costs upon us. And some of the criminalistic addicts who did enter the maintenance program would continue their former life style with its attendant depredations upon society, while absorbing the cost of maintenance as well.

In addition, the $15,000 figure does not include the indirect costs of the on-the-premises system. It does not include the social cost of the inevitable diversion from the system, the political and symbolic costs of locating the clinics, and the welfare costs caused simply by the fact that for many attending an on-the-premises system would be so time-consuming that it prevented gainful employment. Finally, any kind of heroin maintenance system, regardless of whether a prescription or an on-the-premises system, involves certain inherent costs which must be considered along with those already mentioned.

## THE COSTS OF ANY HEROIN MAINTENANCE

Among the costs of all maintenance schemes, we must consider the political disadvantages of any government-controlled system which distributes addictive drugs. We have already heard charges that methadone maintenance is a type of genocide and an effort to manipulate large numbers of minority group members through government tranquilization.[33] Even if one rejects these charges as extreme and unbalanced, there

32. Bjorklund, "Estimates of Costs of Heroin Maintenance in California," pp. 1–2.
33. Ronald Bayer, "Heroin Maintenance, the Vera Proposal and Narcotic Reform: An Analysis of the Debate 1971–1973," *Contemporary Drug Problems* 4, no. 3 (Fall 1975): 313–14.

is legitimate cause for concern. Anyone interested in limiting governmental power over the individual should worry about programs which will keep sizable numbers of citizens dependent upon the goodwill of officialdom to avoid withdrawal and being deprived of their supply of an addicting drug.

This problem is a disadvantage of those methadone maintenance programs which already exist, but they are more aggravated with respect to heroin for two reasons. Because of heroin's presumably greater ability to attract addicts, more addicts will be dependent on the goodwill of government, and because of heroin's presumably greater desirability, those addicted will be more accommodating to their supplier's wishes.

## Maintenance and the Addict's Health

The fact that the very nature of heroin maintenance involves giving heroin to addicts raises another issue. In the long term, heroin use, especially through intravenous injection, is not good for the addict's health. As we have noted, the British addicts, when they were receiving legal heroin, had a death rate even higher than that of American street addicts.[34] So long as they continue intravenous administration, addicts will risk collapsed veins, hepatitis, and a whole series of physical ailments. Moreover, even though heroin seems relatively nontoxic, at least as compared to alcohol, we do not yet know the long-term physical effects of heroin addiction, even on a stabilized dosage and apart from the method of administration. The relatively sparse anecdotal evidence on this issue is not sufficient. The few case reports indicating that the long-term physical effects of medically stabilized heroin addiction are not serious cannot make up for the lack of controlled studies or careful examination of an adequate sample of users.[35]

The physical effects of heroin are by no means the only health problem. It is likely that many of those maintained on heroin will not be able to stabilize their doses, despite the efforts of the maintenance clinics. As a result, many addicts may be left alternating between a heroin deficit and a heroin euphoria as their tolerance outstrips and then falls behind the amount of the drug they receive—perhaps supplemented by street heroin.

The situation may even be more complex. A number of America's leading experimentalists in the opiate area have pointed out that heroin, when the dosage is gradually escalated, does not continue to produce euphoria and that, in the higher dose ranges, tolerance to the euphoric

---

34. Gerry V. Stimson, *Heroin and Behaviour: Diversity among Addicts Attending London Clinics* (New York and Toronto: John Wiley & Sons, 1973), p. 7.

35. O'Donnell, *Narcotic Addicts in Kentucky*, pp. 23–30. Musto and Ramos, "A Follow-up Study of the New Haven Morphine Maintenance Clinic of 1920," pp. 1075–76.

effect of heroin develops more quickly than tolerance to certain unpleasant effects. As a result, in the place of euphoria "come negative mood changes such as irritability, suspiciousness, hostility. . . . Sooner or later a state is reached at which disphoria predominates, [and] the interval between doses are more marked by withdrawal type discomfort."[36]

Presumably the physicians running the maintenance programs will attempt to stabilize the addict's dosage at not too great a level so as not to compromise his psychological adjustment and his ability to hold employment. It is likely that in doing this they will be met by complaints that the dosage is not high enough—since despite the ill effects, many addicts still increase their doses as much as they can.

In England, when the clinics were prescribing heroin, the amount of the drug prescribed was a matter of negotiation, often adversarial, between the staff and the addict. In this negotiation, the staff had to meet inconsistent requirements; it had to exert social control over addicts in the program; it had to meet enough of the addicts' wants so that they did not drop out of the program entirely; and it had to avoid the therapeutic undesirability of giving the addicts ever increasing doses.

The duty of physicians to help their patients does not fit in well with a system of heroin maintenance that is designed in great part to keep addicts from imposing costs upon the rest of us. At the very least, the tension between the physician's ideal of helping his patient, his role as policeman, and the desires of the addict for more heroin will result in serious staffing and administrative problems in any heroin maintenance program run under our medical model.

## Enrolling Nonaddicts

The administrative problems in running any kind of a heroin maintenance system are likely to put more truth into the myth that every heroin user will become addicted. The most obvious reason for this is that many nonaddicted heroin users may prefer even an inconvenient on-the-premises system to their present lives. Some may simply become addicted, knowing that they will then be candidates for maintenance. Others may be able to talk their way into the maintenance program while not yet addicted—though of course addiction will soon follow, at least if the program is an on-the-premises one.

We know that membership in a methadone program has been considered by welfare authorities in some areas as tantamount to an inability to work. It is likely that heroin maintenance will also attract seekers of

---

36. Avram Goldstein, "Heroin Maintenance: A Medical View. A Conversation between a Physician and a Politician," *Journal of Drug Issues* 9, no. 3 (Summer 1979): 343–44.

welfare payments. Indeed, the combined lure of heroin and welfare payments may be that much greater.

Moreover, with respect to those receiving heroin, the argument for welfare may be more persuasive. Addicts maintained on heroin may in fact be less able to engage in productive work than those maintained on methadone, and, if they have to come to an on-the-premises system three times a day, this may be true, independent of any direct drug effect.

## Prolonging Addiction

Another cost of any heroin maintenance system is its effect on alternative methods of grappling with the heroin problem. If the life of the junkie were the only alternative to maintenance on legal, cheap and pure heroin, we could probably agree that those on heroin maintenance would be better off. The choice, however, in many cases, will be between heroin maintenance and no addiction at all.

Despite the once-an-addict-always-an-addict myth, we know that many addicts give up addiction after relatively short periods and before they have built up too great a habit. Usually they do this because they fear the disastrous consequences of continued addiction, because of the problem of locating and affording a supply, and because the heroin scene is too much of a "hassle" for them.

Moreover, even among long-term addicts, perhaps a majority "mature out" and give up addiction after the age of about thirty-five. If heroin maintenance is attractive and easy enough to attract addicts into the treatment, it is quite likely to attract them to stay and, hence, to put a great deal more truth in the once-an-addict-always-an-addict myth.

This problem is not nearly so simple as might appear. The practice of simply discontinuing maintenance, say to addicts over forty, would be fought by clinic staffs on medical and humanitarian grounds. And a policy of gradually making it more inconvenient or otherwise discouraging older patients would be even harder to implement. Even if we did terminate maintenance for addicts of a given age—or at the physicians's discretion—the chances are that at least some of those terminated would become street addicts again. Indeed, the percentage who returned to street addiction might be higher than we think. We do not know how much of the burnout phenomenon is caused by age and how much by the overall toll of many years as a street addict. If the latter, the long-term maintenance patient might have energy left for several years of street addiction.

## The Effect on Other Types of Maintenance

The likely attractiveness of heroin maintenance for addicts will have another effect; it will undermine any other kind of maintenance we might use. As we will see, despite the problems inherent in methadone maintenance, large numbers of addicts have adjusted to that drug and seem to be leading productive, noncriminal lives, at a cost per addict considerably less than that of an on-the-premises system and without producing the massive diversion a prescription system would entail.

Although, as a therapeutic matter, they are better off on methadone, it seems quite clear that most addicts would prefer to be maintained on heroin instead. The institution of heroin maintenance, whatever good it would do for those who have refused our present treatments, would be very likely to lure away from methadone even those who could, in fact, adjust to that more convenient and therapeutic drug.[37]

It is likely that any clinic offering a choice between methadone and heroin maintenance would find its methadone rolls undersubscribed. Nor could it insist, as a condition of receiving heroin, that addicts try methadone first. The preliminary period on methadone before switching to heroin might so lessen the attractiveness of the entire program that it would lose much of its appeal to many street addicts. And unless the heroin maintenance scheme were extremely inconvenient, the addict would have a considerable incentive to fail during the trial period on methadone so that he could thereafter receive heroin.

## HEROIN MAINTENANCE AND CULTURAL CONTROLS

Most discussions of heroin maintenance focus on the short-term effects of freeing heroin addicts from the demands of an illegal habit. Rarely do we see any discussion of the long-term effects of heroin maintenance on the social control of heroin use. Yet this is a worrisome problem. The present cultural constraints against heroin addiction, and even against any use of the drug, are probably a major factor in keeping down the present number of addicts.

It is true that maintenance, with its implication that heroin addiction is a sickness, would probably not cause so great a change in our cultural view of heroin addiction as would free availability. Nonetheless, certain aspects of heroin maintenance might lower the cultural aversion to use of the drug.

The mere fact of large-scale legal supply of the drug by the government and by the medical profession might broadcast the message that heroin is not *that* bad. This might lessen the social disapproval of heroin, which acts as a barrier to many who might otherwise try the drug.[38] In addition,

---

37. For a contrary viewpoint, see Meyers, "American Heroin Policy: Some Alternatives," pp. 216–20. Mitcheson and Hartnoll report that, to British addicts, heroin is the archetypal narcotic and that addicts express a preference for it over methadone.

38. Meyers discounts the effects of the symbolism of this policy message; see "American Heroin Policy: Some Policy Alternatives," p. 200.

the fact that an addict could be maintained on the very drug that has caused his problem might make addiction itself less threatening. This might weaken the fear of addiction, which not only prevents many from initially trying the drug but also acts to impel many occasional users to control their intake.

Of course, we cannot be certain of this. As Oscar Wilde wrote, "as long as war is regarded as wicked, it will always have its fascination; when it is looked upon as vulgar, it will cease to be popular." The same may be true of heroin addiction. It can be argued that the more we treat addiction as a sickness, the less glamorous and attractive it might become. If heroin maintenance were easily available to addicts, risking addiction might also become much less reckless and dangerous and therefore less productive of status among a user's peers.

Even if the cultural controls on heroin use and addiction were temporarily weakened, there might be counterbalancing benefits. Both the demystification of the drug, and the increased experience with it that heroin maintenance might bring, could speed the development of cultural controls, which may be the best safeguard against the social damage caused by heroin.

The final problem with heroin maintenance is in fact a broader difficulty which besets any maintenance system or indeed any attempted cure of heroin addicts. Our experience with methadone maintenance has taught us that though stabilization on an opiate is probably a necessary condition of an addict's social productivity and personal well-being, it is by no means a sufficient condition. By the time they enter maintenance, addicts typically are unable to cope with anger, frustration, or anxiety without turning to one drug or another to ease those feelings. Often both their friends and their values are deeply rooted in the addict culture. It is likely that they suffer from a woeful lack of job skills and in many cases they seem unable to delay their gratification long enough to gain any reward less immediate than their drug use.[39]

Of course, the many handicaps under which the addicts labor do not constitute disadvantages of maintenance on heroin or on any other opiate. These problems do, however, add to the expenses of any program which attempts to cope with them, and, perhaps more important, they limit severely the prospects of success at any given level of expense.

If our major goals in maintaining addicts on heroin are the reduction of their criminality and their restoration to productive life, we should be aware that some but not all of their criminality may be due to their addiction and that most have never led what we would call productive

39. For a review of psychoanalyses of addicts in treatment, see Jerome J. Platt and Christina Labate, *Heroin Addiction: Theory, Research & Treatment* (New York: John Wiley & Sons, 1976), pp. 126–46.

lives. The addicts' many problems apart from their drug use are not, of course, automatically solved by maintenance. Though maintenance may permit their amelioration, the existence of these additional problems, which must also be solved before the full benefit of maintenance can be realized, may reduce our enthusiasm for any kind of maintenance system, and especially for the most expensive and difficult variety—heroin maintenance.

## THE "HOOK" SYSTEM

It might be that the more general disadvantages of any heroin maintenance system would be overbalanced by the benefits of such a system, if only we could find some means of avoiding the specific disadvantages of either the prescription or the on-the-premises system. Unfortunately, there seems to be no way of avoiding one or the other, and any combination of the two systems would seem, at the least, to partake of at least some of the disadvantages of each. Indeed, in all likelihood, any combination involving prescription is very likely to be impracticable. There is no reason to think that a system that allowed an addict to possess any prescribed heroin outside of a secure clinic would be tolerable, considering the value of the drug on the street.

More promising are some variations on the on-the-premises system. One distinguished pharmacologist has suggested that heroin maintenance on a temporary basis be used as a "hook" to get addicts into methadone treatment.[40] The theory is that addicts would be lured by the promise of free heroin into registering at clinics where, after perhaps a six month period of maintenance on heroin, they would be switched onto methadone. However, during the heroin maintenance period—delivered by an on-the-premises system—the inconvenience of excessive traveling time, the difficulties of automobile transportation, and many other disadvantages would still be with us. To be sure, these problems would be quantitatively less because, once a steady state had been reached, there would be fewer addicts receiving heroin at any one time. On the other hand, we can expect a larger turnover rate caused by addicts entering and leaving treatment.

Such a plan does not give full weight to the fact that addicts are intelligent human beings. It is likely that many would receive their heroin willingly but drop out of the program when the time came to stop their supply. This would raise the costs of the system, since the startup expenses of medical examinations and determining dosages are much

40. Avram Goldstein, "Heroin Addiction: Sequential Treatment Employing Pharmacological Supports," *Archives of General Psychiatry* 33, no. 3 (March 1976): 353–58.

higher than the average monthly cost per addict in an ongoing maintenance system.

It is true that during the temporary maintenance period the system
might supply the addict with enough heroin to raise his tolerance and need
for that drug so sharply that his habit could be priced out of the market. If
so, he might have to accept the switch to methadone. Apart from the
questionable moral aspects of such a system, the fact is that it is unlikely
to work. Those on methadone maintenance today are able to drop out of
these programs and return to the use of street heroin. And those addicts
who felt tricked into maintenance to begin with would probably be among
the first to leave. The real problem with this type of heroin maintenance is
that it is not heroin maintenance at all. Rather, it is a heroin reward for
undergoing methadone maintenance. It shares all the problems of any
kind of bribery—most important, that those bribed are unlikely to deliver.

Moreover, no one has faced the issue of what to do with the addict who
drops out of treatment rather than be switched to methadone. If we do not
let him back into heroin treatment shortly, we will face problems with the
clinic staff, which may find a punitive response inconsistent with their
therapeutic values. Experience indicates, then, that they will bend the
rules, overlook violations, and occasionally ignore addicts reentering
treatment under assumed names. If we refuse to allow the addict quickly
to reenter treatment after having dropped out, we will be returning him to
the street to impose the social costs of addiction upon us. Finally, a
punitive approach may make the whole scheme that much less attractive
to the many addicts who may not know whether they will be sufficiently
satisfied with methadone—and hence may be less likely to sign up to
begin with.

On the other hand, a permissive approach would also have its problems. The addict could continue indefinitely in heroin maintenance simply
by dropping out and then reentering the treatment. In this case it would be
the addict, not the system, that held the hook.

## OTHER VARIETIES OF HEROIN MAINTENANCE

Other attempts to combine the lure of heroin with the stability of
methadone have also been suggested. Some would reward an addict who
has otherwise met the conditions of a methadone program by allowing
him a shot of heroin. One psychiatrist has suggested that maintenance be
set up to allow the addict one heroin injection per day, while he received
methadone to cover his other wants.[41]

41. Norman E. Zinberg and Wayne M. Harding, "Control and Intoxicant Use: A
Theoretical and Practical Overview," *Journal of Drug Issues* 9, no. 2 (Spring 1979): 126.

Such a plan would have the advantage of proportioning our bribery to the addict's performance. It would also have two serious disadvantages over and above those of the hook system. First of all, it would broadcast a cultural message about the joys of heroin that we do not wish to spread. We probably would be better off using money or sex—two socially recognized reinforcers—as our payment. Second, the problems of stabilizing an addict on one drug are difficult enough. When two different drugs with very different courses of action are used simultaneously, the problems of stabilization become almost insurmountable.

In theory, we might be able to practice heroin maintenance using some less euphoric form of that drug than is available on the street. Thus, we might use an on-the-premises system for subcutaneous heroin; perhaps we could even allow prescriptions of heroin mixed with an additive so that it could not be injected at all and could only be smoked or snorted.

Alternatively, it could be argued that we should not maintain addicts on heroin but on some near relative of that drug. For instance, injectable methadone was used for a while in the British clinics, and there are several opiates longer-acting than heroin but shorter-acting than methadone.[42]

The problem with all these possibilities is that all would be less able than heroin to draw the addict into treatment and less able than methadone to promote the addict's adjustment and health. There is, of course, the theoretical possibility that some untried drug would be more like heroin in giving addicts what they want, but more like methadone in its compatibility with their health and adjustment in society. The problem is, there is simply no reason to believe that any such drug fulfills these requirements, and we would need a great deal of research before we could conclude that one does.

Indeed, the trend seems to be in precisely the opposite direction. If methadone maintenance is improved, the chances are that it will be improved by using even longer-acting opiates. We would thus be relying on the promise of better adjustment and fewer health problems to draw the addicts into treatment, rather than on the promise of a more euphoric drug.

## THE ADVANTAGES OF EXPERIMENT

In view of the facts that our present heroin prohibition system imposes such obvious costs on our society and that, at least, there might be some possible advantage in heroin maintenance, it is surprising that the matter has received so little careful thought. Most advocacy of heroin mainte-

42. Jaffe and Martin, "Opioid Analgesics," p. 507.

nance does not even distinguish between a prescription and an on-the-premises system—let alone go into any more detail as to the specifics of the arrangement.

What is most often advocated in this context is the performance of limited experiment. The suggestion is that we should try heroin maintenance—it is generally not specified what kind—in a very small area which does not have a large addict population. The theory is that this will tell us whether heroin maintenance works and, hence, allow us to decide more intelligently the question of whether our pilot project should be greatly expanded in scope.

It is hard to have much of an objection to this kind of proposal since, if closely watched, it can do very little harm. On the other hand, the chances are overwhelming that it can do very little good. A heroin maintenance scheme, of either the prescription or the on-the-premises type, might be "successful" in, say, Portland, Maine, Lincoln, Nebraska, or a hundred other American cities which do not have a major heroin problem.

In any area where the police far outnumber the addicts and the criminal justice institutions are not already overwhelmed, even a prescription system might work at least temporarily. The police could probably watch carefully those who received heroin from the system, and indeed the addicts would probably be few enough so that each one's heroin supply could be marked with a harmless dye of a particular color, which would allow the police to check on diversion. In areas where the criminal justice system is not already overloaded, those who did divert their heroin could be convicted and punished. Similarly, an on-the-premises system would probably work well in an area where the addicts were few in number and concentrated in a small area. The need for only one small clinic would make the problems of supervision relatively easy, and the small area served would minimize the addicts' travel time.

It should be noted, however, that since the area in which we would run such a heroin maintenance experiment would not be one of major heroin use, the costs of prohibition there would be quite small, too. As a result, the maintenance plan would be undertaken not to lower the costs of our present policy but, rather, as an experiment to see whether the policy could be used in those areas where heroin is a serious problem. The basic difficulty, then, with attempting to learn anything from such a small-scale heroin maintenance program is that the areas we are interested in—our central cities—are so different, both in the nature and in the scale of the problem. Indeed, the very things that make it possible to predict success for these small-scale programs are just those that are not present where heroin use is a major problem.

Moreover, the very fact of being an experiment would make our program very different from the heroin maintenance we could expect to find in an ongoing system. Experiments are typically far better financed than are ongoing programs of similar size. "Pilot" programs are generally very carefully watched by the researchers, and the design of the evaluation systems seems to guarantee that proper procedures will be followed. The people who run such programs are usually the most highly motivated and conscientious, and the Hawthorne effect can be relied on to help produce good results.

It is only after the routine is established in large-scale programs that we will be able to draw any useful conclusions from observing heroin maintenance at work. Not only are the chances of success at a reasonable cost slim indeed, but by the time we have convinced ourselves that the plan cannot work, we may have done considerable harm in our efforts to lower the social costs we are now enduring.

## CONCLUSION

Heroin maintenance is, in many ways, like euthanasia. It is perhaps a good idea if all the details can be worked out. Unfortunately in both cases, it turns out that there are sticky problems that simply do not yield to the kind of line drawing which a legal—and social—system such as ours must do, and, in both cases, the problems appear to be intractable. To use a metaphor, each solution to either problem seems like too small a blanket on a cold night. It may be good enough to cover part of the matter adequately, but when it does it leaves other parts dangerously exposed.

If enforcement of heroin prohibition, free availability, and heroin maintenance all must be rejected as solutions to our heroin problems, does this mean that there is nothing we can do? The answer, it is hoped, is no. There may be no panacea and no way of making dramatic improvements in our situation. Nonetheless there may still be some things we can do. These will be the subject of the final chapter.

# 5 ⬛⬛⬛
# *THE LAW*
# *AND THE USER*

**W**e have now looked at the likely results of making heroin freely available and at the probable costs and benefits of heroin maintenance. After this examination, we may still prefer heroin prohibition, for all its faults, to either of those innovations. Our present policy, however, involves a good deal more than the criminalization of supply, which is the hallmark of any prohibition.

Because of the publicity devoted to exciting cases cracking huge drug rings and arresting one Mr. Big or another, we sometimes forget that the impact of the criminal law on the heroin problem is not limited to its effect on the supply side of the market. The law, in addition, bears directly upon the user himself, and not merely by making it more difficult and expensive for him to obtain his drug.

It is true that once it is decided that prohibition is the preferred policy for heroin, decisions as to the legal treatment of the user represent a kind of fine-tuning of that policy. Nonetheless, since the crimes incident to heroin use—including possession of small amounts of heroin—result in far more arrests than do the crimes of trafficking,[1] it is important to look at these user-oriented policies in some detail. Indeed it may well be that changing these will turn out to be the most practical way available to lower the overall social cost that heroin imposes upon us.

---

1. Weldon T. Johnson and Robert Bogomolny, "Selective Justice: Drug Law Enforcement in Six American Cities," in *Drug Use In America*, app., vol. 4, pp. 523–34.

## ADDICTION AS A CRIME

There are several ways in which the criminal law might conceivably be brought to bear on the heroin user. Perhaps the most obvious way would be to make addiction itself a crime, and for much of the period since the Harrison Act the laws often did just this.[2]

Since most police, judges, and legislators thought that all users quickly became addicts, they regarded addiction and use as, for the most part, synonymous. And even those who made the distinction usually supported concentrating upon the addict, on the ground that this policy applied criminal justice resources to that class of heroin users who presented the most serious social problem.

Then, in 1962, the United States Supreme Court held that statutes which punished addiction as a crime were unconstitutional. The Court took the view that addiction was a disease, and hence, like a "punishment for having a cold," punishment for addiction was "cruel and unusual," within the meaning of the Eighth Amendment to the Constitution. The Court's reasoning was buttressed by a view of the heroin addict which embraced the classic stereotype in its extreme form:

> To be a confirmed drug addict is to be one of the walking dead. . . .
> The teeth have rotted out, the appetite is lost, and the stomach and intestines don't function properly. The gall bladder becomes inflamed; eyes and skin turn a bilious yellow; in some cases membranes of the nose turn a flaming red; the partition separating the nostrils is eaten away; breathing is difficult. Oxygen in the blood decreases; bronchitis and tuberculosis develop. Good traits of character disappear and bad ones emerge. Sex organs become affected. Veins collapse and livid purplish scars remain. Boils and abscesses plague the skin: gnawing pain racks the body. Nerves snap; vicious twitching develops. Imaginary and fantastic fears blight the mind and sometimes complete insanity results. Oftentimes, too, death comes much too early in life. . . . Such is the torment of being a drug addict; such is the plague of being one of the walking dead. [Robinson v. California, 370 U.S. 661 (1962)]

The justices, of course, could not have maintained such an unrecognizable portrait had they paused for a moment to try to reconcile their image with the obvious fact that many of these "living dead" manage to steal or otherwise raise $100 per day for sizable periods.

Nonetheless, a Supreme Court decision is the law. As the late Justice Robert Jackson once wrote of himself and his brethren, "We are not final

2. Lindesmith, *The Addict and the Law*, pp. 5–12. Platt and Labate, *Heroin Addiction*, p. 39.

because we are infallible, but we are infallible because we are final."[3] As a result, if we are to make someone a criminal because of his heroin use, we must do so without treating addiction itself as a crime.

In some ways, this is for the best. Even if it were constitutional, a law criminalizing heroin addiction would raise serious problems. Not only is addiction often a matter of degree rather than an all-or-nothing condition, but the determination of whether someone is addicted generally involves extremely intrusive techniques of enforcement. To enforce such a law, police either would have to hold and take bodily measurements of all but the few suspects who showed gross withdrawal symptoms, or, alternatively, would have to have medical personnel inject suspects with opiate antagonists and determine whether this precipitated the symptoms of withdrawal.

## THE CRIME OF HEROIN USE

A law which merely forbids heroin use avoids some of the problems inherent in antiaddiction laws. The Supreme Court has made it clear that, as a constitutional matter, the legislature may forbid the use of heroin—even by an addict—even though it cannot punish the "sickness" of addiction.[4]

We need not go into detail here to explain what appears to be a pettifogging distinction. It is true that punishing a person for a symptom of his disease makes no more sense than punishing him for suffering from the disease. The justices' unwillingness to follow their view of heroin addiction to its logical conclusion is perhaps attributable to their own quite reasonable lack of confidence in the picture of addiction they had adopted.

Moreover, the use of heroin is an act, while addiction is a kind of status, and our criminal law prefers to punish someone for what he has done rather than for what he is. One reason for this is that we regard a person as having more control over his actions than over his condition.[5] For instance, a heroin addict must of course be an addict, but on any given occasion he does not have to use heroin. Though most do, some do not, paying the price either by suffering withdrawal symptoms or else by accepting medical help in slowly detoxifying.

In addition, defining the crime is usually easier where the crime consists of an act rather than a status. As we have seen, addiction is often

---

3. *Brown v. Allen*, 344 U.S. 443, 540 (1953).

4. *Robinson v. California*, 370 U.S. 660, 667 (1962).

5. See, generally, Herbert Packer, *The Limits of the Criminal Sanction* (Stanford, Cal.: Stanford University Press, (1968), pp. 332–64.

quite difficult to define, while use of a drug simply means taking some of it into the body.

The major problem with making criminal the act of using heroin is that such a law is extremely difficult to enforce. It is unlikely that the police would actually observe anyone in the act of shooting up and, though a urine test for the metabolites of heroin can easily reveal whether someone has used the drug within the past seventy-two hours, urine testing is not a very good enforcement device. Such tests are extremely difficult and unaesthetic to compel. Though blood testing can serve the same purpose, compelling a suspect to produce body fluids is a search which seems close to the limits of permissible government intrusion.[6]

It is true that police are authorized to administer such tests to suspected drunken drivers, but we generally regard that intrusion as a special case. The drunken driver represents an imminent danger to the lives of others, quite unlike the danger we apprehend from the heroin user. Moreover, the theory that driving an automobile on the public highways is a privilege, not a right, helps justify our forcing drivers to submit to sobriety tests. We require that drivers take such tests under certain circumstances in return for the state's granting them the privilege of driving on the public roads. Obviously, no such reasoning permits us to seize the heroin addict in his home or on the street and subject him to tests.

Finally, any test for heroin use which shows only that the subject has used the drug sometime within the past three days will raise a host of legal problems. For instance, such a test will not necessarily determine whether the use has occurred in the municipality, county, or state where the arrest has taken place—a matter which may be of considerable legal significance.

For these reasons, in some states a related law against "being under the influence" of heroin has been utilized as a major weapon against heroin users. Litigating this issue is generally easier than proving that illegal use had taken place within the jurisdiction and avoids the conceptual difficulty of basing a charge on "internal possession" under a law against posession of heroin. Thus the police can make their case by showing that the suspect had recently used heroin and was arrested while nodding.

Cases of "under the influence" generally lack any direct chemical evidence of use. Rather, the arresting officer testifies that the defendant was seen sleeping or nodding, that his movements were sluggish, that his pupils were large and did not react well to light, that he bore on his body a fresh puncture mark, that he refused a urine test when it was offered, and, perhaps most crucial to the prosecution, that he did not smell of alcohol.

The uncertainty of guilt in those cases without urine or blood tests shows that the problem of proof is not completely solved by criminalizing

6. See *Schmerber v. California*, 384 U.S. 757, 760–5 (1966).

use rather than addiction. Nonetheless, in some areas, prosecutions for being under the influence of heroin are extremely common. In Los Angeles, it is by far the most common heroin offense prosecuted. Part of the reason seems to be a local tradition—since other areas of California prosecute other use offenses far more often. In addition, there are two major legal advantages to bringing this charge. Under California law, being under the influence is the only common heroin offense that is a misdemeanor, so that processing costs are held to a minimum. Moreover, the punishment for this crime is a minimum sentence of ninety days imprisonment, so that the sentencing judge has no discretion to be more lenient.

## Possession as a Criminal Offense

Because of the difficulties in enforcing laws against using or being under the influence of heroin, we most commonly criminalize the heroin user through prohibiting the possession of any usable quantity of heroin. Here the problems of definition are minimal, and the searches necessary to prove guilt are much less intrusive than the examination of body fluids which is often necessary to prove heroin use.

Of course, punishment for possession of a drug is an imprecise method of getting at the user. As applied to the possession of large amounts, such laws are not aimed at the user at all but at the trafficker. And, since one can possess a drug without using it, the application of the law to the possessor of small amounts may criminalize some who do not use heroin.

On the other hand, in those cases where a nonuser is in possession of a drug, we may regard his conduct as at least the equivalent of use. Either he is involved in the supply of the drug or else he is holding it for a user, thus aiding and abetting him.

## Ancillary Offenses

The final means of criminalizing the heroin user occurs through what are called ancillary offenses. Typically these offenses, such as loitering for the purpose of narcotics use, "narcotics vagrancy" (which involves "being present without lawful business at places narcotics are used or sold"), and possession of a hypodermic syringe or other "drug paraphernalia," are offenses which not only are akin to the use offenses but often involve some element of public decency and aesthetics. Enforcement of these laws often has two major functions. It clears the streets of those whom the police (and usually the neighbors) regard as unsightly, and is a means of harassing heroin users so that perhaps they will move elsewhere. Such offenses are seldom mentioned in discussions of those criminal laws which bear upon the heroin user because they are usually minor crimes akin to public drunkenness. Nonetheless, they account for a great number of arrests and constitute a significant fraction of the total impact the heroin user fears from the criminal law.[7]

## The Extent of Use Offenses

Considering the importance of use offenses, it is amazing how little we know about their actual enforcement. The matter is extremely difficult to study for several reasons. There are virtually no national statistics, since the FBI collects and publishes comprehensive data only on "Index offenses" such as homicide, robbery, rape, and burglary. Most police records are not available for inspection, and even where they are, the task of collating them is time-consuming and expensive. Finally, summaries of police activities generally do not even break down drug arrests into those involving marijuana (the largest category) and those concerned with other drugs, let alone among the other drugs. Nor do they typically distinguish between trafficking and use offenses.

Nonetheless, the National Commission on Marijuana and Drug Abuse did collect some useful information, which, although ten years old, is still probably the most reliable we have. The commission's study of a random sample of drug arrests in six American cities admittedly leaves many questions unanswered and is delusively precise in its results. Nonetheless it gives the reader some feeling as to the place of heroin use offenses in our criminal justice system.[8]

First of all, arrests for use offenses are extremely common. Of the 500,000 drug arrests in 1971, slightly more than half involved drugs other than marijuana, and of this half, again slightly more than half the arrests involved opiates—presumably mostly heroin. So far as we can tell, about 50 percent of the opiate arrests involved seizure of a small amount of the drug and were most likely arrests for possession. In all, arrests for opiate use offenses outnumbered those for trafficking by about 11–1.

Of those arrested for opiate offenses, 26 percent were employed full-time, while another 5 percent or so were students. Twenty-two percent had had no previous contact with the police while another 23 percent more had had only minimal contact. About 40 percent of the use offense arrests were dismissed. Of those convicted, 90 percent pleaded guilty (presumably for some consideration); and of those convicted 48 percent were sentenced to some incarceration, though we do not know the length of their terms.

Even this brief summary indicates that a sizable amount of energy is expended on the attempted enforcement of heroin use offenses. It is

7. Johnson and Bogomolny, "Selective Justice," p. 505.
8. Ibid., pp. 502, 528, 509, 516, 549, 564, 574.

possible, a priori, that this effort is well spent—and indeed that we should make even greater efforts to enforce use offense laws. To decide this question, however, we must ask in somewhat more detail just what we expect to accomplish through such a policy.

## USE OFFENSES AS RESTRICTIONS ON SUPPLY

To some extent, of course, punishment of the heroin user can be supported as an aid to our prohibition of supply. Where a seller who also is a heroin user is imprisoned for his use, he is put out of action, just as if he had been caught selling.

Sometimes this happens accidently, without police knowledge, merely because a goodly percentage of heroin users, and perhaps especially of those users who come to police attention, also sell the drug. On other occasions, where the police are unable to apprehend a seller for his sales, they may deliberately build their case against him, based on his violation of a use offense law.[9]

Those laws which attempt to criminalize the heroin user by forbidding possession of the drug may also be used to punish the small-time seller. If such a dealer is cautious enough to avoid selling to a police agent or informant and can conceal the location of his stash, he may be extremely difficult to apprehend for trafficking. When such a seller makes deliveries, he will attempt to possess only a small amount of heroin at any one time— below whatever amount is necessary to raise an inference of sale. As a result, if the police are to catch him, they will have to do either a good deal of undercover work to make their case of sale, or else simply apprehend him with a small amount of the drug and secure his punishment for the user-offense of possession.

The laws criminalizing heroin use may help restrict the supply of the drug in other ways, as well. A user caught and threatened with punishment for his possession of heroin may be more likely to cooperate with the police, name his source, and perhaps even work actively to make an "informer-buy," monitored by narcotics agents and complete with marked money and recording devices. Indeed, police often defend laws against heroin use primarily as devices whereby they may "squeeze" information and cooperation out of users to aid the fight against trafficking.

Laws against possession of heroin may also be helpful in allowing the police greater leeway to search and discover physical evidence of trafficking offenses. Our search and seizure laws require that before the police may invade the privacy of a suspect, they must have probable cause to believe that he is violating the law. It often happens that despite

9. Moore, *Buy and Bust*, pp. 138–40.

their suspicion of trafficking, the best police can do is to obtain probable cause to believe that their suspect has committed a use crime. In such a case, then, the use offense will legitimate a search which thereafter may turn up admissible evidence of sale.

If our only concern were to reduce access to heroin, it would make sense to include among our many enforcement strategies the attempt to apprehend, prosecute, and punish as many users as we could. The more we conceive of heroin as the cause of massive amounts of urban crime and other social ills, the more important it will be to utilize all means, even relatively inefficient ones, to reduce the supply of the drug.

The argument for such a course is that each contribution to the suppression of trafficking would do some good, and that, like chicken soup as a cure-all, "it couldn't hurt." The problem is that unless one believes that man was put on this earth solely to suppress heroin, one must recognize that investing considerable amounts of scarce law enforcement resources to make marginal reductions in the availability of the drug can, and does, hurt. The question then becomes whether the restriction of heroin supply brought about by any particular means—here by prosecution of use offenses—is worth what it costs.

Actually, of course, the question is more complex than this. The question really is whether the restriction of the supply of heroin—plus whatever other benefits are produced by the criminalization of the heroin user—outweigh the disadvantages of this policy.

Indeed, the reasons given for criminalizing heroin use do not generally include the effect of this policy upon the availability of the drug at all. Rather, the criminalization of the heroin user is most often seen as a method either of deterring use or of incapacitating criminals.

## USE OFFENSES AS DETERRING HEROIN USE

In all probability, few people would justify prosecution of heroin users on the most simple view of general deterrence—that we should punish those we catch so that others will fear the arrest, prosecution, and punishment we impose upon heroin users and, hence, avoid using the drug themselves. It is hard to deter the use by addicts, whose immediate desire for heroin presumably outweighs the contingent and fairly remote threat of punishment should they be caught. And those nonaddicted users able to gain access to the drug generally can arrange to possess and use the drug privately, with such a low risk of police detection that our threat to punish them is not sufficiently credible.[10]

10. The group of controlled users studied by Bertram S. Sackman maintained their supply of illicit drugs without police interruption. Sackman, "Angela's Band: An Ethnography of Disciplined Heroin Users," November 1976, draft, mimeographed.

This is not to say that the laws against heroin use have no coercive effect. We as yet know very little about the operation of deterrence and the variables which affect its strength in particular cases or upon different subgroups in the population. It might well turn out that laws against heroin use do have some effect on the beginning user. Especially in those areas where heroin use is not endemic the threat of police investigation, publicity and appearance before the juvenile court may be a makeweight to help a young person refuse an otherwise tempting offer of a chance to experiment with the drug.

More likely, however, whatever deterrent effect results from prosecuting heroin users is expected to be less direct. Such punishment raises the level of harrassment that users receive from law enforcement and the surrounding society. It interrupts whatever employment or personal stability they have managed to achieve and tends to make their lives, health, and welfare that much worse.

This effect is most noticeable with respect to addicts. The sorry state to which we reduce them serves several major purposes. For the nonuser, it helps to reinforce the societal image as to the consequence of heroin use or, more precisely, to maintain the cultural controls against such behavior. In addition, it exerts a pressure upon the nonaddicted heroin user to make him be more careful to avoid addiction. Finally, an unknown number of addicts may regard the threat of arrest and prosecution during periodic "drug sweeps" as the last straw, in addition to all the other problems their addiction causes them, and this may then spur their efforts to give up the drug.

The arrest and prosecution of the heroin users may do more than make an example of them for the general deterrent purpose of dissuading others from heroin use; it may also exercise a special deterrent effect upon the future behavior of those we apprehend.

Once we recognize that the once-an-addict-always-an-addict myth is just that, it becomes clear that both the nonaddicted user and the addict have some control over their conditions. A user of either type may stop using heroin once he has been apprehended because he may realize that, now that he has been identified, he will be more closely watched in the future. He may appreciate, as he had not before, just how painful and unpleasant are prosecution and conviction on heroin charges and he may conclude that the punishment for a subsequent offense will be even more disagreeable. Finally, the intervention of the criminal law will add one more painful and unpleasant element to the addict's life, which, added to all the other "hassles" he endures, might be enough to tip the balance and drive him into giving up heroin use—either with or without formal drug treatment.

There are two major difficulties with supporting the criminalization of the heroin user as a means of deterring heroin use. Since the use crimes generally involve some kind of private activity, the great majority of both addicted and nonaddicted users can escape detection. As in all consensual, or nonvictim, crimes, the police are handicapped by the lack of a complainant, by a shortage of resources, and by the constitutional restrictions upon their power to search and arrest. More important, however, is the fact that restrictions on supply are more cost-effective in lowering use than are restrictions on use itself. For instance, the impoverishment and general debilitation of many addicts, which we hope will deter both heroin use and addiction, is more closely related to the high price the compulsive user must pay for the drug than to the criminalization of use itself.

The marijuana laws provide a dramatic example of the relative effect of laws against supply as compared to those against use. While all fifty states have laws against the supply of that drug, in recent years eleven have removed their criminalization of small-scale possession and use. Several studies have been made of the effect of repealing the criminal penalties for use, and each has concluded that repeal had no discernible effect on the number of users or on their frequency of use. In those states which repealed their laws creating use crimes, marijuana use increased no more than it did in comparable states which continued to apprehend and prosecute users.[11]

Similarly, the major way our heroin laws lower heroin use is by restricting the supply of the drug. Law enforcement makes it expensive for anyone to use heroin and, particularly for the nonaddict, makes the drug difficult and dangerous to obtain. Compared to this effect, the prohibitions on use, though expensive to implement, are of relatively minor importance.

## INCAPACITATING THE HEROIN USER

In all probability, today, the primary justification for criminalizing the heroin user is neither the marginal effect of this policy upon the supply of the drug nor any general or special deterrence of heroin use. Rather, the primary purpose of such laws is usually thought to be incapacitation, the isolation of the user through imprisonment. The argument here is not that the incarceration of the user will prevent his repeating the crime of heroin use. As studies of drug use in our jails and prisons reveal, imprisonment does not do this very well at all.[12]

The most common argument for imprisoning heroin users is that this is the best way to lessen the injury they do to society. For this purpose, it is

11. Robert R. Carr and Erik J. Meyers, "Marijuana and Cocaine: The Process of Change in Drug Policy," in *The Facts about "Drug Abuse,"* pp. 176–8.
12. Nicholas Munson et al., "Prisons," in *Drug Dealers—Taking Action*, by Richard Blum and Associates (San Francisco: Jossey and Bass, 1973), pp. 171–200.

not important whether their heroin use in fact causes them to wreak their damage. Even if one decided that involvement in criminality produced heroin use rather than vice versa, that would make no difference. To the extent that some people do a considerable amount of social harm, locking them up for any reason will prevent their victimizing others—or at least others outside prison.

When we thought that all users were addicts and that all addicts were thieves, we could regard it as not very important whether we imprisoned them for their heroin use or for their thefts. We could believe that this relatively small group of individuals would be up to all sorts of mischief anyway and, hence, that their incarceration, whatever the reason, was worthwhile.

This is not quite so shocking as it might sound, so long as those imprisoned had, in fact, committed the heroin use crime for which they were convicted. Very different considerations apply in determining whether to enact a law forbidding an act than in judging whether to convict a person of committing that act. A much rougher judgment is permissible in the former case.

After all, we may recognize that not every possessor of a sawed-off shotgun is going to use it for a criminal purpose—but still forbid such possession because of a rough judgment that, considering the lethal nature and easy concealability of the weapon, a sufficient percentage of its possessors would be criminally inclined. If, after the law has served fair notice of the legislative decision, someone is nonetheless found beyond a reasonable doubt to have been in illegal possession of a sawed-off shotgun, he may properly be punished. This is very different from convicting him because he is criminally inclined, or because he is only moderately likely to have possessed a sawed-off shotgun.

In the case of heroin users, the judgment as to their criminality is not always such a rough one. Probably the most dramatic demonstration of the reduction in crime that may be obtained by their imprisonment took place in 1971 in Santa Barbara, California. There, the police mounted a campaign to make arrests on use offense charges, and, in two months, fifty-four addicts were imprisoned. Immediately, the number of both burglary and bad check offenses reported to the police declined about 50 percent.[13]

Although in the next year a similar effort was also followed by a large drop in the property crime rate, the Santa Barbara experience seems to be atypical. Similar programs instituted in other California cities have met with considerably less success. Sacramento police, in 1976, set up a special task force which made some 930 arrests on use offenses. Although the conviction rate on these was around 90 percent, property crime did not appear to decline at all. Los Angeles had a similar experience, and

13. Bjorklund, *Alternative Heroin Control Policies* vol. 1, pp. 129–30.

even when Santa Barbara attempted to repeat its drive against users in later years, the effort was not notably successful.

One may speculate as to why the Santa Barbara authorities had been able initially to achieve successes so much greater than those of other cities. Part of the reason, perhaps, is that in Santa Barbara law enforcement agents came across a particularly criminalistic—and quite active—subculture of heroin addicts. It is also possible that for some reason the police in Santa Barbara had been less able than those elsewhere to arrest heroin addicts for the property crimes they had been committing. This would explain why in other cities such programs aimed at heroin addicts were much less successful. In those cities, more of the most criminalistic heroin addicts were already in jail for their nondrug offenses.

There may be one other reason why we cannot expect many repetitions of the success of the initial Santa Barbara experiment. There is some evidence that it was produced by wholesale violations of suspect's constitutional rights. At least that is the conclusion one would draw from a discussion of the subsequent Santa Barbara efforts which reported that, in 1976, judicial insistence on protection of heroin users' constitutional rights lowered the conviction rate so greatly that the impact of the program on crime was barely noticeable.

Despite this, it is likely that the involvement of heroin users in property crime is still the strongest reason for the enactment of use offenses. One calculation indicated that, over a seven-year period in Santa Barbara, each conviction of an addict prevented twelve larcenies and four burglaries.[14] Even though Santa Barbara may be atypical, we do know that a relatively small number of heroin addicts commit a very substantial amount of property crime. Though we still do not know what percentage of addicts fall into this category—and the percentage may not be nearly as large as many believe—it does appear that criminalistic addicts constitute a significant percentage of the total addict population. As a result, it is likely that the removal from circulation of any sizable number of addicts will result in some lowering of the crime rate—at least so long as the means of selecting the addicts for removal are not biased in favor of removing those who commit the fewest crimes.

On the other hand, where the law prohibits use rather than addiction, the problem becomes more difficult. An increasing percentage of heroin users today are moderate, controlled users, most of whom—along with some addicts—do not pose any special risk of property crime. We would have to know more about the means of selecting users for arrest and prosecution before we could determine the effect on property crime of enforcing heroin use offenses against users in general.

---

14. Votey, "Detention of Heroin Addicts, Job Opportunities, and Deterrence," *Journal of Legal Studies* 8 (1969): 585.

## THE QUARANTINE ANALOGY

Arguments for isolation of heroin users do not rest entirely on the property crimes they commit. Another quite different theory uses the public health analogy and advocates isolation of heroin users because they are the "carriers" of addiction to future generations.

This approach is often premised on the view that, since heroin addiction is a disease, and since the use of the drug is propagated from one person to another like an epidemic, we may use the most coercive method of public health—the quarantine—against its spread. In theory, this quarantine would prevent the communication of the disease so that, after some peroid of isolating the carriers, heroin use would disappear just as smallpox has.

Unfortunately, the differences between heroin addiction and smallpox doom this analogy. While the public authorities can immunize whole populations against smallpox when they fear an outbreak of that disease, we have no practical way of immunizing anyone against a willingness to use heroin.

Moreover, since the smallpox virus has no hosts other than man, we could wipe it out permanently, once we were able for a short period to make sure that no one had the disease. Even if we were able to eliminate heroin use in our whole population, use of the drug could spring up again whenever it became available, people knew how it could be used, and prospective users thought they might benefit from using it.

Though most beginning heroin use today is characterized by spread from one person to another within a peer group, the arrival of a new resident with access to and knowledge of the drug can initiate a whole neighborhood. And, as the British discovered, heroin use can spring up quickly from a very small base.[15]

A little thought, moreover, reveals just how impractical would be the implementation of the quarantine approach. Addicts generally continue to use heroin off and on over a substantial period and, unlike the sufferers from most communicable diseases, neither die nor are cured relatively quickly. As a result, if we wish to isolate heroin addicts, we will have to imprison them for approximately twenty years—from about age eighteen to the "burnout" age of between thirty-five and forty.

To appreciate the strain this would place on our present prison system, we should note that our prisons presently hold about 380,000 convicts serving a median time of less than four years.[16] If we had to imprison, say,

15. R. de Alarcon, "The Spread of Heroin Abuse in a Community," United Nations *Bulletin on Narcotics* 21, no. 2 (July-September 1969): 17–22.

16. U.S., Department of Justice, Bureau of Justice Statistics, *Prisoners in State and Federal Institutions on December 31, 1979*, National Prison Statistics Bulletin, February 1981.

380,000 more addicts for twenty years each, it would necessitate about a fivefold increase in our prison capacity. If we included users as well as addicts in our quarantine, we would further double the number of those we isolated from the public.

Finally, even if we were willing to pay the cost of imprisoning the "carriers" and spreaders of opiate addiction, we must remember that typically they are beginning users themselves. There is no hope that enforcement authorities can find out who they are in time to quarantine them effectively.

## THE HOSPITAL ANALOGY

The disease analogy provides another justification for isolating heroin users. Here, however, it does not matter what benefit we apprehend in their isolation. Although the incarceration of heroin addicts may indeed prevent their committing property crimes, spreading addiction, or imposing any other costs upon society, this need not be our purpose. Rather, we may be moved by the fact that certain heroin users—addicts and those "in imminent danger" of becoming addicted—are sick people who, due to the nature of their illness, will not accept treatment voluntarily.

For this reason, another institution of the healing professions becomes appropriate—involuntary commitment to a hospital. Moreover, since the analogous treatment of the mentally ill is not regarded as criminal in nature, the addict may be committed against his will through the use of civil process, without requiring the state to meet the more rigid requirements imposed in criminal prosecutions.[17]

Interestingly, though the Supreme Court has held that the constitution prevents criminally punishing the sickness of addiction, it has taken a different view where the state's aim is civil commitment. The addict may constitutionally be hospitalized in a prisonlike structure, provided that the aim of the government is therapeutic rather than punitive.[18]

In theory, such incarceration is not so serious a deprivation for the addict as would be imprisonment after a criminal conviction. He is spared the stigma of a criminal record; is confined in a hospital rather than a prison; and must be released as soon as cured.

This reasoning neglects several facts, however. The stigma of treatment as a heroin addict seems at least as great as that of a criminal conviction. The hospitals to which we commit heroin addicts look very much like prisons, complete with guard towers. In fact, they are often "converted"

17. William H. McGlothlin, M. Douglas Anglin, and Bruce D. Wilson, *An Evaluation of the California Civil Addict Program*, National Institute on Drug Abuse, Services Research Monograph Series (Washington, D.C.: Government Printing Office, 1977), pp. 4–6. *In re De La O*, 59 C. 2d 128, 28 Cal. Rptr. 489 (1963).

18. *Robinson v. California*, 370 U.S. 660, 666 (1962).

from prisons for this purpose. And, since we cannot guarantee a cure for heroin addiction, the addict may, as a practical matter, be confined as long as his treaters wish.[19]

Probably the most serious drawback to our civil commitment laws is their withdrawal of procedural protections from the accused heroin addict. Since the commitment of addicts for treatment is regarded as civil rather than criminal in nature, the person charged enjoys no constitutional right to trial by jury, or to the privilege against self-incrimination. He may be "convicted" without the prosecution's shouldering the burden of proof beyond a reasonable doubt. Rather than enjoying the rights of a criminal defendant, the accused heroin addict may be imprisoned after proceedings which extend to him the far lower procedural guarantees given the defendant in an automobile accident suit.

Moreover, the heroin addict subjected to civil commitment is denied the constitutional protection from statutory vagueness which demands a relatively precise definition of his offense, or—more accurately—his disease. Involuntary treatment is not confined to heroin addicts—a term which is somewhat indefinite itself—but also typically embraces those "in imminent danger of becoming addicted."

Although the lessened procedural protections allow cheaper and more expeditious processing of addicts in the courts, civil commitment is not often used. Some twenty-seven states have laws which provide for this disposition; yet only two, New York and California, use it for any significant number of addicts, and even these use it for only a small minority of their addict population.[20]

There are several reasons for failure to utilize what appears to be a very convenient scheme. Many people who could not be classed as civil libertarians have supported the view that even addicts are entitled to procedural protections before being imprisoned—at least so long as the facilities in which they are held look more like prisons than hospitals.

Financial as well as moral reasons restrict the use of civil commitment. Although we do not know how to cure addicts in our narcotics hospitals, the treatment efforts which the authorities are obliged to make there cause these facilities to be even more expensive than prisons.

## THE COSTS OF ENACTING USER OFFENSES

Regardless of whether one's justification for bringing the law to bear upon the heroin user is the effect of this policy in restricting the supply of the drug, deterrence, or isolation, there are serious costs to the effort. First of

---

19. David B. Wexler, "Therapeutic Justice," in *Drug Use in America*, app., vol. 4, pp. 453, 459.

20. McGlothlin, Anglin, and Wilson, *An Evaluation of the California Civil Addict Program*, pp. 10–13.

all, we should at least consider the pain we inflict on the user himself as one of the costs of such a policy. Ignoring this, in the words of Franklin Zimring, puts us in the situation reminiscent "of the man who was advised that the best method of increasing his horse's efficiency was violently to castrate the animal with two bricks. When he asked, 'Doesn't that hurt?' his mentor responded, 'Not if you don't get your thumbs in the way.' "[21]

It is true that the restrictions on supply which make heroin expensive and difficult to obtain do make life more painful for the addict; in fact, they probably cause the addict far more misery than does enforcement of use crimes. But, although they lower the quality of the addict's life, restrictions on his supply are a given in the system, unless we adopt either free availability or heroin maintenance. It is quite another thing to work deliberately to increase the unpleasantness of the addict's life; and if we do this, we should consider whether it sufficiently serves our purposes.

Disrupting the User's Adjustment

Enforcement of use offense laws may be costly to us as well as to the heroin user. To the extent that the user is not addicted or, if addicted, is living an otherwise law-abiding life, any use of the criminal law against him is likely to do both him and society more harm than good.

The arrest of the noncriminal user or addict may damage his social relations and cost him his job. By exposing his use, it may label him a dope fiend and make it difficult for him to find future employment. An arrest may disturb the adjustment which had provided the user with an alternative to criminality, decrease his stability, and increase the likelihood of his committing other crimes. Finally, a term of imprisonment will introduce him to other heroin users, including the most criminalistic. If he is not already a member of the junkie subculture, the experience, as well as his new friends, may make his entry easier.

It may even be that the constant threat and occasional actuality of arrest increases the criminality of some junkie addicts as well. We know that many addicts, including some in the junkie subculture, do give up heroin without direct coercion, but we sometimes forget that ceasing heroin use may require as much effort as continuing. An arrest, prosecution, or incarceration may actually disrupt this process and put off further the time when the addict finally gives up his drug.[22]

Of course, the case for imprisoning heroin users is strongest with respect to most criminalistic addicts. They are the ones we most want to

---

21. Franklin E. Zimring and Gordon J. Hawkins, *Deterrence: The Legal Threat in Crime Control* (Chicago: University of Chicago Press, 1973), p. 43.

22. Lindesmith, *The Addict and the Law*, p. 38.

cease heroin use. Although making their lives more unpleasant may prevent some from giving up heroin, it will probably help drive others into abstinence—with or without the help of treatment. And, even if we do not succeed in driving them into giving up heroin, we benefit from their temporary isolation in prisons to the extent that they would otherwise be at large committing property crimes.


## Selective Enforcement

There are problems, however, with justifying laws against heroin use by their application to criminalistic addicts. Even if lifestyles of such addicts make them the heroin users most likely to attract police attention, they are considerably outnumbered by other heroin users. As a result, any law establishing a use crime will inevitably force the criminal system to deal with substantial numbers of occasional users and noncriminalistic addicts.

To avoid this, we must rely upon the police to enforce selectively the laws prohibiting use, to concentrate upon the criminalistic heroin offenders, and to ignore socially adjusted or occasional offenders. The problem is that the police decision process is not completely accurate and cannot be made much better without introducing into it a good many of the procedural protections which we provide in our trial system. As a result, the police enforcing any kind of a use prohibition inevitably will sweep into their net many otherwise noncriminal users or addicts.

The meager evidence we have on this issue makes it likely that the police decision process is less accurate than one might assume. A study of the enforcement of the "under the influence" law in Los Angeles has indicated that about 20% of those against whom such charges are filed, and of course, a larger percentage of those arrested for that crime, were not in fact under the influence of heroin at the time of their arrests.[23] Moreover, of those who were under the influence of heroin, according to the same study, the great majority, perhaps over 90%, were not addicts in that they did not show even relatively subtle signs of withdrawal.

Part of the reason for such poor selectivity by the police was their inadequate training. Often in arrest reports they cited, as supporting evidence of the under-the-influence crime, the fact that the subject had a "staggering walk," used "thick or slurred speech," or was "aggressive" or "incoherent," none of which are signs of heroin intoxication.[24] Moreover, occasional users are more likely to come to police attention

---

23. Ed Weiss, "'Under the Influence of Heroin': Enforcement of Section 11550 of the California Health and Safety Code in Los Angeles" (manuscript on file, Stanford Law School, 1982).

24. Ed Weiss, "Under the Influence of Heroin," p. 8.

than addicts because their tolerance is lower and they therefore react more noticeably to a given dosage of heroin and because they have not developed the "street smarts" of addicts in avoiding detection.

In addition, selective enforcement itself should also be seen as a major cost of criminalizing the heroin user.[25] It is undesirable to allow the police to pick and choose among a sizable group of people and to decide whom they will and whom they will not arrest for a serious crime. Such an arrangement—which is all too common in American law—leads to a feeling of unfairness among those selected for prosecution; to bribery and corruption of the police; and to the covert use of all kinds of discriminations—including race, class, and "appropriate" attitude toward the arresting officer—which we would not condone if they were overt. Further, this practice leads to the development of a semipermanent underclass of offenders who subsist at police sufferance. They cannot complain of police mistreatment, and this, in turn, encourages the police to use against them a whole series of abusive tactics. Not only are these tactics in themselves a threat to our values, but they also accustom the police to engage in improper activities that, on later occasions, may be applied to the rest of us.

## Criminal Justice Resources

Perhaps the most important cost of attempting to enforce the laws against heroin use crimes is the resources this effort requires. To the extent that these resources are devoted to serious criminals who would eventually consume the same trial and correctional space when apprehended for their "addict crimes," this puts no additional strain on our criminal justice system. However, the law enforcement resources going into the prosecution of heroin users who are not otherwise criminal—and even perhaps those applied to the many heroin users who are only petty offenders—are made unavailable for use against more serious criminals, including heroin traffickers.

We have already seen that our very limited criminal enforcement resources will never be sufficient to cut off completely the supply of heroin. If the criminal resources devoted to the heroin problem are relatively fixed, they should be spent where they are most cost-effective—and resources devoted to inhibiting the supply of the drug are likely to be more cost-effective than drug enforcement aimed at the user.

This matter is particularly urgent where the resources devoted to suppressing drug trafficking are decreasing, as seems to be the case in most of the United States. A recent General Accounting Office study of heroin enforcement reported:

25. Packer, *Limits of the Criminal Sanction*, pp. 290–92.

The Chief Assistant State Attorney for Dade County (Miami) believes law enforcement is both "outmanned and outgunned" to deal with the drug problem. He cited a recent case involving a wiretap that could have resulted in apprehension of many more high-level violators. It was curtailed because the police ran out of money.

In New York City, the recent financial crisis resulted in the layoff of 5,000 police officers. According to the chief of NYPD's narcotics division, the cutbacks affected drug enforcement just as they affected other types of police work.

There have been recent cuts in drug enforcement activity in San Francisco, and, according to the head of the police department's narcotics unit, only 20 officers are working narcotics presently, down from 60 officers at one time. This is despite the fact that drug activity does not appear to have decreased in the city.

The narcotics division of the Phoenix Police Department has refused to join a multiagency task force in the city. The head of the unit stated he cannot give up one or more officers to the task force when he is struggling to get more resources to satisfy the division's own responsibilities.

A 1977 survey by the California Department of Justice showed that 77 percent of local police agencies in the State indicated they do not have adequate equipment for drug enforcement. An assessment by the same department in 1976 concluded that "local agency commitments to drug enforcement have declined while drug abuse is increasing."[26]

In addition, the federal aid for local drug enforcement has also decreased under the pressure of budgetary constraints. Grants for drug law enforcement from the Law Enforcement Assistance Administration, the primary source of federal enforcement aid, dropped 79 percent, from $23.5 million to $5 million, between 1972 and 1977.

The police are not the only part of the criminal justice system suffering from a shortage of the resources necessary to perform their appointed tasks. Few people who are not directly involved in the trial of criminal cases can appreciate the degree to which our court system is already overcrowded. A recent editorial in a local newspaper gives details on a typical situation—in this case in one of California's most affluent counties:

One day recently, Judge Stone's calendar listed a record 269 cases. A courthouse holding cell designed to accommodate 20 defendants was jammed with 100. The judge says they were unguarded because the

26. Comptroller General of the United States, *Report to the Congress: Gains Made in Controlling Illegal Drugs, Yet the Drug Trade Flourishes*, General Accounting Office, 25 October 1979 (Washington, D.C. Government Printing Office, 1979), p. 129.

sheriff didn't have enough deputies to assign one to the holding
cell. . . .

Judge Stone estimates it could cost up to $1 million a year to
provide Santa Clara County with enough prosecutors, public defenders and adult probation officers to keep the courts operating efficiently, which is to say justly. He doesn't know where the money will
come from and, at this point, neither does the Board of Supervisors,
which is facing the prospect of a budget deficit. . . .

A million dollars isn't going to build a new jail, but $1 million would
go a long way toward clearing the Superior Court's criminal trial
calendar, thus reassuring the public that the criminal justice system
isn't about to collapse.[27]

This and worse is the case throughout the nation. The police are unable to
investigate all but the most serious crimes; the court-processing institutions, the prosecutors, the public defenders, and the judiciary are all so
burdened that between 85 and 90 percent of cases must be disposed of by
plea bargains, which leave neither side nor the public satisfied. Obviously, in this situation we should consider carefully the necessity of each
category of cases that adds to the strain upon our court system,
appreciating the fact that each addition is not only costly in itself but also
diminishes the attention we can pay to all the other crimes.

Finally, our jails and prisons are grossly overcrowded. Additional
prison capacity has been described as the single most urgent need of our
criminal justice system. The President's Commission on Violent Crime
recommended that $600 million be allocated for new prison construction,
but the funds have not been forthcoming. To the extent, then, that heroin
use offenders take up prison and jail space, they may prevent the
utilization of this scarce resource on many offenders whom we would
regard as better claimants for funds spent on incarceration.

## COERCION INTO TREATMENT

It is very likely that we could not justify our criminalization of the heroin
user if we had to rely solely on the usual purposes of the criminal law—
isolation of those who will commit property crimes, deterrence of use,
and the aid this policy provides to the restriction of supply. The heavy
costs in criminal justice resources, human suffering, and freedom entailed
in imprisoning heroin users may well outweigh the advantages of attempting to imprison them.

It is not necessary to decide the issue at this point, however. We are not
confronted here with the stark choice between ignoring and imprisoning
the heroin user, since it is likely that the balance of costs and benefits

27. "Overloaded Justice," *San Jose Mercury-News*, 20 January 1981, p. 6B.

stemming from imprisoning the heroin user can be improved by coercing him into treatment instead.

In a sense, coercion into treatment is a misnomer, since it implies a clear line between treatment and punishment. This, however, is not always the case. As we will see, treatment can have some of the qualities of a punishment; and punishment often has some aspects of treatment. Whenever it is directed toward preventing the offender from repeating his crime, punishment may be seen as a kind of treatment—at least to the extent that we feel continued criminality is not in the interest of the offender himself. Though rehabilitation is no longer regarded as a central purpose of criminal punishment, it nonetheless has a limited place in penology.[28] With respect to some crimes and in particular to some noninstitutional programs, it is both cost-effective and, compared to the alternatives, humane.

There are several reasons why the use of the criminal law to coerce the user into treatment is a much more cost-effective means of reducing both his heroin use and the crime produced by such use, than are the usual processes of the criminal law. Although, like general deterrence, coercion into treatment makes use of the threat of punishment, it does not seek to influence large numbers of unknown prospective users. Rather, like isolation, it acts directly upon those who have already been apprehended. Coercion into treatment has one major advantage over isolation, however; it does not attempt to restrain the offender physically from repeating his heroin use. Rather, it allows him physical freedom and attempts to control his behavior in other, more efficient, ways.

Two well-established parts of our correctional system—probation and parole—make use of similar principles. With respect to heroin treatment, however, there is a difference. Though we have no evidence that the usual methods of probation or parole—counseling and attempted surveillance— have much effect on subsequent criminality, we have good reason to believe that some kinds of heroin treatment can considerably reduce both heroin use and its associated crime, and that they can do this at much less expense than imprisonment.

This is not, however, to say that such a policy is better than ignoring completely the noncriminal user. We will return to that question later. At this point, we need only show that the policy of coercion into treatment works better than do the usual processes of the criminal law against the drug user; and considering the difficulties of using the criminal system in this area, this is not a very strong assertion. Before examining this issue, however, we must first take a brief look at just what we mean by treatment.

28. Francis A. Allen, *The Decline of The Rehabilitative Ideal: Penal Policy and Social Purpose*, (New Haven and London: Yale University Press, 1981), pp. 60 et seq.

## HEROIN TREATMENT

Although the ideal way to stop heroin use would be either to prevent all access to the drug or else to guarantee somehow that no one would want to use it, treatment has more modest goals. It seeks to make those who have been identified as having a "heroin problem" more willing and better able to resist the lure of the drug and, if possible, change them so that they have no desire to use it.

Our efforts at treatment fall into three major categories, each of which has its own advantages and costs. In general terms, they can be classified as outpatient treatment, residential treatment in a therapeutic community, and methadone maintenance.

Outpatient drug-free treatment is in one sense hardly a treatment at all.[29] Usually it involves detoxification if necessary, counseling, and a number of other means of helping and giving psychological support to the addict or user who desires not to return to heroin use. It has two great advantages. First is its cost; it is by far the least expensive of the methods of treatment, costing only some $900 per person per year. Second, even if it is enforced by court order, this kind of treatment exerts far less control over the user's life than do other treatments. Not only does it restrict less the freedom and autonomy of the user, but it lessens the likelihood that the user will be labeled a dope fiend and forced into associations deeper in the heroin culture than himself.

In many ways, coerced outpatient treatment looks very much like standard probation—with medical personnel and counselors replacing probation officers. Like probation in practice, it often exerts very little supervision, and, as a result, outpatient drug-free treatment may not be at all drug-free. On the other hand, our technology makes outpatient treatment different from other kinds of probationary or parole supervision. A probation officer or parole agent cannot generally tell whether his charge has violated the terms of release. Unless the probationer is apprehended by police, there is usually no way the case officer can know whether one of those he oversees has committed a crime. Often the best the officer can do is attempt to monitor the conditions of release, such as not driving a car, refraining from alcoholic beverages, not associating with known criminals, and maintaining steady employment—and he cannot even do these very well. In many cases he does not even try very hard, knowing that it is almost impossible for many probationers or parolees to lead normal lives and still obey the conditions imposed upon

29. Herbert D. Kleber and Frank Slobetz, "Outpatient Drug-Free Treatment," in *Handbook on Drug Abuse*, pp. 31–38. *Final Report, April 1979, Data from the National Drug and Alcoholism Treatment Utilization Survey (NDATUS)*, National Institute on Drug Abuse, Statistical Series F, No. 8 (Washington, D.C.: Government Printing Office, 1980), p. 9, 31–38.

them—conditions which, moreover, are only very indirectly related to the goal of keeping them free of crime.

In the area of heroin treatment, the monitoring is much simpler. The primary fact we are interested in is whether the user has continued to use heroin, and urinalysis can tell reliably whether someone has done this within the past seventy-two hours. As a practical matter, it may be better not to revoke an addict's release because of a few occasions of use, since slips occur even in the most successful cures—and, according to our present data, what we should be most worried about is the development of a compulsive run of heroin use. Nonetheless, the ability to check on whether someone is using heroin is extremely important—not only for behavior control but also because to the extent that the pressure to avoid heroin use succeeds, the values, associations, and other satisfactions which the user may develop can make his return to heroin use less likely and actually effect a "cure."

That is not to say that urinalysis makes easy the problem of coercing the heroin user into abstinence. Outsmarting resourceful addicts is still a difficult task. Note what occurred when one program attempted this:

In the early days . . . it was relatively easy to heat a bottle of clean, usually cold urine—obtained earlier from another person not on drugs—with hot water from the bathroom tap in order to fool the attendant who routinely checked to see if the urine was warm and thus fresh. Measures were taken to prevent this deception simply by turning off the hot water supply to the bathrooms. To counteract this move, patients heated the bottom of the bottle with matches, but the black smoke stains soon gave that away. Currently the patient is ahead in this contest by paying a fellow patient—clean at the time, as mentioned above—to precede him into the bathroom, hide one bottle of part of his fresh urine in a prearranged place and then return another bottle of his remaining urine to the attendant. Recently, however, some of the more strict and sophisticated programs insist on the return of a reasonably full bottle of urine from each patient. Thus the game continues, and a bookmaker will give you odds on the patient staying a step ahead.[30]

Even with urine testing, then, outpatient treatment is not very effective. Most important, it seems singularly unable to affect the behavior of the long-time addicts in whom the criminal justice system is most interested. Indeed, whatever success outpatient treatment does have most often pertains to younger and less established heroin users, who typically find it easier to give up the drug anyway.

30. Preble and Miller, "Methadone, Wine, and Welfare," p. 239.

## RESIDENTIAL TREATMENT

At the opposite extreme from outpatient drug-free treatment, in terms of expense and control over the user's life, is residential treatment. Usually this takes place in what is called a therapeutic community under the control of an organization such as Synanon, Daytop, Odyssey House, Phoenix House, or one of the numerous other such groups which have received a great deal of publicity in recent years.[31] Typically the organization regards addiction primarily as a symptom of a more basic underlying disorder involving personal inadequacy, dishonesty, and weak character. For this reason, the treatment can be applied to anyone with similar character—not only heroin addicts, but any kind of drug abuser and even those, such as occasional heroin users, who may abuse no drug at all.

The drug-free residential treatment program aims to make fundamental changes in the user's personality, values, and ways of coping with the world. It makes use of group processes and a highly structured environment, where the patient usually lives, works, and takes his recreation in the same "house." Often discipline is severe and the interactions are confrontations that are demeaning to the patient—the rationalization being that the program aims "to wipe you out completely, alter your self-image and self-esteem, so [you can] be rebuilt."[32] This rebuilding often continues after cure—indeed, in many cases, cure is promised only while the former patient remains in the therapeutic community—usually treating others.

Although residential treatment programs are, in general, quite resistant to outside evaluation, they do seem to suffer from several major problems. Only relatively few addicts will accept this kind of treatment, even considering the many disadvantages of the life of the heroin addict; the relapse rate after treatment seems to be considerable, except for those who stay on within the organization; and, finally, the treatment is extremely expensive. Residential treatment costs about four times as much as methadone maintenance—though probably still less than imprisonment.[33]

In addition, a number of drug-free programs raise serious moral issues. Often they are directed by a charismatic leader with extremely authoritarian values. Such leaders tend to demand absolute obedience, and harshly punish the slightest infractions. Some drug rehabilitation programs have

31. George DeLeon and Mitchell S. Rosenthal, "Therapeutic Communities," in *Handbook on Drug Abuse*, pp. 39–47.

32. Lucy Komisar, "The Mysterious Mistress of Odyssey House," *New York* 12, no. 45 (19 November 1979): 47. See also Imhof, "Is Odyssey House the Tiffany of TC's?," *Contemporary Drug Problems* 3 (1974): 443.

33. *Final Report (NDATUS)*, pp. 9, 12. DeLeon and Rosenthal, "Therapeutic Communities," pp. 43–44.

developed into cults, very much like those religious groups where members completely surrender their autonomy. More worrisome yet, the autonomy is not always yielded to those who use it benevolently.[34]

This is not to say that such treatment is useless. What data we have indicate that it is about as effective as methadone maintenance in securing a long-term lowering of heroin use. Its comparative popularity, despite its high cost and degree of regimentation, is probably due to the fact that such programs are usually run by community activists rather than by the physicians who run methadone programs. These activists are much more skilled than physicians in recruiting political support, garnering favorable publicity, and even reaching out for clients.

## METHADONE MAINTENANCE

The final major means of treating heroin addiction deserves separate and extended discussion because it is both the most common and the least understood method used today. In a sense, it is not really a cure at all, but can be best thought of simply as a maintenance scheme with methadone, a synthetic opiate, rather than heroin as its basis.

We have already seen that the idea of maintenance for heroin addicts is an attractive one, but that heroin itself is not well suited to this purpose, being too short-acting and too subject to diversion. If another drug could be found without these disadvantages, maintenance on it would be an excellent option. The maintenance drug could be dispensed and taken legally and hence, compared to illegal heroin (though not to the hypothetical legal heroin under free availability or heroin maintenance), extremely inexpensively. Maintenance, then, would allow the addict to escape demands of his habit upon his time, energy, money, and his law-abiding behavior.

Actually, it is somewhat of an oversimplification to refer to all the nonheroin opiate maintenance programs as methadone maintenance. Though methadone is the most common maintenance drug used for heroin addicts, it is not the only one. Under the same heading belong the few programs which have used propoxyphene, also a synthetic opiate, and some experimental programs using, apparently quite successfully, a yet longer-acting opiate called LAAM.[35]

Moreover, methadone maintenance may be more than mere mainte-

34. Robert Sam Anson, "The Synanon Horrors," *New Times* 2, no. 11 (27 November 1978): 28–50.
35. Walter Ling and Jack D. Blaine, "The Use of LAAM in Treatment," in *Handbook on Drug Abuse*, pp. 87–95. For information on the use of Darvon in treatment, see Institute for Social Concerns, "Another Methadone Thing?", *Connections* 2, nos. 4–6 (February-April 1974): 1–16.

nance. Not only may it replace most heroin use so long as the addict stays in this treatment, but it may also be a part of a longer and more difficult process whereby the addict eventually ceases all opiate use.

## Methadone

Methadone, a synthetic opiate developed in Germany during World War II, can, as a first approximation, be conceived of as similar to heroin except for several important differences which affect both the occupational and social stability of the addict in treatment and the ease of diversion of the drug to illegal use.

Methadone is much longer-acting than heroin; its effects last for a little over twenty-four hours—about four to six times as long as those of heroin. Moreover, methadone can be taken orally far more easily than can heroin—and, perhaps more important, can be prepared so that it cannot be injected.[36]

Based on these differences, one would expect several advantages of a maintenance system based on methadone over one using heroin. The longer-acting nature of methadone should produce two major differences. First, it should make an on-the-premises system practical, since the addict in treatment would have to appear for his supply only once a day. Second, it should make it easier to stabilize the addict's mood swings, thus leaving him freer to perform any socially useful activities which require a sustained level of effort. Rather than be subject to constant alteration between a slight heroin intoxication and an equal degree of heroin deprivation every four to six hours, the addict could be placed on the much more manageable twenty-four-hour cycle.

In addition, the requirement that methadone must be taken orally can free the addict from his dependence upon the needle by removing his temptation to take the drug by a more euphoric though less therapeutic route. This not only eliminates the health complications of intravenous injection, but it also contributes to the stabilization of the addict's behavior. Since a drug is absorbed considerably more slowly and gently when ingested than when injected intravenously, the means of administration reinforces the longer-acting nature of the drug in dampening the alterations in mood that are characteristic of heroin use.

## Methadone Diversion

Our ability to prepare methadone so that it can only be taken orally also makes methadone a much less attractive prospect for diversion. At first glance this would not seem to be very important. Because methadone is

36. Kreek, "Methadone in Treatment," p. 59.

long-acting, an on-the-premises system could stop diversion almost completely. Nonetheless, the ability to give addicts a "take-home" supply of methadone is helpful for maintenance programs. A program can use this privilege to reward addicts for good behavior by allowing them to take home two days' to a week's supply of the drug rather than requiring them to report daily to consume their doses.

Virtually all methadone programs insist that, at the beginning of maintenance, addicts make daily visits and either consume the doses on the premises or else take only that day's supply home for consumption at bedtime. Though, of course, this is more convenient than would be an on-the-premises system using heroin, it still is inconvenient for most addicts. As a result, an every-other-day schedule or, better yet, even a schedule calling for only one visit per week is seen as a considerable benefit.

This reward can be given for abstinence from heroin, as shown by urinalysis; holding of steady employment or, if a student, regular class attendance; or any other behavior which is regarded as a step toward reintegration into society. Of course, the obverse side of this reward system is that the take-home privileges can be withdrawn for behavior which treaters feel is a relapse toward the chaotic life of the junkie.

In the early days of methadone maintenance there were a considerable number of accidental poisonings, where the children of addicts came upon a supply of the drug mixed with orange juice and drank the liquid. Soon regulations provided that each addict was to store his take-home supply in a lock box and programs were not to dispense the drug in any sweet-tasting mixture. As a result, accidental poisonings have decreased considerably—though they still occur.[37]

Although the appeal of diverted oral methadone seems to be limited compared to that of heroin, this does not mean that diversion is unknown. Users of methadone get no rush from taking the drug orally and generally regard the experience as much less pleasurable than injecting heroin, but they do get somewhat high from an oral dose. The consumers of diverted methadone may be addicts in methadone programs who supplement their prescribed dosages; street addicts out of programs who switch to diverted methadone when their heroin supply is interrupted, it becomes too difficult for them to maintain their habit, or they feel they must gradually detoxify themselves; and polydrug users who occasionally seek a methadone high. Although a market for diverted methadone does exist, in most areas the problem is not a serious one. The drug is held in far less esteem

37. Joyce H. Lowinson and Robert Millman, "Clinical Aspects of Methadone Maintenance," in *Handbook on Drug Abuse*, pp. 52–53. Much of the procedure is mandated by the federal government. See *Food and Drugs*, Drugs Used for Treatment of Narcotic Addicts, 21 C.F.R. Section 291.505(d)(8)(1981).

than heroin—as evidenced by the fact that illegally diverted methadone sells for less than one-fifth the price of comparable amounts of heroin.[38]

The most important proof of the relative unimportance of methadone diversion is the rarity of primary methadone addicts—those who originally became addicted to methadone. Whatever the value of the drug to those already addicted, oral methadone does not have the attractiveness necessary to lure significant numbers of new users into addiction. This is a matter of considerable significance since one of the major worries raised by any maintenance proposal is the possible creation of new addicts through diversion from the system.

That is not to say that we should ignore the problems of methadone diversion. In at least one area of New York City, a methadone street culture has grown up in which methadone is valued for its euphoric effects and members often divert part of their supply for sale to others.[39] Most observers have criticized the laxness in permitting methadone diversion on this scale, but the problem does not seem as serious elsewhere in the nation.

Moreover, not all of those involved in the diversion of methadone are members of the methadone street culture. Some of those who occasionally either sell part of their methadone supply or supplement their prescribed dosages with diverted methadone have nonetheless stabilized their own lives considerably and are functioning fairly well in society. Even the members of the methadone street culture—the methadone equivalent of the heroin junkie—seem to be somewhat better off than when they were addicted to heroin. As described in a now classic paper by two street ethnographers, their life style is based on "Methadone, Wine and Welfare," but they use far less heroin and commit many fewer crimes than they did before their treatment. Their social productivity, while still unimpressive, becomes much less so when compared to the costs they had imposed on society while they were addicted to heroin.

## Methadone as an Opiate

The similarities between methadone and heroin are, of course, as important as the differences. Methadone, like heroin, is addicting, so that the addict in a methadone program can be "hooked" into treatment.

Regardless of the political or moral problems this may raise, a treatment involving maintenance on an addicting drug does have several practical advantages. It places the addict under strong pressures to appear on a fixed schedule for his dose, which in itself adds a degree of stability

38. James A. Inciardi, *Methadone Diversion: Experiences and Issues* (Rockville, Md.: National Institute of Drug Abuse, 1977).

39. Preble and Miller, "Methadone, Wine, and Welfare," pp. 229 et seq.

to his often chaotic life. Moreover, at each appearance of the addict, the program staff may monitor his progress. They may question him about his work status; subject him to urinalysis to determine his nontherapeutic drug use; talk to him about his problems; and help him in securing employment. Since, as noted before, many addicts in maintenance are willing to modify their behavior to gain a methadone supply more easily and to secure various other rewards, such treatment can have a major impact on the addict's behavior.

The fact that methadone is an opiate cross-tolerant with heroin also gives methadone the important property of preventing the withdrawal symptoms of heroin addiction. (Indeed, methadone in decreasing doses is the medically preferred means for the slow, painless detoxification of heroin addicts.)[40] As a result, the withdrawal symptoms which make it more difficult for heroin addicts to cease use do not affect those maintained on methadone, even if they have been supplementing their methadone dosage with illegal heroin. As long as they stay on methadone, addicts are in little danger of developing a compulsive run of heroin use. Since it is just during such a run that the criminality of the addict is most likely to skyrocket, methadone is of considerable importance in reducing the number of crimes perpetrated by addicts.

At one time, methadone was also thought to "block" the euphoric effects of heroin. If this were true, it would constitute another advantage of methadone maintenance in reducing heroin use. Unfortunately it does not seem to be true. The belief probably gained currency because many of the early methadone patients attempted to get high on heroin but failed in their attempts. Their use of relatively large quantities of methadone had probably caused them to develop an increased tolerance to the euphoric effects of heroin, and the relatively low dosage of heroin that they used was insufficient to overcome their tolerance. What was thought to be a "blockade," they soon learned, could be surmounted simply by using a larger amount of heroin—and today an addict maintained on methadone knows he can gain euphoria from heroin provided he uses a large enough dose.[41]

The increased tolerance to heroin that methadone maintenance produces is not a very significant factor in the benefits of the treatment. Indeed, from a social point of view, it is a mixed blessing. The greater amount of heroin an addict on methadone requires to get high raises the price he must pay per "fix." Since the demand for heroin by an addict in methadone maintenance is now far more elastic than when he needed the

40. Robert G. Newman, "Detoxification Treatment of Narcotic Addicts," in *Handbook on Drug Abuse*, p. 24.

41. Kreek, "Methadone in Treatment," p. 59. William R. Martin et al., "Methadone—A Reevaluation," *Archives of General Psychiatry* 28, no. 2 (February 1973): 288, 293–94.

drug to stave off withdrawal, this will lower the number of times he uses illegal heroin. On the other hand, if the addict is going to use heroin occasionally, there is no social good accomplished by forcing him to raise more money than necessary to indulge in his taste.

Nonetheless, though many addicts maintained on methadone do use heroin occasionally, and enjoy it, they use heroin far less often than before their entry into methadone maintenance; and, as noted earlier, they are much less likely to develop a compulsive run of drug use—with its often concomitant property criminality.

It also appears that heroin use by those in methadone maintenance gradually decreases so long as they remain in their programs.[42] Partly this is explainable on pharmacological grounds, but there are other reasons as well. Often those in methadone programs gradually lose their friends and contacts in the heroin-using community; their more regular lives tend to leave less place for heroin use; and sometimes they develop bonds of friendship with their counselors, which causes them to fear the consequences of a "dirty" urine upon their relationship.

## Criticisms of Methadone Maintenance

Several of the most common charges made against the use of methadone focus directly on one of the main advantages of the drug, its addictive nature. There are, of course, moral implications to using our control over the supply of an addicting drug to coerce certain behaviors from addicts. The use of "drug enslavement," even in a worthy cause, may be beyond the powers legitimately exercisable by the state. In the case of the heroin addict, however, we are dealing with someone who, to a greater or lesser extent, is already controlled by a drug. Attempting to use this already existing condition for therapeutic purposes raises very different issues than would "hooking" a nonaddict.

This is perhaps the major reason why we are unwilling to use methadone on the nonaddicted user. He has no habit from which methadone might free him, and we are unwilling to addict him in order to give his treaters a pharmacological handle by which they might control him. It is true that we do not know how to treat the nonaddicted heroin user, but addicting him to methadone is not seen as the answer.

Even if we were prepared to overlook the moral implications of exerting this kind of pharmacological control over sizable numbers of citizens, the political aspects of the decision are significant. Since a large percentage of heroin users are either black or Hispanic Americans, this

---

42. Avram Goldstein, "The Status of Methadone Maintenance," in *Problems of Drug Dependence*, Proceedings of the 37th Annual Scientific Meeting, Committee on Problems of Drug Dependence (Washington, D.C.: National Academy of Sciences, 1975), p. 43.

method of control is vulnerable to attack on the ground that, in the words of one Black Panther leader, "We don't need the government making more *good* citizens. Methadone is just genocide, mostly against Black people."[43] This argument is extreme as applied to maintaining heroin addicts on government-supplied methadone. It is less so as applied to "hooking" mere users.

The opposition to treating heroin addicts with another addicting drug is at the core of the most frequently made charge against methadone maintenance, that it is not a cure for heroin addiction at all, but rather a means of switching the addict from one addiction to another. Though to a considerable extent true, this is beside the point. The fact that methadone maintenance is not a cure for addiction should not be determinative so long as it improves the addict's life and health and lowers the cost he imposes on society.

This criticism does point up one problem, however. The longer an addict is maintained on methadone, the higher the cost of his treatment to the society and the greater the interference with his freedom. Moreover, granting that methadone does far less harm to the addict's health than would street heroin, there may still be certain long-term health complications from the drug's use. If so, the longer the time the addict spends on methadone, the greater the likelihood he will be subjected to whatever harm the drug does.

It turns out that methadone, though primarily conceived of as a maintenance drug, can also help an addict give up opiates entirely. The widespread view to the contrary is premised on the earliest studies of methadone maintenance, which showed an extremely high relapse rate among those addicts who had detoxified and withdrawn from their maintenance programs.[44] It now appears that, with time, a sizable percentage of addicts maintained on methadone can stabilize their lives and then withdraw from treatment without returning to heroin use. That is not to say the process is an easy one. Psychiatrists have described a particular clinical entity involving a panic reaction to the withdrawal of methadone's support. And, even where this does not occur, the addict may have several false starts in his attempt to give up methadone. Often these result either in readdiction to heroin or in a situation threatening enough to cause a return to methadone maintenance for a while. Nonetheless, a number of addicts in maintenance do eventually give up both their methadone and their heroin use and, thereafter, remain opiate-free.[45]

43. Alec Dubro, "Methadone Is," *Liberation* 20, no. 2 (January-February 1977): 12.
44. Edward Senay et al., "Withdrawal from Methadone Maintenance," *Archives of General Psychiatry* 34, no. 3 (March 1977): 363–67.
45. Barry Stimmel et al., "Ability to Remain Abstinent After Methadone Detoxification," *Journal of the American Medical Association* 237, no. 12 (21 March 1971): 1216–20.

## The Limits of Methadone

There is no doubt, however, that methadone is not penicillin. Entirely apart from its inability to effect miracle cures, methadone maintenance suffers from another, more serious disadvantage.

Typically, the patient with an infection has only that wrong with him; if that is cured, he is well again. The heroin addict, on the other hand, may labor under many additional handicaps to his social functioning—such as the lack of a high school diploma, functional illiteracy, the absence of a work record or any legitimate occupational skills, and the inability to receive help from any friends in a better position than his own. Whether or not these obstacles are traceable to his heroin addiction, they will remain after he ceases his heroin use.

As a result, some heroin addicts do not greatly improve their functioning when in maintenance programs. Even those who obey all the rules as well as they can and do not join the "methadone, wine and welfare" subculture may hardly be accounted successes in treatment. Though their criminality and heroin use may cease, or at least be markedly reduced, they may never become productive citizens. Similarly, to the extent that an addict's criminality is not caused by his addiction, even successful treatment for his drug problem will not lower his predation against society. Indeed, the freedom that methadone may give him from the demands of his heroin habit may allow him to commit crimes at an increased rate.

Probably the most important difference between methadone and penicillin, however, is the fact that, except for a very few allergic individuals, no one objects to being treated with penicillin. Though we may consider methadone a much better drug than heroin for the addict, he may prefer heroin, and hence not wish to be treated. Indeed, probably the greatest problem in making methadone maintenance more successful is that many addicts prefer their life on illegal heroin to that in methadone treatment.[46]

Part of the reason may be pharmacological. Since methadone is not injected, it does not produce the much desired rush; and, on the stabilized doses usually used, methadone often does not even produce much of a high.

The nonpharmacological aspects of methadone maintenance may be even more objectionable to the addict. No maintenance scheme can satisfy the needs met by the subculture of heroin use, the values of the heroin addict, and the junkie life style. If methadone maintenance were merely irrelevant to these needs, it would perhaps be more popular among addicts. In that case, they could be in maintenance and continue their former lives in all other respects. This is not the case for several reasons.

---

46. Preble and Miller, "Methadone, Wine, and Welfare," p. 237.

Entry into a methadone program flies in the face of some cherished values of the heroin user. It involves a surrender—or at least an accommodation—to "the man." Moreover, the treatment programs generally exert a constant pressure to give up the life style and values of the heroin addict.

The willingness of many heroin addicts to accept treatment means that those entering methadone maintenance, like those entering the other treatment modalities, will constitute a biased sample of heroin addicts. Those addicts who enter voluntarily are most likely to be those who derive the least in psychological and physical satisfactions from heroin; find it most difficult because of age or class backround to cope with the heroin scene and its life style; have the most difficulty in obtaining heroin at that time due to a shortage of income or a dearth of the drug; and, because of their education or job skills, face the most attractive prospects for their life once free of heroin addiction. These addicts are also the ones most likely to be accounted treatment successes.

This is not to say that methadone is worthless as a treatment for other addicts. It does, however, mean that the success rate of methadone treatment will probably be less for them and that they will less often be voluntary patients—a matter to which we will return shortly.


## The Effectiveness of Methadone Maintenance

The major test of methadone maintenance lies in the success or failure of the many treatment programs using this approach. Unfortunately, however, the published research does not allow us to draw very precise conclusions as to the efficacy of methadone maintenance in practice.

To begin with, the treatment is relatively new; the first evaluation of a methadone program was published only about a decade ago. Although, by the standards of previous social experiments, great attention has been paid to independent scientific evaluations of methadone programs, the evaluations vary greatly in their methodology and reliability, a problem compounded by the enormous differences among the programs that exist in almost all sizable American cities.

As we have noted earlier, some programs are not even very careful to make sure they are dealing with addicts to begin with. They may enroll occasional heroin users, and perhaps even a few who have never used heroin but are attracted to the programs because they like the "patient" life style, the welfare payments that in some areas go with it, or the status of being a "former" heroin addict.[47]

---

47. Fleetwood, "Psst . . . Kid, Wanna Be a Junkie?", pp. 68–82. Fleetwood's criticisms have been criticized. See Ronald Bayer, "Methadone under Attack: An Analysis of the Popular Literature. Appendix: Methadone and the free press: Documents from a Case in Controversy," *Contemporary Drug Problems* 7, no. 3 (Fall 1978): 379–400.

Some programs give out methadone and provide virtually no other services; others regard methadone primarily as a method of "hooking" an addict into treatment so that they may work on his underlying psychological and social problems—antedating as well as caused by his period of addiction.

Programs differ in the dosages of methadone they use. Some monitor the responses of their patients carefully, while others sometimes use too high a dosage, leaving their patients slightly dizzy or sleepy much of the time. Some programs pay far more attention to preventing diversion of their methadone than do others, and there is, in general, a wide variation in the amount of control different programs exercise over the lives of the addicts they enroll.[48]

The relation of methadone programs to the outside society also varies greatly among areas and programs. Some programs are met with hostility by the surrounding community, the police, and the local social service agencies; some are aided by them; and some are rendered less effective by too accepting an attitude on the part of welfare agencies, which simply treat any methadone patient as unemployable, regardless of his prospects for a return to a productive life.[49]

Probably the easiest way to summarize the differences among methadone programs is to say that some programs are run by bureaucrats and timeservers, who abound in all walks of life. Others are run imaginatively by people who care about their patients.[50] One program even introduced a "clean urine" raffle to give its patients an extra incentive to stay off heroin.

For one reason or another, different programs enroll different kinds of addicts. As we have noted, some candidates for methadone maintenance are far more promising than others, and the percentage of these "easy to cure" addicts enrolled will often determine the apparent effectiveness of a program.

Our research on methadone maintenance nevertheless indicates that it is the most cost-effective treatment we have today for heroin addiction. The addict receiving this type of treatment is often much better off than on heroin—with respect to both his well-being and ours. That is not to say that this treatment permanently helps all or even a majority of addicts. Probably the figure is closer to 40 percent. Considering all the costs and benefits of the other treatments and punishments at our disposal, this seems to be about as well as we can do.

48. Platt and Labate, *Heroin Addiction*, pp. 260–307.

49. John Blackmore, "The Use and Abuse of Methadone," *Police* 3, no. 1 (January 1980): 50–51.

50. Charles P. O'Brien and Lorenz K. Y. Ng, "Innovative Treatments for Drug Addiction," in *Handbook on Drug Abuse*, pp. 195–96.

The Bakersfield "Experiment"

One of the most interesting efforts to measure the effectiveness of methadone maintenance took advantage of a "natural experiment."[51] In September 1976, the only methadone program in Bakersfield, California, was closed down. Since the nearest program was seventy miles away in Tulare, the great majority of those registered in Bakersfield were withdrawn from methadone, and joined no other such program. As a result, they could be compared with those in the Tulare maintenance program at that time, who continued to have that option open to them.

When the two samples were compared two years after the Bakersfield closing, a number of interesting facts were revealed. Of the men in the Bakersfield group, 73 percent had been arrested during the two-year period, while in Tulare only 43 percent were. Fifty-five percent of the Bakersfield men had become readdicted to heroin, "using a narcotic daily during some period after discharge," while only 32 percent of the Tulare men had become readdicted. The Bakersfield men also led in in the category of dealing in drugs (62 percent versus 32 percent), while lesser, though still significant, differences appeared in their number of property crimes committed, percentage employed, and amount of alcohol abuse. At the end of the two-year followup, most differences between the samples still favored the Tulare sample. At that time, the Bakersfield sample had a far higher percentage on probation or on parole (51 to 21 percent), a lower percentage employed full or part-time (58 to 72 percent), and twice as high a positive urinalysis rate (30 to 15 percent).

A number of other interesting findings also emerged from the study. Although there were fewer women than men in the two samples and, hence, the findings are perhaps more subject to error, it does appear that the women terminated from the Bakersfield program, in all but one respect, fared worse than their sisters in Tulare. This one respect, however, is interesting. The amount of property crime committed by the Bakersfield women was far less than that of the Tulare women. Probably the difference is accounted for by the fact that addicted women are likely to have a major alternative to property crime or drug dealing. They can raise the cost of their habits through prostitution.

There are reasons, moreover, to suspect that the benefits of methadone maintenance were understated by the study. At the time of the termination of the Bakersfield program, one of the periodic heroin droughts occurred, which had the effect of lowering the amount of heroin used and the consequent property crime in the Bakersfield sample. A number of the indices were affected by the fact that the percentage of men incarcerated

51. William H. McGlothlin and M. Douglas Anglin, "Shutting off Methadone: Costs and Benefits," *Archives of General Psychiatry* 38 (1981): 885.

for over thirty days was twice as high in Bakersfield as in Tulare and, hence, the Bakersfield sample was free less of the time to engage in socially costly activities. Finally, though the Bakersfield and Tulare samples were very similar on most dimensions prior to their entry into their respective methadone programs, there was one major difference between them. The Tulare sample was far more criminalistic. Before entering into methadone maintenance, the Tulare members averaged some $7,200 per year from property crime while those from the Bakersfield sample averaged only $3,900. (The Bakersfield sample, on the other hand, seemed to make more of its living dealing in drugs—some 56 percent as opposed to the 36 percent in the Tulare area sample.)

The final interesting finding of the study replicates that of most other methadone studies. Both samples, upon entry into methadone treatment, showed a very sharp drop in the costs they imposed upon society. These differences dwarfed the differences between the two samples at the time of the Bakersfield termination—when members of both had been in maintenance for some time. Thus, income from property crime in the Bakersfield sample fell from $3,900 to $400 a year on entry into the methadone program, while in Tulare it dropped from $7,200 to $1,700 a year.

Overall, the study attempted to sum in dollar terms the social costs imposed by the addicts during three periods: immediately before entry into methadone maintenance; while on methadone maintenance; and at the time of the interviews two years later. The cost of treatment, arrests, incarceration, property crime, and the like yield the figures shown in table 3.

TABLE 3

| Status or Behavior | Bakersfield | | | Tulare | | |
|---|---|---|---|---|---|---|
| | N-M* | M-D** | D-1*** | N-M | M-D | D-1 |
| Mean Social Cost: ($ x 1000) per year | 120 | 61 | 52 | 170 | 82 | 56 |

N = Narcotics; M = Methadone; D = Date of closure
*Period from first daily use of narcotics until entrance into methadone maintenance.
**From entrance into methadone maintenance until date of closure of the Bakersfield clinics.
***Period from date of closing of the Bakersfield clinic until interview, approximately two years later.

In other words, while the closing of the Bakersfield program probably imposed a small additional cost upon that area because of the discharge of those addicts already in maintenance, the major cost of the termination was elsewhere. It made methadone maintenance unavailable to produce the much larger cost savings that come from treating new entrants into the program.

## COERCED TREATMENT

Although our methods of reducing addiction to heroin (though often increasing addiction to methadone) are not so effective as we would wish, it is probably still in our interest to treat the great majority of addicts. As compared with imprisonment, treatment is both economical and effective—not so much because our treatments are so enormously successful and cheap but rather because, as applied to heroin addicts, the usual processes of the criminal law seem to be singularly costly and ineffective.

Even if the addict remains in treatment only a few months and, hence, is accounted a failure, treatment may work to better his life and reduce the social damage he causes. At the very least, the demands his treaters place upon the addict both to reduce his heroin intake and to live a less criminal, more regular, life, will work to lower the number of crimes he commits during his brief period on methadone subject to the discipline of a residential program or even in drug-free treatment. Though, of course, this reduction might be even greater were he imprisoned for the same length of time, the far lower cost of treatment may make it a better buy for society. This is especially the case so long as our overcrowded jails and prisons would not permit us to imprison the majority of heroin addicts for very long terms anyway.

Our quantitative information on the criminality of heroin addicts support this view. If the addict commits six times as many property crimes when he is using heroin daily as when he is not, any means of preventing daily (or more accurately, compulsive) heroin use would reduce his criminality by five-sixths. Any treatment then that costs less than five-sixths of the amount we pay for imprisonment might be, in terms of crime prevented, a better buy. Even residential treatment, the most expensive form of heroin treatment, costs considerably less than five-sixths the cost of imprisonment.

To be sure, a small percentage of addicts in treatment still manage to use heroin compulsively. But this effect is at least balanced by the fact that treatment has several advantages over imprisonment. We can treat addicts—even involuntarily—for a considerably longer time than we could imprison them. Our treatment interferes less with their autonomy and inflicts less pain upon them; and treatment is more likely than jail to encourage life styles and values which make both heroin use and crime less likely after the legal or medical intervention has ceased.

The greater cost effectiveness of treatment over imprisonment remains even where the addict is coerced into treatment by the threat of imminent imprisonment. Though probably not as effective as with purely voluntary patients, coerced heroin treatment may nonetheless make major changes in the life of the addict. Often he will cooperate fully in his treatment—to his and our benefit—even though he would not have entered voluntarily. On one psychological level, he may have even desired the coercion.

In one way or another, each of our treatments makes a return to heroin less likely. The residential drug-free community obviously accomplishes this through close and constant supervision. Outpatient treatment, though less effective, can use the threat of imprisonment after too many "dirty" urines, together with various other pressures, to lessen the probability of a return to the junkie subculture. Finally, methadone maintenance may use the discomfort of withdrawal as a "chemical prison" to compel the addict to remain in treatment and, hence, make efforts to restructure his life.

This practice of using the threat of imminent imprisonment to coerce those who have been convicted into ceasing a type of behavior is not at all unknown to the criminal law. It may occur even where the behavior to be prevented is not itself a crime but rather is felt to have produced criminal activity. Cessation of that behavior may be made a condition of probation, enforced by the threat of immediate imprisonment should the condition be violated.

Thus, after conviction, a probationer may be ordered, on pain of imprisonment, to abstain from the use of alcohol, or to keep away from his former wife. Or, rather than be an order not to do something, the condition may require positive action from the probationer geared toward preventing a repetition of his crime. He may be required to undergo psychiatric treatment, or to attend traffic school.

This is not to say that probation conditions are always successful. Some conditions, such as that the probationer not associate with known criminals, may be impossible for many urban youths to fulfill; often such conditions become devices for harassment, which make the reformation of the probationer more difficult; and, finally, should the conditions be too onerous, the probationer or parolee may simply abscond rather than accept punishment when he makes his regular visit to his case officer.

Nonetheless, in the case of the violator of a heroin use offense, a probation condition that he enter heroin treatment seems a reasonable one. Considering the alternatives, our treatment, enforced by the threat of probation revocation, is effective enough to be worth the effort. Moreover, where the law is used to coerce treatment aimed at a cessation of behavior which itself is criminal—such as heroin use—the case for the condition of probation is at its strongest.

Yet another aspect of coercion into treatment is the fact that it is more economical of trial resources as well as of imprisonment space. In the drug area we have developed a large number of diversion programs where an arrestee who has consented may be referred to a treatment program before any adjudication of his guilt.[52] If he completes his treatment, the charges will be dropped, and the enforcement system will have achieved its result without adding to the clogging of the courts. If the user does not complete his treatment satisfactorily (remembering the relatively low expectations of many treatment programs), the prosecution can be reinstated, a conviction obtained, and the user then either imprisoned or subjected to treatment again, supervised by the probation office.

On the other hand, this saving of trial resources does come at a social price. Treatment, as compared with imprisonment, is so lenient that many arrestees, regardless of their innocence, may prefer accepting diversion to litigating their guilt in court and taking their chances on conviction. This may remove a major check on police behavior, lowering the accuracy of the process whereby citizens are selected for arrest. In addition, the ready availability of such an economical means of controlling behavior encourages the government to exert more control over the population, further diminishing the ambit of the individual's autonomy.[53] These arguments against diversion are perhaps of insufficient weight to overbalance the advantages of using this technique, once it has been decided that the heroin user should be criminalized. When that decision itself is examined, the disadvantages of diversion should be weighed in the balance.

With respect to the use offender, then, there are relatively few arguments that a policy of imprisonment is to be preferred to one of coercion into treatment. This raises two questions, however. First, in the case of the heroin user who has been found to have committed a criminal offense, should coercion into treatment still be preferred to imprisonment? (By criminal offense here, of course, is meant a nonuse offense, most likely but not necessarily an "addict" crime, such as a property offense or the sale of heroin.) Second, in the case of the noncriminal heroin user, should coercion into treatment be preferred to complete repeal of use offenses and ignoring heroin use, so long as it does not lead to other crimes?

## The User Criminal

Taking the first question first, we should note that unlike the use offender, in whom we are interested primarily because of the contingent possibility that he is also a criminal, the criminal user has already committed a crime. On the other hand, we have no good way of knowing even in this case whether the addict committed his crime because he used heroin; whether

52. Weissman, "Survey of State Drug Offender Diversion Authorities," *Contemporary Drug Problems* 7 (1978): 533.

53. James C. Weissman, "Drug Offender Diversion: Philosophy and Practices," *Drug Abuse and Alcoholism Review* 2 (1979): 1.

he used heroin because he was a criminal; or whether, in his case, there was no significant relation between the two events.

In the case of the nonaddicted user, the question is easy. We do not recognize any causal relation between his occasional use of heroin and his criminality. Presumably he should be punished as would any other criminal.

The addicted criminal presents a more difficult case. If his criminality is not caused by his addiction, our coercing him into treatment will not reduce his depredations against society. Hence, our treatment resources will be, for the most part, wasted. (Theoretically by treating him we could make him feel better and be less distracted while he continued his criminal career, but one would not be too hard-hearted if one viewed improving his life under these conditions as a misuse of public funds.)

Ideally the addict criminal whose crimes are unrelated to his addiction should be treated no differently from any other criminal. In most cases, however, we cannot tell whether a given addict would still have committed crimes had he not been addicted. As a result, we are probably best off presuming any criminal who is also an addict is sufficiently likely to be a criminal because of his addiction. Even though this will not always be true, it will be true for a substantial number of addict criminals. Although we may be wasting treatment resources by coercing into treatment an addict whose criminality will not be reduced thereby, we are at least wasting a lesser sum than would be expended on the unnecessary imprisonment of those addicts for whom treatment would be effective.[54] If we are to make errors, it would seem good policy to err in the direction of the less expensive—and more humane—ones.

Moreover, in the case of those who commit crimes while addicted, treatment may be more in line with our moral feelings than is punishment. Those whom we would treat are in a sense less blameworthy, because they might not have committed the crime charged had they not been addicted—even though they may be blamed for remaining addicted while knowing that they would have to commit crimes to continue in that condition.

Just as we had trouble fitting the heroin addict into our disease model, there are also problems in fitting him within the usual assumptions of the criminal law. We feel that our criminal system is most appropriate for those who share two characteristics: first, they have free will and hence are completely responsible for their actions; and, second, they are not seen as fundamentally different from the rest of us. Unfortunately, the heroin addict does not fall easily into either of these categories. While to a degree he has freely chosen his condition, it is also true that to a degree he

54. *Treatment Research Report: Effectiveness of Drug Abuse Treatment Programs* (Rockville, Md.: National Institute on Drug Abuse, 1981).

lacks control. And whether he is seen as just like the rest of us is debatable. Like those alcoholics who accept the ideology of Alcoholics Anonymous that they are different in a fundamental biochemical way from the rest of the population, many people look upon the heroin addict as "different."

Even in those cases where our presumption that treatment would lower the criminality of the addict criminal turned out to be contrary to fact, there are several reasons why we might take our error with some equanimity. Though treatment is not intended as punitive, those retributively minded may draw some comfort from the fact that coerced treatment fits the classic definition of punishment; it is a deprivation visited upon a criminal because of his crime. Moreover, the threat of having to cease heroin use and suffer the considerable inconvenience of coerced treatment may exert some deterrent effect upon the addict contemplating a crime. Though this may not lessen his criminality, neither often does the threat of our usual criminal punishments.

The criminal addict, moreover, will be brought a step nearer imprisonment. If he leaves treatment, he will be punished, because we must keep our promises about requiring his treatment. If he commits further crimes while in treatment, then he will be punished because, having been treated, he is no longer an addict criminal moved by a need for heroin, but rather is simply a criminal.

In addition, no legal or moral impediment prevents our also imprisoning the addict as a punishment for his crimes and then coercing him into treatment as a condition of postrelease parole.[55] After all, even if his crimes had been caused by his addiction, they were still voluntary in the sense that he could have undergone treatment earlier and, hence, removed his need to break the law.

However, aside from the relatively few cases where the crime was so serious—such as perhaps a violent robbery—that a failure to impose criminal punishment would be a public scandal, we probably would not wish to spend our limited criminal justice resources on punishing addicts initially. After all, deterrence and isolation, though perhaps often necessary, are inefficient and expensive means of controlling the typical addict crimes. Considering the likelihood that the criminal's addiction to heroin is causally connected to his criminality, it would in most cases make sense to try treatment first.

Forcing criminal addicts into treatment does not necessarily produce the most efficient use of our treatment resources, however. If the reason for our governmentally financed treatment is seen more in conventional

55. William I. Barton, "Drug Histories and Criminality of Inmates of Local Jails in the United States (1978): Implications for Treatment and Rehabilitation of the Drug Abuser in a Jail Setting," *International Journal of the Addictions* 17 (1982): 417.

public health terms—lessening the misery of sufferers from a disease or painful condition—we could do better.

Unless there is some other purpose to be served, it is unwise to expend scarce treatment resources on unwilling patients who have less than the best prospects for cure. In the case of the addict whose crimes are caused by his addiction, however, there is just such a purpose—lowering our crime rate. Even though our limited treatment resources, in health terms, could be more efficiently used on more willing and cooperative patients, the promised reduction in criminality makes it sensible to use these resources on the addict criminal.

To be sure, treatment resources should also be made available for voluntary patients—those who sincerely wish to escape heroin addiction. This can be justified in terms of humanitarian and public health values; on economic grounds, because of their potentially increased productivity; and also because many of them also present a significant criminal problem, even if they have not been apprehended. It is not clear whether this effort should receive higher priority than the treatment of the more criminal but harder-to-cure addicts whom we would coerce into treatment, but both efforts are of considerable importance.

## TASC

One of the relatively few successful federal initiatives in the criminal justice area was directed at systematically coercing addicts into treatment instead of imprisoning them.[56] This program, successful in the sense that many local governments have adopted it even after their federal funding ran out, is called TASC, an acronym for Treatment Alternatives to Street Crime. The evaluations of these programs are even more tentative than those of heroin treatment itself. First of all, they build on heroin treatment and are dependent upon the effectiveness of that treatment—a matter of ongoing research. In addition, TASC also diverts into treatment not only heroin users and addicts but also those abusing alcohol, barbiturates, P.C.P. and other drugs. Moreover, because of the leniency of the treatment, TASC programs often divert those who abuse no drug at all but for whom criminal conviction is seen as too severe, such as occasional users of marijuana. Finally, these programs are only a few years old, and as yet there are no studies which carefully measure the subsequent criminality of those in such programs against those handled in more traditional ways. Obviously, when the effects of TASC upon heroin

56. U.S., Department of Justice, Law Enforcement Assistance Administration, National Institute of Law Enforcement and Criminal Justice, Evaluation of *Treatment Alternatives to Street Crime*, National Evaluation Program, Phase II Report (Washington, D.C.: Government Printing Office, 1979).

addicts are separated from the vast amount of noise and more carefully measured, we will know more about the effectiveness of coerced treatment.[57]

## THE WISDOM OF USE OFFENSES

The decision to rely initially on coercion into treatment rather than the usual processes of the criminal law may perhaps end the matter so far as the addict criminal is concerned. After all, we must do something with him. With respect to the use offender, however, we have the option of simply ignoring his behavior, adopting for heroin what has on various occasions been called the "vice model," "partial prohibition" or "decriminialization" (as distinguished from "legalization").

At the outset we can reject two common arguments against such a course—first, that failing to take action against the buyer or consumer of a substance or service while prohibiting its sale is somehow inconsistent; second, that failing to punish use of an illegal substance or service signals that such use is safe or socially acceptable. A recent report of the National Research Counsel of the National Academy of Sciences answered both these arguments with respect to marijuana, and their obsrvations are equally applicable to heroin:

> At first glance, criminalizing the selling of marijuana might appear inconsistent with failing to punish its purchase. But in the drafting of laws, a line is often drawn between legal and illegal conduct so that the maximum reduction in the proscribed behavior can be gained at minimum social cost. Frequently it turns out that laws aimed solely at suppressing sales are more cost-effective in reducing both the possession and use of a substance than are laws that attempt to suppress possession directly. There are several reasons for this. First, there are fewer sellers than buyers; this permits a concentration of law enforcement efforts where they do the most good. Second, juries are likely to be more sympathetic to a "mere" user, who may be ill-advised, than to a dealer making a profit from the weaknesses of others. Offenses treated under the vice model (partial prohibition) range from gambling—the person who takes illegal bets is guilty of a crime while the person who places them is not—to the offense of selling new automobiles not equipped with seat belts—the seller, not the buyer, is guilty of an offense. Even Prohibition in 1919 never criminalized the possession or use of alcohol, only its manufacture and sale. . . .
> . . . It has been suggested that repeal of government prohibitions might change attitudes related to health or morals, perhaps symboliz-

57. James J. Collins et al., *Criminal Justice Clients in Drug Treatment* (draft copy) (Research Triangle Park, N.C.: Research Triangle Institute, 1982).

ing that health officials certify marijuana use to be safe. The absence of large increases in marijuana use in repeal states, however, indicates that either the change in policy has not had such a symbolic effect, or that, if it has, its causal significance is not appreciable— though it must be acknowledged that changes of this type might take generations to occur.[58]

If the choice were simply between using the usual processes of the criminal law and repealing all laws creating heroin use crimes, it would be easier to opt for the latter solution. The greater cost effectiveness of coercion into treatment, however, makes the issue more difficult. A major problem in deciding this is our lack of knowledge. We do not know enough about the connection between heroin and crime. Though we know that some addicts commit far more crimes when on a run of heroin use than when not, we do not know much about noncriminal addicts or about those who are merely petty offenders, who should not be the subject of serious and expensive attention. We have no idea what percentage of the addict population falls into each category. Nor do we know how likely each kind of addict is to be caught for use offenses by the police and, hence, what the chances are that an addict arrested by the police for a use offense will also be a criminal. Nor do we know enough about the effectiveness of the criminal law in compelling treatment, or the cost effectiveness of treatment on heroin addicts. And of course we know even less about nonaddicted users.

It is especially important that we increase our understanding of how the police select heroin users for arrest. Though there are more users than addicts, there are probably many more occasions of use by addicts. At least, that is the case with alcohol, where the 10 percent heaviest users consume more than half of the drug used. Whether the most heavily using addicts—who are also perhaps the most criminalistic—come to police attention most often for their use as well as for their crimes, however, is not so clear. It may well be that those heroin users and addicts whom the police most often notice are the least successful users—petty criminals or simply the drug equivalent of skid row derelicts. They are users of heroin and perhaps a sizable number of other drugs; who occasionally are addicted, but they do not present a serious criminal problem.

If it is too difficult to select accurately the criminal addicts from the noncriminal users who also come to police attention, another problem arises. Do the advantages of treating the former group outweigh the wastage in arresting and processing the latter, even considering the high cost of both criminal and treatment resources?

---

58. National Research Council, National Academy of Sciences, *An Analysis of Marijuana Policy*, Washington, D.C. 1982, pp. 12–13.

Although we would probably be better off not attempting to suppress use by the nonaddicted user, the heroin addict presents more serious problems. Here the risk of other crimes is higher and less contingent. For various reasons, including Supreme Court interpretations, we cannot draw this distinction in our formal criminal law; hence the issue then involves the question of whether, considering our interest in suppressing the crimes that addicts often commit, we are better off trusting the criminal justice system to allocate its resources so as to make the retention of use offenses worthwhile for us. Whether the police and courts can do this depends on their ability to catch and punish addict criminals for the crimes they commit, as well as on their ability to select from among heroin users those most deserving of intervention. Obviously, in different areas the criminal justice system will differ in its ability to perform these tasks, but in those areas which in fact have any significant amount of heroin use the institutions of criminal justice are so overcrowded that we can have very little confidence in their abilities.

The effect of all these unknown factors upon the cost and benefits of coercing heroin users into treatment cannot yet be determined. Nonetheless, it is clear that the costs of treatment itself are significant, and that those heroin users who have been coerced into treatment programs not only have higher than average rates of attrition but are, on various other grounds, the hardest to treat and the worst prospects for success. We have also noted that the narrowest category of users we should coerce into treatment are those we have just discussed—those whose addiction has caused them to commit the typical addict crimes—thefts and heroin supply offenses. These addicts, whose cure would most likely result in a considerable lowering of their criminality, should have the first claim on our law enforcement and on our treatment resources as well.

Similarly, it is clear that the last priority for our treatment resources should be those unwilling subjects who are not otherwise known to be criminals. Not only are they harder to cure than the willing subjects, but their treatment offers us less promise of crime reduction than in the case of the addict criminals.

It is not only treatment resources which may be misapplied to unwilling noncriminal heroin users. Coercing them into treatment may also waste our scarce criminal justice resources. Since the major reason we are interested in criminalizing the heroin user in the first place is that we believe he commits addict crimes, there is at least some reason to save ourselves the trouble and expense of arresting and processing heroin users who are not otherwise criminals.

In short, based upon our present data, we cannot be sure whether we would be better off ignoring all use offenses and coercing into treatment only those addicts who have been caught committing crimes. Such a practice may be more or less cost-effective than establishing use offenses and coercing into treatment all apprehended users—criminal and non-criminal addicts and nonaddicted users as well.

There are, however, reasons for preferring a system that coerces addicts into treatment only where they have committed other crimes. In terms of the freedom and autonomy that concerned John Stuart Mill, such a course is far more acceptable than is the use of criminal law against individuals whose primary harm is to themselves.

Note how different the case is for the addict caught committing a property crime than for the noncriminal user or addict. Those addicts who have committed crimes because of their addiction to heroin have shown that they cannot handle that drug without causing harm to others—thus removing their drug use from the category of self-harming conduct and making it the business of society.

Nor can they fashion an excuse out of the fact that our criminal law has so raised the price of heroin that many otherwise law-abiding addicts must commit crimes. Once we reject both free availability and heroin maintenance, our restrictions on the supply of heroin become a given. If the heroin addict commits crimes to feed his habit, it is regrettable that we have made his habit so expensive, but this is necessary for other reasons and need not change our treatment of him.

Another benefit in removing use offenses from our criminal law would be a better solution of the awkward problem of the nonaddicted, occasional heroin user. Of course, if he commits property crimes, or any crimes that are not use offenses, he should be regarded as no different from a social drinker of alcohol or a complete abstainer. Since we do not regard occasional heroin use as a causal element in any significant amount of crime, we do not regard him as less responsible because of drug use, or believe that his coerced treatment would lower his criminality.

It is sometimes said that it does not make sense to coerce the occasional user into treatment because we cannot treat him. If this were so, an advantage to eliminating heroin use offenses would be an avoidance of the anomaly that the addict criminal would receive the more lenient disposition of coercion into treatment, while the noncriminal user, whom we could not treat, would have to be either punished as a criminal or else coerced into "treatment" which both the treaters and the patient recognized as an exercise in hypocrisy.[59] This would affront our ideas either of justice or of honesty.

The view that we cannot treat the occasional user, however, is perhaps an oversimplification. It is true that considering occasional use of heroin, unaccompanied by any other pathology, to be a sickness overstrains our disease model, and without a disease, the concept of treatment is

59. William H. McGlothlin, "Criminal Justice Clients," in *Handbook on Drug Abuse*, pp. 203–9.

inapplicable. Nonetheless, what we mean by treatment is in part a kind of behavioral control. It may be for the good of the user and it may also be for the good of society—but subjecting such users to urinalysis and other controls to attempt to make sure they do not use heroin can be effective. The argument against this course is not that it is ineffective, rather it is that such a course may be wasteful and inhumane.

Where the nonaddicted user commits no crimes other than his use itself, we cannot treat him for the purpose of reducing his criminality. By hypothesis he has not been shown to be a criminal. Nor, considering the relatively low likelihood that any given user will later become an addict, does it make sense to coerce him into treatment to prevent his getting more deeply involved with heroin. Not only will our treatment often have the opposite effect, but, considering the urgent and immediate demands on our criminal justice and treatment resources, it would be inefficient to expend them against such a contingent possibility.

One further advantage of withdrawing the criminal law from the otherwise law-abiding heroin user is more speculative in nature. Over time, this policy may permit the development of informal social controls, which may be more effective than the legal controls we attempt to impose on heroin use. This is not likely to happen in the very near future, as the social controls on most heroin use today are weak indeed. Yet, no one looking at the results of our present heroin policy, or any changes in that policy that we can think of, can regard our adjustment to the drug as a satisfactory one. If we ever are to reach some much less costly accommodation to heroin, the development of informal social controls over its use may well be a major factor in the improvement.

It is possible, of course, that the development of informal social controls that allow people to use heroin without injury may never progress sufficiently to permit the adoption of a heroin policy that greatly lowers the overall cost of the drug to our society. Nonetheless, we must make choices about our policy toward the substance—even though our information is in many ways inadequate. A short step in what may be the right direction may be the best we can achieve today—especially since we can retrace our steps and criminalize use again should the results be unsatisfactory. The choices are difficult and none is very promising. In such a position, the important thing is to do the best we can.

# AFTERWORD

*T*his book has been devoted to examination of the costs and benefits of different policies toward heroin. For the most part it has ignored the political obstacles, which make it likely that even if some dramatic change could improve the situation, the disturbances this would cause to our equilibrium might make such a move politically unfeasible.

Any heroin policy will benefit some people while hurting others, and it is possible that those to be hurt may be able to summon enough political support to block those who hope to benefit from a change. Our present policy hurts our institutions of criminal justice (though of course not all those who work in them), those who are addicted, and those upon whom addicts prey—at least to the extent of any additional depredation caused by their heroin addiction. Free availability would, in many ways, improve the lives of our present addicts and of those they victimize, as well as the integrity of our criminal justice processes. On the other hand, it would hurt those who would then become addicted and who would not otherwise have encountered heroin. It would also hurt those who, in one way or another, would suffer more from the public health and personal aspects of a greatly increased addiction rate than they do from the many ramifications of our present heroin policy. Heroin maintenance would injure those who would have to foot the bill, those who live in the vicinity of a heroin distribution center, and those who become addicted through diversion from the system, while it would improve the lot of our present addicts and those whom they victimize.

Of course, naming in general terms who will and who will not lose by

differing heroin policies is not the same as attempting to gauge the impact
of a given heroin policy on any particular group. Black and Spanish-
speaking communities include the largest number of both addicts and
their victims and hence the largest proportion of those presently disad-
vantaged by heroin prohibition. On the other hand, though heroin
maintenance would mitigate these problems, the congregation of addicts
it would cause would lower the quality of life in the area and perhaps also
increase the attractiveness to youth of heroin use and addiction. Finally,
though free availability might solve many of these problems, in some
ways it would represent a greater threat to the black and minority
communities than does the present system, since many of those who have
to struggle hardest to succeed in our society might also be lured by cheap
and easily available heroin.

The political aspects of heroin policy are not the only problems, of
course. The nature of heroin and the capacities of our society to cope with
it seem to promise that the drug and the social problems related to its use
and control will be with us for a considerable time to come. Heroin is,
after all, a most inconvenient substance. Both its social meaning and its
pharmacology seem almost to have been designed to give trouble to a
pluralistic democratic society which lacks massive police resources,
maintains a strong tradition of individualism, and values the search for
personal pleasure and fulfillment.

The social meaning of heroin to those who use the drug—that the
beginning user is reckless and brave, and that the experienced user is an
outlaw, unconstrained by the usual demands of the dominant morality—is
a major factor in the damage the drug causes to society. Contrast this with
the much less troublesome social meaning of cocaine—that the user is
"cool," "with it," and open to experience.

The pharmacology of heroin compounds our problems as well. The
rewarding nature of use and the high potency of the drug help ensure that
the early user may begin easily and cheaply, while the onset of addiction
and the rapid buildup of tolerance tend to make the maintenance of a
heroin habit more and more difficult, demanding, and expensive. Not only
does the short time-course of the drug make legal maintenance of it
extremely difficult, but one might even conjecture that its anti-anxiety
effect increases the ability of those under its influence to accept the risks
of apprehension that go with criminality.

That is not to say, though, that the problem will be as serious for the
foreseeable future as it has been in the recent past. There is always the
hope, proven forlorn many times in the past but a theoretical possibility
nonetheless, that without any deliberate change in our policy large
segments of the population—and especially of the subgroups in those
areas where the drug is most available—will turn away from heroin use.

We are also making progress on our own and are slowly learning a great deal about the treatment of addiction and indeed about many compulsive drug-taking behaviors. As yet, this field of knowledge is in its infancy. We have hardly begun to discover which kinds of treatments work best with which kinds of addicts. It may well be that the therapeutic community is most appropriate for some; that relatively minimal treatment over and above monitoring is the most cost-effective solution for others; and that maintenance on some opiate is the best means for the rest. Once we can allocate the individual to the most appropriate means of treatment, we may find that the success rates increase for all our interventions.

Even within the area of maintenance there are issues which are only now receiving investigation. Matching the subject to the proper dosage so that he will stay in treatment without undue difficulty and yet be able to function at his fullest capacity, developing new longer-acting opiates, improving ways of relating to patients (there are indications that small cash rewards for clean urine or other steps toward social integration may be highly cost-effective), enlisting the families of addicts in the treatment process, and working out methods of having those in maintenance pay all or part of their costs all seem promising.

Though the use of narcotic antagonists to block the effect of heroin has thus far not proved very successful—simply because the addict can easily stop taking his medicine when he wishes to use heroin again—there is hope that longer-acting antagonists can be developed. At least in theory, these would have great advantages in the treatment of some addicts—and might be combined with various other means of treatment for many.

We are learning a good deal about the mechanics of coercion into treatment, as well. It turns out that even something so simple as escorting an addict from the courtroom to the treatment program makes a great difference in the retention rate. And we are learning that although a considerable degree of patience may be required to cope with many addicts, this can prove worthwhile in the long run.

There is also some hope that we may develop outreach programs which contact addicts or users before they come to official attention. In one experiment, youth workers were able to catch a heroin epidemic at its very beginning and without significant coercion talk many of those who were becoming dependent into treatment before the worst personal and social effects of addiction had surfaced.[1] Our society does not seem either very interested in or good at this technique. It involves intervening at the lowest level of community organization, and it involves political as well as therapeutic questions—but it does seem worth considerably more exploration than it has yet received.

Although there is hope that the cumulative effect of many small improvements may eventually lower greatly the cost of heroin in our

1. Patrick H. Hughes *Behind the Wall of Respect,* The University of Chicago Press, 1977.

society, it looks very much as if no dramatic change will rescue us from the problem. Admittedly the drug area is full of surprises. Who would have thought five years ago that Western Europe, which long seemed virtually immune to the drug, would consume more illegal heroin than the United States—yet it did in 1982. Similarly, seven years ago, no one would have predicted that cocaine would bring more money into the illegal market than heroin. In recent years the uniqueness of heroin has declined noticeably. It has become clearer that heroin is only one of many harmful drugs, and that the United States is only one of the nations to which it causes harm. Remembering this may give us a perspective on the problem—but it does not make solutions and improvements easier to find. Perhaps this should come as no surprise. After all, if the heroin problem were an easy one, we probably would have solved it by now.

# INDEX